Book from England     2005

With love
To Rita

Love Mel

D0758045

# AN ORDERLY MAN

The terrace looking west. June 1982.

# AN
# ORDERLY MAN

## DIRK BOGARDE

CHATTO & WINDUS
THE HOGARTH PRESS
1983

Published by
Chatto & Windus Ltd
The Hogarth Press
40 William IV Street
London WC2N 4DF

All rights reserved. No part of this publication
may be reproduced, stored in a retrieval system,
or transmitted in any form, or by any means, electronic,
mechanical, photocopying, recording or otherwise,
without the prior permission of Chatto & Windus Ltd.

British Library Cataloguing in Publication Data

Bogarde, Dirk
An orderly man
1. Bogarde, Dirk    2. Moving-picture actors
and actresses—Great Britain—Biography
I. Title
791.43'028'0924    PN2598.B647

ISBN 0 7011 2659 0

First published March 1983
Second impression March 1983
Third impression April 1983

© Labofilms S.A. 1983
Photoset in Bembo by
Rowland Phototypesetting Ltd
Bury St Edmunds, Suffolk
Printed in Great Britain by
Redwood Burn Ltd
Trowbridge, Wiltshire

For

E. L. L. Forwood

# ACKNOWLEDGEMENTS

I am indebted to Chatto & Windus Ltd for allowing me to use extracts from their letters written to me. Also to Mrs G. Goodings, Mrs A. Holt, and the executors of "Mrs X's" estate in America.

As always, most particularly, to Mrs Sally Betts who has managed to make some order out of my typescript in record time.

D. v. d.B.

# CONTENTS

# List of Plates

## COLOUR PLATES

## MONOCHROME PLATES

# I

I am an orderly man. I say this with no sense of false modesty, or of conceit. It is a simple statement of fact. That's all. Being orderly, as a matter of fact, can be excessively tiresome and it often irritates me greatly, but I cannot pull away. I sometimes think that I would far prefer to live slumped in some attic amidst a litter of junk, dirty underclothing, greasy pots and pans, paints and canvases strewn about everywhere, an on-the-point-of-being-discarded mistress weeping dejectedly on the stairs, fungus on the walls, and an enormous overdraft at the bank or, better still, absolutely no money at all. Unvarnished, music-less, Puccini.

But it just wouldn't work for me. I have to live in an orderly manner; I'd tidy up the attic in a flash, scrub the pots and pans, stack the canvases, exterminate the fungus, label the paints and send the mistress back to her mother. Or husband. And keep what money I had, as frugally as a miser, in a sock beneath my mattress. Orderly is what I am. You only have to see my plate at table, when I have dealt with asparagus, kippers or an artichoke, to know this: neat bundles of chewed stalks; bones and skin precisely laid aside in immaculate little blocks; tidy piles of leaves stacked as carefully as Dresden saucers.

All this is done quite unconsciously. I am not aware that I discard my rubbish in so fastidious, not to say elegant, a fashion. It simply happens. There they are. No scattered heaps of detritus or masticated vegetable matter. Neat, tidy, organised packets on a pristine platter. I often wonder, why? I look with quiet astonishment at my contribution to the dustbins.

What instinct makes me behave in this extraordinary fashion? Is it something which I have inherited from my father: a man who was always correct, contained, persistent and fully planned all his life? Or is it some hideous subconscious fault which a psychiatrist would hold against me as a sign of some monstrous flaw in my otherwise apparently serene make-up. God knows. But it is always there, and it has ruled my life from my earliest days. Precision, order, plan.

★   ★   ★

I live, and I must live, according to a pattern which I have made for myself, and fill it in with great care. I take grave risks with it, of course: bend it, turn it, sometimes even turn it quite over, re-arrange it, re-design it, but it is always within its frame, just as a stained-glass window is bounded by the strong pillars of its stone arch.

If a risk seems to me to be too dangerous (that is one which might shatter the whole amazing fabric itself), then I swiftly modify the risk and find another way to go about the altera- tion, seeking a less satisfying, less exciting, but far safer way of placing the bright fragments of life. No Nicholson or Suther- land am I: rather a Burne-Jones or Millais. In short, I am not abstract, I am realist. I think.

Often pinched by doubt.

But, after all, one cannot, at sixty-two, look back down the corridor of one's life and not have *some* doubts about the journey one has made. The doors which one opened are now all closed. The doors one did not dare to open remain shut. The corridor is dark; only ahead is lighter. So one turns and proceeds in that direction. To go back is madness. To turn left or right, at this stage, is both exhausting and dangerous.

However, there was not the least shadow of a doubt in my mind when we crunched gently up the rutted track towards this house one golden November day twelve years ago. Not the very slightest. From the moment that we turned off the narrow road up the lane between giant olive trees and wound up the hill among spiky amber grasses, jutting rocky outcrops, crimson brambles, sparkling little springs of crystal water in verdant bog, all under a sky the colour of Fabergé's blue enamel, I knew that the track was the right track and that my pattern was intact. And that the house, framed in its saffron vine and a large orange and lemon tree, was just about to fit into that pattern as smoothly and effortlessly as a foot into a well-worn slipper. After months of trailing about France, and before that most of Italy, I knew that I had found my ideal without once having set a toe across its threshold. It was instinctively, physically, and most important, spiritually, the exact fragment which I needed to complete my orderly pat- tern. There it was, glowing brightly in the sun. Waiting for me to embrace it and fit it into my life. Which I did.

Fitting *myself* into it proved, on the other hand, to be quite another matter. Crossing the threshold that morning for the very first time, I discovered that the ground floor consisted of three separate quarters. A kitchen with a vast canopied fireplace, a stone sink in one corner and a set of dusty sequinned drums and a music stand set in the centre of the tiled floor. Next door, down a couple of steps, two lofty stables, one for sheep, one for carts.

On the second floor, arrived at by a curving slate staircase, a sitting-room with an upright piano and a photograph of Che Guevara; beyond it three small bedrooms and a pitch dark bathroom. On the same level, just beside Mr Guevara, a door led up two steps into a sort of black pit, which had a stove and a sink and could have held two people in a grave emergency, and one in extreme discomfort. Above all this, running the length of the entire house, was a vast room which had recently been the hay loft. That's all. I admired the circular windows in the hay loft and the view from them of the massed olives below, and the sea shining some way off like a sheet of silver paper. I was instantly in love.

If the house did not quite contain the accommodation which I knew I should require for this permanent abode, it did contain the space. In my mind I rapidly decided that the ground floor should be opened up to form one enormous fifty-foot room, retaining the kitchen part, arching through the separating stable walls. The ceilings were all, most fortunately, on the same level; the floors rather attractively, I thought, on differing ones. Where the stable door was, presently swinging in the gentle autumn wind, I would have a window made. I should retain the canopied fireplace, convert the hay loft, put in an extra bathroom, and come to terms with the black pit at some later date. The house had limitless possibilities, only my bank balance was restricting. So I must go carefully at the start, and with the invaluable help of Mr Loschetter, my architect, and a rough set of scribbled sketches in his notebook, the ideas conceived between us all rapidly became almost-possibilities. Almost fact indeed. Loschetter nodded sagely and assured me that, as long as I did not desire a swimming-pool, marble stairs, plate-glass windows, wrought iron, and central heating throughout, it need not cost me a fortune. I asked only that the house be made large enough within its walls to provide the accommodation I required and that it should, above all else, retain the character which five hundred years had bestowed upon it. The arches which we would make through the downstairs walls must be irregular, the floors not completely level, the windows must be in sympathy with the ones which already existed, and the plaster must have the texture of centuries instantly imposed upon it. He was suddenly relieved and almost affable. He later confessed that he had heard that I was in "the movies" and expected to have to gut the house, build a sauna and a swimming-pool, and string Venetian lanterns from every ceiling. When I asked him what he would have done had I insisted on these bits of kitsch, he said sharply that he would have "quitted the job".

He stayed, thankfully, and promised that everything would be perfectly ready and in order by the time I arrived back from my work on "Death in Venice" in Italy, which was soon to start. He had no qualms, a splendid workforce of well-trained craftsmen, understood my sympathetic feelings for the house, would only use the most ancient of materials, and assured me that I could have every confidence in him. I had. It was all very orderly. Just what I wanted.

Except that I had not yet got it. A small point; but important.

From that day in November until the middle of January the battle to secure the house raged. The Bank of England stumbled about, blind to the fact that I was desperately anxious lest some other person might make an offer right away and move in. Papers and forms wandered through the air between London and Rome, where I was at that time living in a rented villa above a slum village, and I drove desperately across Italy almost weekly to show good faith and to re-assure the doubting owner that I was serious and all would be well. Eventually, after a great deal of desperate haggling, battling, pleading and struggle, the money was released from the vaults and the house was within my grasp. Numb with relief, I then went into the French phase. That is to say, I discovered that my limited knowledge of that language was of no use at all when it came to dealing with the French law, taxes, the rights of way, plumbing, septic tanks, boundaries and, above all, I speedily learned, something called French Logic. An example? Well: you are ill in bed and wish to have it re-made lying, as you are, in a rumple of sheets and discomfort. The nurse, if she is French, will explain politely that she obviously cannot re-make your bed as you are at the moment occupying it. French

4

Logic. My sense of order was constantly outraged, and I was thrown daily into a state of anguish and disarray, from which I was sure I would never recover.

Fortunately I realised, very quickly indeed, that I simply had to come to terms with things as they presently stood, and to tread my new path with calmness, caution, humility and, above all, patience, love and tolerance. If I were to live the rest of my life out in France, as I sincerely hoped I would, and yet still behave as if I were living in England, then I would very shortly come to grief.

I had seen it happen to so many exiles who had made the journey before me. Lonely, isolated, wistful, clinging in desperation to shrinking pensions, the BBC World Service, old London newspapers and the enervating company of the other expatriates at bridge and cocktail parties. That was no sort of life: one might just as well have gone to live in Sidmouth or Cheltenham.

Here I was, facing a new life pattern, one of my deliberate choosing, one which I had dreamed of having for as long as I could remember, certainly from my very earliest days when we came over to France each summer for the cherished holidays which marked me for ever with a deep and undying love for the country. And long ago I had decided that one day, when the time was right, I would seek out a place of my own there and stay for good.

The time was now, the place had been sought and found, and I was on the very brink of making the great change, so . . . all my preconceived and accepted ideas and notions must be set aside for they would not fit into the scheme of things, or into my new pattern of life which I hoped was stretching out ahead of me like an unwalked map. If I tried to fit them in, if I tried to adapt or bend them at this point of the journey, I'd be lost.

So. Calm down. Listen. Watch, try to understand what takes place, how things are done, how things are *not* done. Reason with it all, and, above all else, try to see the French point of view: for it is their country you are about to enter, and they know it far better than you do and how to make it work for them. After all, you are not starting negotiations to purchase a holiday caravan; you are negotiating for a new life. Yours. So you'd better take it all very seriously indeed. Even the logic. Just remember that second chances don't come so easily at forty-nine.

5

All this went through my head as I lay sleepless in my hotel bedroom the night before I was due to present myself at the local Notaire's office in a neighbouring village, to set my name to the deeds of the house and surrender my cheque, just wrestled from the Bank of England, which amounted to a great deal more than half my life savings. My bonnet, if not actually at this moment over the windmill, had been thrown high. Time to take things very seriously indeed: to remain calm, to be orderly.

Order restored, somewhat, I turned on my side and attempted sleep.

★　★　★

In a cutting wind, brilliant sunshine, and a thick tweed coat, I was outside the Notaire's office, with Forwood, at precisely five to nine the following morning. Loschetter and his wife Clair, who had now most agreeably taken over all the fussing legalities since she knew the ropes and spoke faultless English, were waiting, smiling and stamping fur-booted feet. As the village clock clanged the first stroke of nine, we entered the Notaire's bureau and all at once a sudden hush of sanctity and gravity descended about us like a pale shroud.

A shadowy room, wood-panelled. On one side, neat and tense in bentwood chairs, the owner and his representative both with dark suits, briefcases and heavy glasses; on the other, our bentwood chairs standing empty on thin legs like insects, waiting. Before us on a high podium behind a large desk, the Notaire, a youngish man with a framed photograph of an unsmiling President flanked by two furled tricolours and a wreath. On our entrance there was a scraping of chairs and the assembly rose in a rustle of blue suits and papers. A silent "Good morning" was nodded and we eased into our seats. The atmosphere was extremely grave. A case of rape, perhaps? Or embezzlement?

No. The purchase of a house. I couldn't imagine why my mouth was suddenly so dry.

Needless to say, it all took a very, very long time indeed and I didn't understand a single word uttered. My sense of order and discipline started to slip. I became completely lost, and although Clair whispered the translations rapidly, I was none

I a  The house, looking from the north towards the sea,
Pointe de L'Esquillon and the Estérel Massif.

b  Some of the terraces and walls, rebuilt. November 1977.

II a  Spring 1971. Clearing the site of the *potager;* fallen walls on the right. Daisy at left.

b  Eleven years later. The cherry trees, from the Long Walk. May 1982.

the wiser, for I was far out of my depth with the legalities; even in English. I only knew for certain that my offer had been accepted and that now, one hour later, they were still discussing the house and its twelve acres with as much intensity and attention to detail as if my offer had been for Versailles and its entire park. Furnished.

Clair suddenly touched my arm to attract my wandering attention.

"Now they will make the renouncement," she said in a low voice.

The room was suddenly hushed. A crackle of papers, rustle of a coat, a chair scraped on the stone floor. A tall, white-haired, aged man, faded and wrinkled, as if he had been stored like an apple in an attic, rose unsteadily to his feet and, raising his right arm high above the silent group below him, renounced his rights to the house and the land which had been in his family's possession for over five hundred years, "for all eternity". Three times he repeated, slowly and deliberately, the words, "Je renonce. Je renonce. Je renonce." The room was still. He turned to look at me with a tired, kind, smile, nodded his head, and sat down carefully. I found it extremely moving.

Clair gave me a pen and, as I signed my name to the deeds, she handed my cheque in a sealed envelope to the old man's son, M. Claude, who was, or had been until that moment, the nominal owner.

Outside in the brilliant sunlight we suddenly came back to life. Hands were shaken, hats removed, and the ex-owner, he of the sequinned drums, suggested a glass of wine to warm us and to seal the deal in all amicability. We crossed the dusty square to the local bar in grateful acceptance. The deliberations had taken so long that the bar was almost full, and the heady scent of thick tobacco and pastis made me realise how badly I needed my glass of rouge, which arrived at the marble-topped table by the stove almost before I had had time to wedge myself into my chair.

"Well!" said Clair, spreading her hands to the glowing heat. "Now you are the patron! You have your house at long last. Do you feel happy?"

"I feel extraordinary. I can hardly believe it after all the struggle and the worry . . . all I want to do is go there immediately and start measuring things."

She looked at me with a gentle smile. "Measure what things?"

"Oh, the rooms, the walls for pictures. I have really only seen the house twice, you know. Now I want to get down to things before I return to Rome."

Clair lifted her glass of wine, raised it in a light toast and said, "Ah, but that is not possible, you know."

I didn't know.

"It is in the contract. You cannot visit the house just as you please."

"But it is mine!"

"Yes, yours, but you cannot take possession until April."

"Why?"

"It is in the contract. The family must not be disturbed and they will vacate in April, when they have found alternative accommodation. So you cannot visit it."

"But this is madness!"

"It is in the contract."

"But I *must* see it again. I have to go with your husband and decide on a hundred things . . ."

She shrugged gently. "He cannot start to do anything for you until April. They will not permit it."

"But it is *my* house!" I began to bleat like a sheep in desperation.

"You understand that the family do not know that their papa has sold the house. And the children will be unhappy. He wishes to break the news of the sale to them very gently, as a *fait accompli*, before he does anything else. There will be many tears, you know."

"You mean he didn't tell them? They don't know that I own the place?"

Clair looked uncomfortable. "No. They do not know yet. He felt it was wiser to do it this way. Now that it is done, it is done. It is all in the contract, you know. Did you read it carefully?"

Not carefully enough, I realised wretchedly. The ex-owner, Jean-Paul, was looking excessively sheepish during this exchange; although he did not understand a word of English, he very well understood my anguish and surprise. As if to try and mollify my anger he cautiously pushed a sheet of crumpled paper towards me, and murmured something under his breath to Clair.

8

"Ah! M. Claude has here a list of all the animals and birds which you will find on your land, is not that very thoughtful of him?"

"I would far rather know where the plugs and switches are, and where I can fit a new bathroom."

"If you look at this list you will see how many splendid beasts you support. Look. There is a badger; you have pheasant. . . ."

I looked at the list in crushed silence. Jean-Paul hastily went to get himself another glass of rouge. Numb with disappointment, I looked down the list.

Badgers indeed were there, partridge, pheasant and rabbits; black, I noted. The hoopoe and the golden oriole came every spring, the cuckoo arrived with the punctuality of a Mussolini train on 16th April, the nightingale a little later, and the swallows a week after. There was a fox in the oak wood at the back of the house, and wild flowers of bewildering species in abundance. I should never lack for water on the hill, for there were clear springs all over the land, and the olive trees numbered exactly four hundred.

But none of this could be mine until the arrival of the nightingale and the swallows. Or the cuckoo.

However, after a very lengthy, and sometimes heated discussion with M. Claude wringing his hands and shaking his long locks about his shoulders, it was finally agreed that I would be allowed to visit the house just one more time, in company with Loschetter or Clair, while his wife was away in Nice and the children were at school. In that time we were to make our final plans and decisions about the alterations, and the time laid down was very exact. From ten a.m. until eleven-thirty a.m. The children would be back at noon precisely to start lunch. One and a half hours to re-plan an entire house. Well: we did it. Order prevailed generally. The next morning we arrived at the house, attacked the problems, took a mass of photographs, and stole away like thieves as the first child, aged about six, wobbled up the track from school on his bicycle. Loschetter would start work sometime in April and I would return, all being well, in July: for "Death in Venice" would fully occupy me until that time . . . and probably even longer. It was a tormenting thought. However, as Forwood wisely pointed out, the house was mine. Loschetter was very sensible, capable and fully understanding, and I had a very big

9

job ahead of me on the film. When it was over the house would be ready, or ready enough, for me to move in in some kind of order. Meanwhile we had plans, measurements, many photographs, and we could spend our time, during the shooting of the film, making lists of the furniture, packed and stored somewhere in London, which we would require or reject. First things first. The house was secured, so now back to Rome and the demands of Visconti, Thomas Mann, and the ghostly shade of Von Aschenbach who was waiting tentatively in the shadows of my mind.

★   ★   ★

One morning in the middle of July, sitting alone, as was my habit throughout the making of the film, so that I could contain complete concentration, Forwood arrived at the door of my little beach hut on the Lido, with a telegram. It was from Loschetter to say, very simply, that the house was finished and the front door key was hanging on a nail behind the orange tree.

The film was, at last, slowly drawing to a close. In a week's time I knew that we should have finished the main shooting in Venice and would move up to Germany to shoot the opening shots of the film in some abandoned cemetery and, later, a railway station. This move would take at least a couple of days, which would be the first free days away from my alter ego, Von Aschenbach, that I had had since he had come to join me in early March. I resolved that we would use those two days by driving to the house to see what had been done and to make the final plans for the arrival of the furniture from England, for although the film had overrun its original schedule by many weeks, the light was clearly at the end of the tunnel and August, or the early part of that month, must see it finished.

Grudgingly, for he was appalled that I could allow any personal problems to come near me at such a time, Visconti allowed me to make the trip on the clear understanding that I should break the threads of my concentration for only forty-eight hours. I promised this faithfully, and we drove through the night a week later, to France, and on the morning of July 21st, in blinding heat, I found the front door key on its nail behind the orange tree and pushed open the heavy wooden door into the house.

And there it was. Just as I had always hoped it would be. Loschetter had been as good as his word. Inside, the whole house sparkled in a fresh coat of whitewash, the dingy khaki plaster had gone, the drums had gone, the canopied kitchen and the two crumbling stables were now transformed into a long, cool, elegant room, fifty feet in length, linked by gently irregular arches. Ancient tiles covered the once dirt and concrete floors, the stable door was a graceful window, the giant beams had been stripped, sanded and cloth-washed with white, the whole place was light, serene as if it had been thus for centuries.

On the floor above, Che Guevara had gone, along with the upright piano which had almost filled the small room; the black pit was less black under a coat of white paint, and a shining new cooker standing in the centre of the floor gave it an almost immediate feeling of space and light. But it was still too small, and I wondered how Antonia would manage when she arrived from Spain to "settle me in", as she and Eduardo had promised. However, for the moment, that could wait. I went on up to the hay loft and found to my delight that it was now a set of three pleasant bedrooms and a bathroom. We were complete. I looked out of the round windows, which had been retained, and down across the olives and the huge untended vine. Hollyhocks in all colours nodded on tall spikes, lizards dozed, and Labo, the stray dog which I had found in Rome, ran about the tussocky grass far below, putting up rabbits. It was all exactly what I had hoped.

Downstairs, in the long white room, sitting on a box and drinking a beer from the bottle, I looked about me and wondered how it would look with all the furniture which was soon to be on its way from England. Would it fit? Would all the planning which had gone on over the months with lists and graph paper and detailed measurements of chairs and pictures have been a waste of time, or would every item slip comfortably into its allotted place? The room looked as if it would easily contain every stick which I had chosen to bring abroad.

Before I had left the last house in England, I had had a vast sorting-out of all my goods and possessions, knowing that never again, come what may, would I have a house of forty rooms; for this was the "cutting down" period, the two suitcases and small flat plan. Except that the present house, small as it was, was certainly not a flat, and there were already rather more than the two allotted suitcases of my theory that from now on I must travel, so to speak, light. And live simply. A great auction had been held of all the surplus stuff. Books, furniture, paintings, glass, china and God only knows what else. For two days the housewives of Guildford and Godalming fought hysterically to outbid each other for items which ranged from a Minton tea set of sixty pieces to a wicker hamper containing two tin plates, a wooden towel rail and a hurricane lamp. The dealers arrived in heavy overcoats and picked through my dud Old Masters, carting several away in exchange for comfortable cheques, and the hysteria mounted as did the money. I was bemused, amused, and only saddened that I had been forced to part with so many books, some two thousand. But two thousand books bundled into boxes took up room, and there was, I felt certain, nowhere that they would fit in the new life somewhere then vaguely ahead of me. But I saved the best and the favourites, and planned to start again, from scratch, when I finally settled down. So what would arrive in the vans from England would be a very much cut down list of possessions, things which I had cherished for many years and which would fit into my new life-plan easily and comfortably.

But what of the people? The friends, the acquaintances, the figures who had decorated, embellished, enriched, filled out my life before? I had made no selection of them: there had been no auction of surplus-friends. Would they come all this way to join me in my long white room? Would there, as it were, be a Cast of Players to fill the Set which I was thoughtfully planning with my bottle of beer on this still, hot morning? Impossible to say at that stage. But of one thing I was quite certain: there would never again be any more Beel-Bendrose-Nore-Sundays. Twelve or sixteen people for luncheon, tea, and dinner. Those days were finished, and a good thing too—absurdly extravagant, tiring, and self-indulgent.

Twenty years of almost constant entertaining had become finally exhausting. There had been long weekends, from Friday to Monday, as well as the famous "Sundays" and this, of course, could not be done without help, and help was "Staff". And staff were more people in the house, and more problems. Battles in the staff sitting-room, smoothing ruffled feelings between an hysterical parlour maid and a furious cook, allocating jobs and territory—who fed the dogs, laid the tables, ordered the food, turned down the beds, did the laundry, cleared the fires, brought in the logs, cleaned the brasses or ironed my shirts? There were also often serious problems to face in the staff room, which only a qualified psychiatrist could properly handle. What to do if three out of five people wanted to watch "Come Dancing" on the TV, while the other two wanted to stay with "Panorama"? Buy another television set. Simple. So one did. Many people preferred not to eat what we ate in the dining-room. Risotto Milanese, Coq au vin, Osso bucco, Lapin aux pruneaux, or even Bratwurst and cabbage; that sort of thing. I hasten to add that we did not only eat these continental delights, there were also English dishes like Steak and Kidney and enormous barons of beef and so on. But one had developed a liking for slightly more exotic dishes during one's travels, which were considered as "muck-ups" or "too spicy" by the staff sitting-room, so they had to have a separate menu. Days and nights of cottage pie, baked beans, fish pie, fish fingers, chemical sausages, eggs and bacon or horrendous "fry-ups" of old Brussels sprouts and mashed potatoes drenched in margarine and fried until carbonised.

Of course it all meant a great deal more work, and a great deal more expense: at times it seemed that we subsidised the frozen food manufacturers, and the two big refrigerators were jam-packed with junk-muck that had been advertised nightly on the television. However, I tried to be scrupulously fair, and the problem was not daunting on condition that one realised that an early death from cholesterol poisoning was the staff room's personal choice. Not mine. Food therefore was a simple matter. Even I could manage to play Herod at the discussions on Friday nights when the week's menu was normally planned. But it all took time. One did not need the psychiatrist for that. There were darker problems which lurked about behind the green baize door.

One morning the housekeeper sobbed, in great distress, that the gardener's boy, all of sixteen and dim with it, had chased her round the kitchen table with the bread knife. She was doubly outraged because at the time she was wearing her best "negligee". There was the cook who had been in service with Queen Mary and who insisted on a personal maid for herself to bring up her morning tea and massage her legs which, she said, were frail with years of standing at a stove just "slaving". She also, on one memorable occasion, ordered ninety-eight white pillow-cases from Harrods: for the staff bedrooms. I never knew why. Another cook was brutally shot in her large backside by a ricochetting bullet fired from a double-barrelled gun by her eight-year-old son (strictly forbidden to have a gun as he had already shot two of the cats during the summer) just two hours before a Christmas dinner at which we were to sit sixteen, and there was a Portuguese couple who threw enormous parties, in my absence, ate mountains of food, drank vast quantities of drink, and lay about all over the drawing-room in highly immodest positions, all of which were unpleasantly, and clearly, revealed in a scatter of Polaroid snapshots which one of them, dazed on Mouton Rothschild and Chivas Regal, had unwisely forgotten underneath a cushion.

Those were the rich and gaudy shades of life's brilliant pattern; and I knew, sitting in my long, white, empty room, that I wished for a less vivid and disturbing set of colours. Muted, simpler; patternless in fact.

Of course, there were glorious exceptions to these aberrations. The Zwickls from Vienna had stayed with me in complete harmony and love for ten years until the temptation offered by a millionaire in Palm Beach overcame their sensibilities and off they went. There was hiatus then, of course, but after the storms, which lasted a number of wearying years, Antonia and Eduardo arrived, bringing serenity and order, from Valencia, where they were now waiting patiently for my call to arrive in France, for they had decided generously, long before, to throw in their lot with me when I left England, and to wander about Europe with me until such time as I found the place in which I wanted to spend the rest of my life. And here I was, sitting in it, drinking my beer, remembering the past, and looking forward to a bright, clear, uncluttered, orderly future. But the friends? The Cast for the Set which lay before me . . . would they come back? The fare was expensive, the distance far, the house humble, there was little to do, no swimming-pool, no television, no English newspapers, no sea lapping a foot from the terrace. Hardly a terrace. Yet. A shepherd's house, up a goat track, and worst of all, no guest room. That would be the "cruncher"; for no one could stay.

It was a "cutting off" all right. A complete change of tempo and life. I was greatly interested to see how I would cope with it, let alone the curious group of well-loved friends who thought that I had taken leave of my senses anyway. Some would come back, out of curiosity, others might brave the trip from affection and, perhaps, pity, for I was broke now, to all intents and purposes, with a tight and limited budget ahead. But of one thing I was certain; my family, which I cherished above all, *would* arrive, and somehow if they passed it as sensible and sound, then I would know that all was well. And I was pretty sure that they would approve and that my father, in particular, would be delighted. He had approved of the idea from the very start although he had shown vague, if amused, doubts as to my ability to carry the plan through. But here I was, starting it. First move accomplished. In the high July sunlight I wandered round my acres feeling well satisfied, if a little astonished at my own temerity.

It was mostly what I call goat-land, that is to say, broom and thyme, coarse grass, jagged boulders with here and there boggy patches of brilliant green where little springs bubbled among wild watercress and bulrushes. And all about was the gnarled age of the olives, some as old as the house, others as young as one hundred years. Walnuts flourished, elms, and behind, rising high up the rocky hill, a wood of towering oaks. The house stood four square to the winds on a small plateau shouldered on three sides by the mountains which would protect it from the worst of winds, and facing down over the plain beyond which lay the sweep of the sea, Corsica, and beyond that, Africa. This land, I thought with happiness, would look after itself. I should have sheep to graze it, perhaps even goats, which are good at that sort of thing. We'd have chickens and ducks as well. I'd clear and dig the overgrown *potager* to the east, and grow leeks and potatoes, lettuce and radish, and maybe, because I couldn't quite see myself without them however tight the budget was to be, flowers for cutting. I had it all planned out, easily. Here there would never be acres of velvet lawn to cut, as there had been at Nore. No box hedges to trim, no roses (two hundred in the last rose-garden; to be pruned each March), no herbaceous borders to tend and dig, no gravel paths to rake and weed, no ponds and waterfalls, no fruit trees to prune and spray, no greenhouses to air and fumigate. It would be the simplest possible existence: a few pots of geraniums here and there, a scythe for the grass immediately about the house, and the little *potager* bursting with fresh vegetables, mint, chives, garlic and tarragon. There was already a great rosemary hedge around it, and a bay tree of incredible girth. We would be self-sufficient in time, with our own grapes and olives and water from the stone well, eggs and chickens and, perhaps, when the time came, our own mutton and lamb . . . I might even keep a pig. The orderly man *had* taken leave of his senses.

I was completely unaware at the time, of course, that I was suffering from almost total exhaustion. The five months of work on "Death in Venice" had been the hardest I had ever known for stress and mental strain; daily I had struggled with a personality of my own invention who had overwhelmed me to such an extent that every single function I performed in my daily life was as he would have done. I was never without his influence at any time, even in sleep. Therefore on one single day in a completely different environment, with very different problems to face, with a mind and body briefly released from his demanding personality, I lost my head and sense of balance and, at the same time, my invaluable sense of order.

I was looking at my possessions that day, not through rose-tinted glasses, but through glasses of every known tint and hue in the spectrum. Nothing, I was to find, would be as I had thought and planned. But for the moment, that supremely happy moment, I was as confident as I could possibly be. Sure, brave, secure, without apprehension. What folly!

But that was all then. And I am, as I said earlier, doing what I should *not* do, looking back, or going back, which is madness, except that it is a joyful madness.

Satisfied, satiated, and a little giddy with so many pleasures, we locked the empty house, hung the key on the nail behind the orange tree, packed the dog into the car, and headed back to Italy.

The day before we had set off from Venice for the trip, Visconti had suddenly decided that he preferred a railway station in the port of Trieste to the one which he had originally chosen in Munich. It was closer to Venice, more rococo than the Munich one, and there was an extraordinary restaurant in the back room of an alimentari near the docks which he insisted I must not on any account miss. So to Trieste we drove, secure in the knowledge that within two or three weeks "Death in Venice" must finish and the word could go out to the furniture vans in London that they should start the journey bearing all my worldly possessions to the shepherd's house up the goat track. I settled myself into my seat, and almost as soon as we had crossed the frontier at Ventimiglia, Von Aschenbach was once again plucking softly at my sleeve, a little resentful that for one day I had almost completely banished him; but so insistent, so strong was his personality, that it was he, and not I, who drove into Trieste in the lengthening shadows of that late afternoon.

## 2

I don't, at this moment, remember exactly who wrote "The best-laid schemes o' mice an' men gang aft agley". Or words to that effect. I rather think that it was Burns. But it really doesn't matter much now, for, happily, it never entered my head on that blazing August morning when Eduardo, Antonia, Forwood and I shuffled about in the shade of the trailing, unkempt, vine. (It was already hot at seven-thirty a.m.) Eduardo, as usual, had a cigarette hanging from his lower lip; Antonia, in fresh floral apron, flapped a brand new duster at flies; Forwood was messing about with the vine, and I stood staring down the track, willing the container vans with all the furniture to arrive from England.

We had come together the evening before at the Colombe d'Or; they from Valencia, Forwood and I and the dog from Bolzano, in northern Italy.

It had been their first glimpse of the house that morning at seven, and Antonia, with the grace and tact of so many Spanish women, professed that she found it all "Lovely!" and that the black pit, which I had kept till last, "wasn't *so* bad", and she'd make a kitchen out of it by nightfall.

I confess that I was a little startled to re-discover the bright new cooker in the centre of the floor, and even more surprised to find an enormous refrigerator gleaming in white enamel, high as a man, and very expensive, standing proudly in the middle of what would, I hoped, later be the dining-room, both like children awaiting confirmation. They seemed to me not to have any kind of connections: but since I know as much about electricity as I do about hang gliding, I put my surprise aside; in case it should turn to unease. I was really most orderly about everything. And nothing was to spoil the pleasure of this long-awaited event: the arrival of my goods and chattels from England after a year or more in storage.

We were not alone, the four of us. Under the lime tree, in a small group, two gendarmes, a man from Customs, and another who had arrived just moments before from Nice, and who was to represent the Beaux Arts. They stood together smoking and murmuring.

The gendarmes, I assume, were there to check that I was not smuggling hashish or worse in my wardrobes, and to check, minutely, each item against the inventory held in their hands. Each piece which entered France had to be accounted for. The chap from the Customs was there with a large pair of metal clippers to break the seal on the vans; the gentleman, who wore pince-nez, and stooped a little, there to check, against *his* inventory, the pictures, lest I should smuggle them out, or sell them. It was all most correct; the scent of Gitanes hung in the air and I rather longed for a cup of coffee.

But then, oh, blessed sight! They arrived. Gleaming yellow through the trees. Like elephants ambling slowly towards a water-hole, the two great container vans came up the track, thrashing against the low-hanging branches, nudging carelessly at the tree trunks on either side, rolling easily over the boulders and potholes, they came to a halt by the house as we moved towards them.

With that splendid over-importance all minor officials wear as easily as their shiny uniforms, the gentleman from Customs clambered on to the trucks, and with a great deal of unnecessary ceremony, clipped the steel wire seals which had, I suppose, been placed there in England.

"I wonder," said Antonia, hands clasped in happy expectation like a child watching a conjuror, "what will come out first?"

The doors swung wide and there, in crates and bundles and great disarray, lay the tumbled contents of my house. The vision we got that morning was one of wreckage. Total.

There is no point now, all these years later, in going into detail over the dismal and distressing sights which we stared at in disbelief. No point in remembering Antonia's anguished cries as one shattered piece of porcelain after another was carried in sacking cloth and laid in the sun; no point in remembering the life-size lead garden figure, smashed at the knees, and jammed, blind eyes to heaven, in the shards of what had been an elegant Carolian table, or the tea chest so lovingly packed, and upon which we got to work with care, certain that it would contain the best of a Meissen collection of wild birds. What it *did* contain, wrapped in yards of sticky paper, cotton wool, and newspaper, was fifty electric light bulbs of varying strengths. Intact. The Meissen parrots, both pairs, were smashed beyond repair, as were all the rest. And so it went on. Kitchen utensils spiked through oil paintings, every frame on every picture, chipped or worse; all the plates were bundled, loose, in old blankets and had rumbled and splintered themselves across the Channel. Only Antonia's sudden cries of woe as she discovered another piece in ruins broke the grim silence as we unloaded the wreckage.

We had managed to clear half the first container when one of the gendarmes suddenly folded his inventory, stuck it into his tunic, touched his cap politely to us and suggested, in a low voice tinged with sadness rather than scorn, that if the British really did want to join the Common Market, they'd better manage things better than this.

There wasn't much I could say to that.

He and his companion straddled their motorbikes and bounced down the track followed, very shortly afterwards, by the stooping gentleman from the Beaux-Arts who shook his head in despair at a painting which appeared to have been impaled on the prongs of a garden fork, and by the Customs man who said that he'd come back one day soon. If I'd been into drug smuggling that day I'd have made a hell of a killing.

But we went on doggedly, and wretchedly, unloading, for the vans had to be back in Nice that evening.

Antonia, sensible creature, collected some assorted cups and said she'd go and make coffee. I handed round beer, which we had bought in the village with some other bits and pieces to tide us through the day, and just as we were about to sling a rope round a large chest of drawers which we were going to haul up through one of the top windows, for we had suddenly discovered that nothing larger than a tea chest would ever be negotiated round the sharp corner on the lower stairs, Antonia called softly from an upper window; there was no electricity.

Anywhere.

Plugs we had; switches in abundance; but every wire in every ceiling had been neatly cut off, one millimetre in length, by the previous owner, and somewhere along the line the builders, who had striven so hard to break through the three-foot deep walls and open them up into graceful arches which I had wanted, had also severed the main cable. And plastered it tidily away. We had not the least idea where it could be. We hadn't got any coffee either.

It was August, the middle of the biggest French summer holiday. Not a hope of finding an electrician, let alone one who knew where the main cable might run. We continued unloading the vans as fast as possible, all thoughts of a refreshing bath banished, no comforting coffee, no light, and presumably no heat to cook a meal.

My splendid sense of orderliness was still with me. But badly fraying at the edges. I passed the now loathsome refrigerator constantly, and the idiot cooker, and carted pictures, blankets, chairs and God knows what else past them all day, placing each object exactly where we had planned they should go from the long evenings' work with graph paper and rulers. Everything, that is to say everything that was not smashed into small pieces, fitted into place eventually, and a sort-of house began to take shape. I felt rather comforted. At least we had all got there, even if not all of us were entirely unmarked or unscathed. And my comfort increased greatly when a perspiring Eduardo discovered a gas cylinder, half full, under the kitchen stairs. Triumph! All we needed now was a gas ring and a bit of rubber tubing and we'd have a hot meal that evening.

Which we did; sitting among the chaos of the long room, forking at bowls of hot tinned Cassoulet which we'd bought that morning, and admiring everything around us by the light of six candles someone had found rolling about in a drawer.

"Is a big adventure, no?" said Antonia, cheerfully drinking white wine from a cup. And that's exactly what it was: at least we had got our beds into place, found sheets, and the lavatories worked perfectly.

I decided that I'd think of the greater problems tomorrow.

There were to be rather more than I'd envisaged.

⋆   ⋆   ⋆

Somehow it all got settled, in a rough and ready kind of way, a few days later.

A cable was looped round the house like bunting, and the lights went on. The refrigerator and cooker took up their respective positions, and in time, we got some more or less hot water, and Antonia started to cook—her main problem being the re-discovery of her cooking utensils which were adrift in every conceivable part of the house. In spite of all the initial problems, the destruction of the collection of Meissen, a sudden and alarming feeling that one might have done the wrong thing and realised the error a mite too late, the search for coat hangers, wooden spoons, saucers, picture hooks, glue, and the dire efforts to deal with the one and only telephone in inadequate French, in spite of all these, and many more things, I wandered about in a state of mild euphoria.

On the other hand it could have been diagnosed as amnesia.

But after the last six months or more of living with Von Aschenbach, with his sadness, loneliness, fastidiousness, his cold precision, I did, quite honestly, feel a lifting of a tremendous burden. There is no other word for it. Cliché though it may well be. I had a lightness about me, which I recognised from having once possessed it many years before; there were sudden surges within of supreme joy and happiness, which caused me to skip like a goat (when no one was looking). They did not occur very often (they don't at forty-nine, after all) but when they did they were intense and glorious. I was released. Von Aschenbach had gone. For ever.

While others were busy dusting and polishing, sweeping and nailing, I would go with the dog, Labo, and walk about my rough land, pressing through bramble and broom, touching sun-hot boulders buried in thyme, caressing olive trees of vast girth and great age, drinking from the little springs which bubbled in mats of verdant green, marvelling that all this should, at last, be mine.

How could I possibly know, in this state of amnesia, for that is surely what it was I fear, that all I touched, saw and drank was not as it seemed? What would have happened to this sudden and new-found joy with which I was suffused had I been told that the four hundred olive trees of venerable age and impressive girth had been neglected for more than thirty years; and were slowly dying? That the sun-hot boulders, wreathed in their collars of thyme, were not boulders at all but parts of long-tumbled terrace walls? That the sparkling springs from which I drank so romantically came not from the bowels of Provence but from leaks in the giant reservoir, which held the water for Cannes, high in the hill behind me? That the bramble and the broom concealed acres of once-tilled land on which had grown jasmin, roses and artichokes?

What should I have done then?

I have no way of knowing because no one did. I found it all

III a  The front door, leading on to the terrace.

b  The terrace and the vine, looking east. June 1982.

IV a  Looking towards the old kitchen. The central section was the original sheep-shed.

b  Looking from the old kitchen down to the cart-shed. Now all one long fifty-foot room.

out, painfully, for myself. By which time my amnesia had faded and reality had grabbed me by the throat.

After a week of sitting hunched in various armchairs eating our meals, it did, finally, dawn on me that a dining-table might be just the thing we needed. Why I had overlooked this vital item I cannot now remember. All I do recall is that the splendid Sutherland table, around which so many people had sat, at which so many discussions were held, decisions made, marriages repaired and, sometimes, broken, and which I had had for a great many years, was sold with all the rest of the "excess baggage" at the auction in Guildford, as being unsuitable for a cottage.

So a table was the next, and indeed most pressing, item, plus an electric drill of some kind, since every nail one hammered into the stone walls did a tremendous U-bend or sprung, lethally, back into one's face. Therefore pictures stood stacked in rows everywhere, and Eduardo couldn't hang a shelf. Antonia ranged her modest supply of cooking implements in a cardboard box, and our clothes stayed, mouldering, in our suitcases.

So: a table and an electric drill.

The local antique shops were useless to me on my limited budget, and, in any case, mostly sold rather over-glazed bits of Louis-anything. Along the main road there was a rather raffish shop, however: it had its fair share of over-glaze and fake Sèvres, but also it had lower floors on which were crammed a great variety of goods. This seemed my best bet.

At first, the Madame inside took me to be an American, with my dreadful accent, and showed me, with a flinty eye, all that was most desirable to the well-heeled and ignorant. When it was explained that I was English merely, and poor, she shrugged, and led me down to the basement which was filled with, as far as I could see, broken bits and pieces, sagging, springless chairs, and an unattractive odour of decay. But, in the midst of this, I discovered a table. Big enough to sit eight, ten at a pinch; hefty, wooden, covered, at that moment, in tattered shards of dirty American oilcloth which had been nailed down its edges. It was, frankly, a pretty unattractive sight. And I made clear to Madame that I considered it so, in order to put her off any possible scent of interest she might be picking up. I could see, in the knowing eyes, under the imposing yellow wig, figures flicking through her cunning

mind like those in a fruit machine. I sought other pieces of
junk, poked about among terrible paintings, a wicker-work
bedhead, a batch of cracked plates in a tin bath bearing the
words "Hotel", and finally, in as laconic a manner as possible,
I asked her the price of the table.

She'd been yawning, so I caught her by surprise. She said
suddenly: "600 Francs", which was a little under sixty pounds
in those days, and I, pulling at a filthy strip of chequered
oilcloth, asked her if it was made of pine.

"Oh yes!" she cried. "It's all pine. I swear."

I told her I'd think about it, because it was larger than I had
wanted and I had a serious problem in my house with a
dangerous, unnavigable, bend in the staircase. She shrugged,
asked where I lived, and that was that.

A little before dawn, or so it seemed to me, the following
morning, Antonia called up to my room from the terrace that
there were a "lady and a gentleman" with some wood for me.

It was the table.

Madame had made a determined effort to see that it would,
no matter what, go round my unnavigable corner in the stairs
by demolishing the thing. There it lay, in the back of her large
shooting-brake, in about ten pieces, legs, stretchers, planks
still a-flutter with torn strips of oilcloth.

I don't know why I didn't stop her. Perhaps because she was
much taller than I, and the yellow wig gave her a majesty
which unnerved me. In any case, she threw wide her arms,
assuring me that the table would now fit perfectly.

Her "gentleman" meanwhile carted pieces of lumber past a
horrified Antonia, and the dining-room, for an hour or so,
became a carpenter's shop while he re-pegged the bits, and
hammered them home. Once up, it was perfectly clear that it
would never be got down the stairs again unless an axe was
used.

Madame, meanwhile, accepted coffee in an odd cup, and
cast an acquisitive eye about the bits and pieces in the long
arched room. She made me some not too bad offers, but I
refused them all politely, saying that I was not allowed to sell
anything on account of everything being listed on the Inventory. This she accepted, in a disagreeable way, and we went
once more to the dining-room where it was obvious to all and
sundry that the table was, indeed, a table and not a bundle of
old sticks, but, more important, that it was far too low, and no

chair would pass under it. This did not bother her in the very least. Holding out a plump palm for her six hundred francs, she assured me that tomorrow morning she would arrive with "four little glass things, which you use under grand pianos. They will give you all the height you need. And I won't charge." And left.

The table was a sorry sight; Antonia's face sorrier. With tears which she did not bother to conceal, she stripped the pieces of oilcloth away, revealing a wooden top covered in bottle-ring stains, and said that it was the very stupidest thing I had ever done. Eduardo said something useless to her like "Cheer up, Cookie," and started to sweep up shavings.

Order, my order, swept back. "Now look here!" I said. "I'm sick of eating crouched in armchairs and I wanted a pine table and here it is."

Antonia looked at me heavy with reproach. "If you eat from this table, sir," she said, "you will die instantly from stomach trouble. It is filthy. Filthy. All grease."

For three solid hours we scrubbed the damned thing. I removed a full tin mug of rusty nails from the sides, we burned the oilcloth, and scrubbed the wood again and again with a very strong bleach. And when we sat down to supper we sat at a too-low table, sideways. But a table made from solid walnut.

Not pine.

Madame arrived the next morning, not early as she had promised, but just before luncheon, while we were applying the first coat of polish to her bit of treachery. She had not found the little glass things which you use under grand pianos, but had brought, instead, a length of old wood which she said I could have free, cut into blocks, and le voilà! And then she saw the table.

"It's not pine!"

"No."

"It's walnut! Solid walnut!"

"So we have discovered."

"You have cheated me! I gave it to you for nothing!"

"You swore it was pine."

"How could I tell! Under all that filth."

"How could I?"

She left in a rage, bouncing down the track so that not a shock-absorber could have remained intact.

A few months later she was found in her garage, headless,

handless, footless, and run over five or six times by her own car. It was strongly rumoured in the village that she "entertained" Arab youths from time to time, and this was the unpleasant result. The house and shop have remained empty and derelict ever since.

But I still have the table. On wooden blocks. Free.

★   ★   ★

September came: the heat abated, the grapes started to turn, wasps droned among the heavy bunches, the morning grass was silvered with dew, and the great French holiday was over. Which meant that people started coming up the track to get things sorted out generally.

Electricians arrived and wired us up so that probable electrocution was not always as inevitable as it seemed it might be, but they never found a trace of the cut main cable, which stays a mystery to this day.

Plumbers came, mercifully, so that we no longer had to fill the baths with the shower-spray, a form of entertainment I cannot recommend.

A very strong man came with an electric drill big enough to bore holes through a battleship, so that pictures got hung, and a less monastic atmosphere prevailed in the whitewashed rooms and passages, and carpenters arrived to put up shelves and cupboards, hooks and hangers, followed by the plasterers in newspaper hats (to keep the plaster out of their hair, but not out of the rooms themselves, to Antonia's vexation) and covered unsightly pipes and built bookcases, in old tile and brick, so that gradually we eased into a promising, bright, and rather more comfortable life without the hazard of falling headlong over piles of books. What with a table on which to eat, pictures at which to look, and baths which flowed full and hot from real turn-on taps, we felt pretty well off.

I bought another table, this time of metal, an old restaurant table, large enough to seat eight. It stood on the terrace, and there one ate, while poor Eduardo and Antonia sat hunched at a fold-down flap thing in the black pit and I made plans, on sheets and sheets of paper, to convert the present woodshed and the olive store above it, which abutted the house, into a self-contained flat for them. This gave me great pleasure, but seemed, oddly, to make them rather uneasy. I couldn't quite work out why, but put it down to exhaustion, from which, in one way and another, we were all suffering. In any case, I knew that they had promised to stay with me for six months, to get me settled in, and then they would return to Valencia where they had bought themselves a small flat. However, stubbornly optimistic, I felt certain that if I built them a perfectly splendid little house up here, with this amazing view, this soft air, and gave them land for a garden, well: perhaps they'd stay a bit longer. They had been wonderfully loyal and good in agreeing to come with me from England and stay where I stayed. Rome had enchanted them. Venice they had loathed deeply. Except for the fact that they could go to Mass at the drop of a hat, almost anywhere. And they had liked all the churches and the bells but disliked, with vehemence, the damp, the water, the drains, and the people. Since Venice is all water, drains, damp and people, they had a fairly miserable time of it. Apart, that is, from Mass.

But how, I wondered, could they not love this present situation as much as I? No damp, no drains—almost none we even needed—and no people for miles. And Mass practically on tap in the neighbouring villages.

At supper, on the tin table, moths flopping round the oil lamp, a soft wind rustling the vine above, the darkness beyond infinite, save for the distant lights of Grasse on one side, and the rope of diamonds which wound itself along the Corniche far across the bay on the other, I felt almost certain they would fall under the spell, as I had done. Given time . . .

"Do you think so?" I asked Forwood.

"Couldn't possibly say. All people are different," he said. "But one thing I do know for certain is that if we are only allowed, say, well, five years here, it'll have been worth it."

The telephone suddenly rang: such an unusual occurrence in the house that for a moment I couldn't remember where it was, and panicked about in fear that it might stop ringing. It didn't, I found it, and it was my sister, Elizabeth, on a rather crackling line from Sussex, to say that our parents were safely on their way and should arrive at Cannes station early the next morning. Greatly elated, for I had not seen them for a year at least, I hurried up the stairs to the black pit to tell Eduardo who was stacking the supper plates and who told me that Antonia thought that very possibly she was seriously unwell.

Now I understood the unease I had detected.

Sudden shock usually spins me immediately into banalities.

"Eduardo! How do you know? Are you sure?"

"Not sure, no. But there is something . . . not so big, like this only; we knew in Rome."

"In Rome! But that's months ago, why didn't you say then?"

Eduardo shook his head. "We were not so certain, and you had the film before you, such a big job, so we waited. But now we have been to some doctors."

"Where?"

"Here. In Grasse. Instead of doing our French lessons. They think maybe."

"Then you must return home at once. Discuss this with your own doctors; you can't mess about with a thing like this in a language you can't even speak."

"It is difficult, and people here have been very kind. But I agree."

"Well, go downstairs and telephone Valencia and start getting things moving."

Eduardo lit a cigarette nervously. "It will take some time, to make appointments with the specialists, all thing like that, but I will do so, and we will go as soon as your parents leave."

Antonia had, tactfully, stayed out of the way, but now she came into the black pit to accept my embrace of gratitude, and also my reprimands.

"It will be well, sir, you see. But please do not tell your parents, it will spoil all their holiday, and we shall go as soon as they do."

So we agreed. Antonia and Eduardo knew, and loved, my parents well, for they had, as it happens, been "broken in", or whatever the phrase is, by them while I was making some frightful film in Budapest, and with my enforced absence the four of them, and my ever-loyal secretary, had managed very well indeed in the large house in England. I knew that they wanted my parents to enjoy their short stay, and that it would, as Eduardo said, take him time to arrange appointments. So for the time being, and it would be no longer than a week, we would concentrate on the holiday only. Now that we *all* knew there was a problem made it a little easier to cope. A burden shared. After that . . . well, we'd have to wait and see.

★　　★　　★

The Flanders Express was dead on time the next morning at Cannes. My parents were suddenly there before me; incongruous in tweeds and Burberry's among the hustle of shorts and summer frocks.

"It was bitter in England, yesterday. Oh! It's all so beautiful, Ulric! Can you feel the sun? It hasn't been as hot as this all summer at home; mildew on the roses: the garden's a wash-out."

They had little luggage, but I was glad to see that my father carried his old wooden paint-box and a small, folding easel.

"Oh yes! Couldn't leave this behind very well. You know, I never *did* get that green of the olives right in Rome. It's extraordinary!"

"Well, you've got four hundred specimens to choose from at the house, so it's just a matter of careful selection."

"Good heavens! Four hundred. Take me ages. But of course this is Cézanne's light, isn't it? Maybe that'll help me."

"Cézanne was a bit more towards the Var, some miles away really. This is Bonnard light. That do?"

My father slung his paint-box into the boot of the car. "I'll settle for Bonnard," he said.

The house was, as I had hoped, a great success, even roughly furnished as it was. My mother refused to take off her hat until she had seen every room, accompanied by a delighted Antonia, arm in arm, and my father begged, with eloquent signs of dire thirst, a beer immediately.

"It's a bit early, Pa. You sure?"

"Certain. A lovely glass of French beer. Stuff they're selling us in England really is piddle, you know. Awful muck."

My mother called down from their bedroom. "Ulric! Come up and look at the view, the mountains, you can see the sea and all the little boats."

"I *am* looking at it, my dear," he called, "through a lovely glass of beer."

We sat at the white tin table on the terrace, Labo leaping and squealing with pleasure at the remembrance of an old friend whom he had not seen since the far-off days of Villa Fratelli in Rome.

"Got a present for you, dog," said my father. "Where's my little hold-all? Get it for me, will you? All the presents are there."

A ball for Labo and four sticks of sulphur to put in his water bowl, and worm powders, a tin of hair lacquer Antonia had asked for particularly, Players cigarettes for Eduardo, and a half-a-pound of wine gums for me.

"And those are the real ones. None of those squashy substitutes. Look!" he said holding one scarlet shape against the sun. "There you are, 'PORT'. I don't know why 'SHERRY' is green all of a sudden, but I expect you'll find them just as good as they used to be. And here are some seeds: Canterbury bells, Shirley poppies, lupin, sweet peas, wallflowers and foxgloves. Must have a few foxgloves somewhere."

Looking out across my bouldered acres, where only teazle, thistle, broom and bramble seemed to flourish, I felt a sudden stab of panic. Had I gone absolutely mad? Made a gigantic error from which escape would be costly if not impossible? Could this long-deserted land ever be made to flourish again? Could it ever produce anything as ravishing as a foxglove? A Canterbury bell? At this tender moment of the day, just before noon, the September light spilling gold across the wilderness, it reminded me, with depressing clarity, of Chobham Heights, or, at best, a remote corner of the Shetlands.

During the last three weeks I had watched, with ever-increasing anxiety, the many workmen who dug deep into my earth in search of lost water mains, electric cables, and drains. My anxiety stemmed from the fact that everywhere they dug, the top soil, if that is what it could be called, lay ten inches deep only, and was limestone shale and dust. Below (for which they needed great picks and electric drills) it was solid rock, or as solid as made no difference. I was, after all, living on the side of a moderately high hill. Nothing, I was assured by one of the workmen, would flourish here without constant help. It was barren land fit only for the olive and the cypress, and in any case the Mistral, a particularly savage and unpredictable wind, blew straight down the Rhone Valley and hit the house dead centre. In the summer it scorched every leaf; in the winter it froze them.

I was in for a very agreeable time. Without Canterbury bells and foxgloves, it would seem.

"I'm sure you'll get round that somehow," said my father. "Things did grow here once, I imagine, and you have plenty of time on your hands to get things to rights, and of one fact I feel pretty certain; you haven't made a mistake in the house or the view. Magnificent! Just grow olives if the land beats you. I would."

My father, as far as I knew, had never so much as lifted a spadeful of earth in his entire life. Except, perhaps, on one or two occasions when we had had to bury a pet cat or a dog. Even a goldfish in a matchbox. But otherwise he was strictly a non-gardener.

My mother's distress each time he constructed *another* small bridge over a drain, or sawed down large branches from a tree which he felt obstructed his view, was often acute, for it was she who gardened with Old Charley, or Nick, or Mr Pierce, or whoever would come up and do "the heavy work". My father took his easel and his paints and drifted away into well-deserved relaxation. However, he did enjoy constructing hideous little hump-backed bridges out of bricks and concrete, and was a fiend with a saw and an apple branch. But that is as far as he went, and although we could, indeed we did, *step* across the tiny little drains over which he spent such hours of labour bridging, and had to cart away his wretched branches to cut up for firewood or kindling when he had all but wrecked the orchard, no one said anything, even our mother, because we all knew, very well, that working at "The Times", as he did, was a very demanding business. He deserved his relaxation.

His advice today, however, seemed very sound. If the land beat me, as I strongly suspected that it would, then I should concentrate on the olives. They'd been there for centuries bearing their crops and, apparently, flourishing. I should make them do the same for me. Exactly how, at that moment, I did not know. I had some hazy idea that it was a sort of Christ-like business: disciples, and loaves and fishes. Ageless somehow. Figures seemed to drift before me in flowing homespun, baskets on arm, bare feet treading beneath the venerable trees, culling the ripe fruits with slender Veronese hands. A Biblical style of life which had, in fact, existed long before that Book had even been written. Timelessness. Calm. Absolute rubbish: of course. Like so many of my fantasies. Had I been told then and there, that morning on the terrace, with my father swigging his French beer and swatting wasps, that my Biblical image would be cruelly shattered by the inescapable fact that the harvest took place in the four bitterest months of the year, December to March, that I'd spend my time, not wandering in homespun, bare foot, from burdened tree to burdened tree with a basket on my arm, but crouched on my knees in an anorak, sodden, frozen, fingers white with ice, gathering up the blasted little fruits one by one, mice-nibbled, worm-ridden, in a howling mistral, I might easily have caved in, moved to an hotel and pressed buttons for Room Service for the rest of my life.

As it was, thankfully, I was ignorant of the facts, and order wavered back; the great trees silver in the light reassured me of my dream, and my mother arrived on the terrace obviously delighted by what she had seen in the house, and the exceptional courage and determination of her eldest son. Or so I hoped.

"Well: I've seen it all. It's extraordinary. And how wonderfully all the old stuff from England fits. So awful about the Meissen birds, I could weep."

"Well," I said. "There's a lot to do yet, but it's beginning to feel like a home, don't you think?"

"Oh yes! And when you've laid the carpets it'll be much more comfortable."

"Oh. No carpets."

She looked at me uneasily. "No carpets? Just those rough tiles everywhere?"

"Just the tiles."

"But not in the long room, surely?"

"Yes. It's that sort of house."

"What sort of house? Ulric, open me a beer, darling, will you?"

"A shepherd's house. Simple. It stays that way."

"With no carpets *at all*?"

"No."

"The beautiful green one you had in the drawing-room in England?"

"Sold it."

"I see," she said, but clearly didn't. She sipped her beer. "I think it'll be hell in the winter. With no carpets."

"A bit of rush matting," said my father suddenly. "That would be all right. And some curtains of course."

"Ah no. No curtains."

"You *must* have some curtains," he said in surprise. "People looking in—awful."

"Shutters."

"You mean nothing in the bedrooms? Not even in the lavatories! You *must* have curtains in the lavs."

"Why?"

"Well . . ." he fidgeted a bit, stroked his nose with a finger. "Rather inhibiting."

"But who's to see you? Only trees, they won't inhibit you, will they?"

He shook his head. "Well, Margaret, how will you feel? Blackbirds and so on peering at you. Fearful business."

"It seems very strange to me," said my mother and stared vaguely up into the vine.

"I've fixed a sort of curtain in your bedroom actually; you are in mine, I've moved into the little room Gareth is having as his. I've put up a big bedspread. Just stuck up with nails, but it'll keep out the early light anyway."

"Well, that's a blessing," said my father, and finished his beer.

That evening I found the upstairs lavatory window neatly covered with Tuesday's edition of *The Times*.

My father was a very stubborn man. I discovered, many years after, that he was known, by some of the more irreverent members of the staff of that journal, as CD; which, literally translated, meant "Constant Dripping Wears Away the Stone". That was Pa.

## 3

IN 1892 Oscar Wilde wrote *Lady Windermere's Fan*, the first trains arrived at Johannesburg from Cape Town, Lottie Collins sang "Ta-ra-ra-ra-boom-de-ay", and my father was born in a pleasant villa in what was then a small village outside Birmingham, called Perry Barr. I was born in a nursing home in Hampstead in 1921 and did not really get to know him until one blustery April day twenty-three years later. Perhaps I should say that I did not get his approbation until then, when I marched up the steps at Sandhurst Military College as a fully fledged, shining new young officer ready, and even willing, I rather think, to die for my King and Country. Only we were already calling both those things "Democracy".

It probably seems a long haul for approbation, or even getting to "know" your own father, but that's how it went.

I had seemed, frankly, a dismal failure to him up until that time. His dream, as a stubborn man, from the moment that I drew breath in that Hampstead nursing home was that I should be trained, and trained hard, to follow him into the sanctity and majesty of "The Times". I was, however, just as stubborn as he, and nothing on earth was going to persuade me to climb upon that red brick altar in Printing House Square on which, my mother so often said sadly, he had sacrificed himself and his family.

Of course that part wasn't true. My mother had been an actress and rather preferred the twopenny coloured to the penny plain in speech.

However, that was to be my destiny. I resisted passively. Hopeless at school except at things like art, pottery, and bookbinding or metalwork, greenery-yallery bits of effort which would obviously be of no use whatsoever to a future in "The Times", he sent me off to the Sun Engraving Works in Watford to learn all about photogravure, where all I managed to do, in the time I was there, was to see "Snow White and the Seven Dwarfs" twelve times and make friends with a printer and his wife who bred budgerigars. Then, in final desperation, my stubborn father sent me to Chelsea Polytechnic to study art, since that was about the only fairly reasonable thing in which I had made an effort to excel.

This time things went slightly better: I was lazy; spent most of my time in the Royal Court Cinema or The Classic in the King's Road, but got excellent reports by doing *all* the term's work almost overnight. Among others, I had two splendid teachers, Henry Moore and Graham Sutherland, neither of whom saw in me the spark of actual genius: in fact many years later at luncheon in his house in Menton, Sutherland admitted that he felt certain I'd do "something quite good". But that it was certainly *not* to be in painting. However, I managed to ease my way towards theatrical design, in a slightly underhand manner, by being exceedingly pleasing to the lady who ran the Drama Society. My aim was in sight. The Theatre.

That's where I wanted to go, and where I was determined to get. My father was appalled. No job for a man, nor for a gentleman. No job, in fact, at all.

But in fairness, with the war looming just across the last peaceful cornfields of Europe, he sent me off with a pound a week in my pocket, for one year. In which time I had to have made my mark "definitively" or, and here his persistence was so remarkable, do as he said and start from scratch again: as an office boy on his sacrificial altar.

Well: I made my mark "definitively", in a very small way, in that year, and somewhat to my surprise he agreed that I could continue. Stubbornness had met stubbornness. But the war put waste to that agreement, as well as to many, many others. The fact that I had even managed to survive the Army did, I think, amaze him. That I should actually *enjoy* it astonished him.

That I was doing it, in fact, for him and for his long-sought approbation I don't think he ever knew, although from the moment that we met after my splendid parade, crisp in my new uniform, wearing the same Sam Browne belt that he had worn in his war, I knew him for the very first time as my father and he knew me as his son. It was a private, unemotional, extraordinarily deep feeling. And thankfully it was never lost. It would have been unthinkable to have failed him.

He viewed the years which followed the war, the years of my being a "film star", with detached amusement, really hardly taking them seriously at all, although he was pleased that I was making what he called a "go" of it and rather

35

enjoyed the trappings and things which come with film success: trips abroad, fast cars, and the fact that he could now manage to afford a "decent" red wine instead of the cheap stuff he had had to put up with before.

But at the very beginning I had not been at all certain that this would be so. The week in which my very first starring picture came out he dismayed me greatly.

There were posters everywhere, feet high sometimes, which pleased me in a rather smug way. Not very long ago I had been only a demobbed ex-officer hoping to get a job as a Prep School teacher, so the posters looked rather comforting, smothered, as they were, with my name in huge letters and that of my co-star, Kathleen Ryan.

One morning the telephone rang: it was my father. He sounded grave. Something, I felt certain, unpleasant had happened at home.

"I'm at the office."

"Well yes, so I imagined. Nothing wrong at home, is there?"

"No. You've seen the posters about this film of yours, I suppose, stuck up everywhere?"

"Oh those. Well yes, actually, I have."

"I just thought that I'd tell you that I have just come through Charing Cross Underground a few moments ago. There's a *mile* of them there, everywhere you look, place is simply littered with them."

"Oh. I see . . . yes . . ."

"I suppose," he said quietly, "you realise that you have brought the family name down as low as you possibly could?" And rang off.

Things which distress me very much, but about which I can do absolutely nothing, I tend often to try and smother into oblivion: not a good fault, I agree, but then I have never been a militant for hopeless causes. There was nothing that I could do about my name. I had altered it to some degree, and it had been printed a number of times already in a couple of television plays and a stage play. Too late now to try and scrape it off the posters plastered over half of London. So, after an anguished hour of worry, I put it from my mind and tried to pretend that the unhappy conversation had never taken place. It was never referred to again by either of us until many years later in a restaurant in Madrid when, for some reason, I suddenly felt brave, or emboldened, enough by the years to repeat the story in his presence.

His amazement was a glory to behold. Normally a very shy and retiring man, it was unusual for him to show much feeling in public.

"But good gracious! My dear boy!" he cried. "It was just a joke! Do you mean to say you've been fussing away about that all these years. It was just a silly little joke!"

"Well, it didn't feel like one at the time, I can tell you."

"My dear boy. Listen. Charing Cross Station is the *deepest* station in London, on the whole Underground line, didn't you know? Good gracious me! I really think you had better order another bottle, don't you?"

I did as he suggested, and the unease which I had carried about with me for many years was all but lost in the general laughter: at my expense, naturally. But all but lost is what I mean. I was not absolutely sure: he was, I knew well, capable of being genially mischievous.

My mother, on the other hand, was absolutely without mischief. She was far too Scots honest for that, entirely without guile, naive at times, at others extremely shrewd, she blazed with courage, and called a stick a stick. Not that it always pleased people, and sometimes got her into trouble which she shrugged off cheerfully.

When she married my father she had been a modestly successful actress with a burning ambition. A year after their marriage my father had to insist, and he was pretty good at insisting as I had found out, that she either stayed married to him or went, alone and forever, to join the Lasky Players in Hollywood who, she said, had offered her a contract. Which I personally doubt. But she was a very beautiful creature and it could have been true. Anyway: she *believed* it to be so. All her life. She stayed with my father. And that was that.

But, if she couldn't be a Great Actress, she was damned certain that at least she would look like one. And she did. She had an amazing eye for colours, for fabric, for fashion, and for finding strange items of apparel in secondhand shops or, her favourite place of all, the Caledonian Market. There she would rescue bolts of strange cloth, mandarin robes, tarnished silver belts and buckles, feathers and flowers and, with a long-suffering Lally kneeling on the floor at her feet, mouth stuffed with pins, grumbling, "Oh! Hold still, do! You'll have a wavy hem," concoct ravishing outfits which, if not altogether *à la mode*, could not be ignored, and in which she looked magnificent.

I remember once, when I was about ten, walking with her in Hampstead High Street. She wore that day, and I vividly remember it to this, a black wide-brimmed sombrero hat, and an enormous black cloak which billowed behind her elegant stride. Someone on a bus shouted, "Blimey! Look! Sandeman's Port!" and people turned to look. No one laughed. She was too splendid for that.

I was abashed that we, or rather that she, had caused a minor commotion. She was absolutely delighted, and strode ahead, eyes sparkling with pleasure, her modest moment of triumph seeming to envelop her like a second cloak.

For triumph, to her, it had been. No actress now: no chance of reaching out to be a Great Star; the Theatre and all its dreams had been denied her. But an audience had not. And by God! She was going to find an audience whenever, and wherever, she could, and if possible hold it. And this she always did, seeking it out, sometimes almost desperately, to the end of her days.

My father watched these dressing-up sessions, as he sometimes called them, with tolerant amusement. He was very proud of her, and loved her profoundly, never fully realising, I think, the deeply buried frustration and resentment lodged in her heart like steel darts and which she was never to lose, or forget, all her life.

Tolerant and amused, proud too, he may have been, but for some of the more formal functions to which they were bidden, from the Opera to Ascot, he insisted that she wear something rather more conventional. Which was not an altogether simple matter on the modest salary which he earned from "The Times". In those days, it was considered that the paper was run by gentlemen for gentlemen, and gentlemen had, of course, private means. Except my unfortunate father, whose only expectation of a fortune had been squandered by *his* father, who had spent it all "exploring the Amazon River". Years before.

But a close, and devoted, friend of my mother's was Yvonne Arnaud, a French actress of great wit, charm and warmth, and possibly, apart from me later on, the closest link she was to have with the theatre. "Aunt" Yvonne dressed only at Worth or Patou; wore those confections once, or at most twice, and then handed them on to Mamma. So propriety, and my father's anxious concern that perhaps his wife might turn up for a First Night of "Carmen" at Covent Garden dressed as a bullfighter, was put to rest.

She may never have been, who can tell?, a Great Actress, but she was a wonderful wife and mother. Our childhood was, it seemed, always summer. She was gay, funny, beautiful and loved us. She cooked and gardened, dealt with wounds and bumps, bad school reports (mine always) and assisted at the births, and deaths, of countless guinea-pigs, rabbits, white mice and stick-insects. Nothing surprised her, everything which made us happy, within reason naturally, she provided. She sublimated all her hidden frustration in her children and her husband, who had been through a hideous war which, although he had not suffered any physical wounds, had left him with almost unbearable memories and griefs, which she alone could ease. Naturally, we were completely unaware of any hidden streams of distress. They were always kept strictly away from us, and life was as serene as it could be; there appeared no cause for any alarms anywhere. Beyond my appalling track record at anything academic.

And then the war. An upheaval of unimagined proportions, not only for us as a family, but for many thousands of others. My unfortunate younger brother was sent off to a Boarding School; my sister and I, in time, went into the Services; Lally had long since left to look after her parents; the big house was sold up; and my parents moved on their own into a glum little cottage some miles away.

My mother embraced the war with open arms. Joined every committee she could find; fitted gas-masks, learned how to set a fractured leg, and everything that the Red Cross ladies could teach her. She arranged accommodation for the lost refugees from London, planted row upon row of garlic, to add some flavour to the miserly rations, cared and tended my over-worked father after his returns from London, and generally found herself so busy that there was no time to think, or for regret. In any case the most important thing of all was that she was needed.

And then the first Allied soldiers arrived in the area, the Free French, Canadian French, Canadians, and later the Americans. Life now took on a really glamorous hue for her. She was everyone's surrogate Mother: writing letters for the illiterate, cooking meals for the canteens, running an open house so that those who were lonely, bored, or had nowhere to go, could read a book in peace, talk if they wished, or bring out the millions of snapshots of wives and children "back home". She was vastly popular everywhere; not only because of the material things which she could supply, but because she was always gay, sparkling, laughing, warm and caring. Very unlike most of the tweedy ladies of the district who did their duty as a sort of moral right to King and Country: without the fun. My mother had a heart big enough for all. She now also had the one thing she most craved all her life: her audience.

And here it was; packed houses every night, adoring, applauding, avid for the stories she would tell about her years "as an actress" which had driven us, her family, to the brink of insanity with repetition, but which all her lonely soldiers had not heard, and didn't mind, if they had, hearing again. She said, often enough, that she was only doing her bit for the War Effort. What she was also doing, and doing extremely well, was holding the stage. Dead centre. And there is no question in my mind that she absolutely adored every minute.

She was very proud that I had managed to achieve a Commission for myself, and every leave I had was a big event: a splendid, for her at least, showing-off of her son. What she was doing, and doing so well, she hoped that other women in her position would do for me in distant lands. Although, to be absolutely fair, one could hardly call Kent, Yorkshire, Northumberland and Cornwall "distant lands". But they were to come eventually, and her generosity *was* reciprocated by other "mothers" from Normandy to Holland and much further East.

My father, overworked, exhausted, lacking sleep from the nightly raids on London which meant that he had to sleep in shelters or his office, wrote to me every single week. My mother wrote once or twice only in the six years. But always added a little scribbled footnote to his letters which, in a very little time, I learned by heart. It wasn't difficult. Short and to the point, it was always the same. "Take care of your dear self, and come home soon. Daddy will have given you all the news. Much, much love, Ma."

But I knew, or the actor in me knew, that she was working;

very happy, fulfilled, and at last finding herself In Demand and, as she used to be billed on her early stage appearances before marriage, "Always Applauded".

But it finished. The War. The curtain came down and everyone went home.

There was no one left on my mother's lonely stage, not even her children, for my sister married as soon as she could, I left for London and a round of job seeking, and only my small brother remained to her, in Boarding School. My father was still wedded to his paper, helping to rebuild it.

What to do in a glum little cottage under the Downs all day? The sound of applause was fading fast. The lights were down. There was no one left who remembered, and no one to listen, once again, to the stories of My Career. Suddenly, with appalling swiftness it seemed, she, in her late forties only, still amazingly beautiful, vivacious and alive, was, to all intents and purposes, alone. She called it "buried". Only my father and my teenage brother now "needed" her.

★   ★   ★

If it was finished for her, it was just beginning for me, and some of the pleasures, to be sure, she shared. Proud that I had made my way in a relatively short time, and that I was in "her profession" and doing well, she enjoyed the periphery of my early career. But it wasn't really enough for her own ego, although she did quite like being known as my mother, and often made sure that people did so. She was about the only one in the family who enjoyed it: my sister got sick to death of her relationship to me, with perfect reason, and angrily said that she had her own identity; my younger brother decided that my career might jeopardise his own, for he, to my mild astonishment, decided, at a very early age, that he too would like to be in the movies and gave a heart-rending story to some tabloid which made it clear that he was "in my shadow". All bunk, of course, and it lasted a very short time before he went off to make a name for himself in another sphere, very successfully indeed.

With time, often too much now, on her hands, my mother joined the local village Drama Society and started producing and, on one memorable occasion, acting. But it didn't last. She simply could not be made to realise that the people who joined the company did so for relaxation after work, as a sort of social pleasure. She looked upon it as a mission. If someone missed a rehearsal through illness, a dental appointment, a lost bus, or a death in the family, she was furious. The Play was All. The company, however, didn't in all honesty think so, and why indeed should they? It was a pleasurable evening out for them in the local hall, with a nice coffee break, home-made biscuits, and a gentle exchange of gossip. Anyway, it was only for fun.

Not alas to my mother, who took it deadly seriously, upset the company, and finally withdrew angrily. And that was that.

On her fiftieth birthday, without warning her, I drove in the morning with some friends to the dark little cottage under the Downs. We arrived about eleven o'clock. The house seemed deserted, windows closed, no sign of life. She was in bed, curled up on her side, the curtains drawn. She lifted her head. Even in the gloom of the room her face was a wreck, and I saw that she had been weeping.

"Darling!" I said. "What's the matter? Are you ill?"

"I'm fifty." The voice was dead with despair.

"Nothing else?"

"Isn't that enough?" she said.

As a matter of fact she was fifty-one. But, fortunately, we none of us knew it at the time.

In under an hour she was dressed, made-up, radiant, and we all went off to Brighton, had lunch at English's, and bought pounds of sweets in the shops along the front, for it was also the day that they came off ration.

A day had been saved by great good fortune, but the acute despair and the depressions which came later, suddenly and alarmingly, were to remain for ever. However, I had taken warning. And from then onwards I did my best to involve her and my father in as many of my film activities as I could. She really wasn't very interested, however. The theatre was what she knew about and loved, not the cinema. And her happiest times were those spent at the Studio, when Stella and Biddy, or Iris and Pearl, took her off to the Hairdressing and Make-Up Departments to turn her into a Great Actress for a couple of hours. In the triple mirrors.

One night, after some long-forgotten premiere (to which I always invited them but to which my father would only go if

42

he hadn't got to wear a black tie) she stood proudly beside me for the photographers' flash-lamps, a moment which she adored above all others.

"Was I all right?" I said. "I think I just pulled it off, don't you?"

"You were marvellous, my darling," she said, smiling and smiling. "But of course, you see, you get it all from me."

★    ★    ★

But that was all a long time ago; now here we were together in my new house in a strange land and she was over seventy: slim of figure, bright of eye, hardly one grey hair on her fine head. And she was bored.

We were reading, or at least my father and I were, the London papers which arrived a day late. She refused to read the "damn" things because, she said, she was on holiday, and could read all she wanted to at home. The fact of the matter was that she kept on losing her reading glasses and just couldn't be bothered to find them. Anyway, all she cared about was how hot, or wet, or cold it was in Sussex. Unless there was a really spectacular murder. But they didn't seem to occur as often as she would have liked.

"You know," she said suddenly, "you were conceived in the Hotel Crillon, Paris."

My father cleared his throat. "Margaret really! What a thing to say! How *could* he know?"

"I'm just telling him, that's all. He's living in France. I wanted you to be born in Paris, too."

I set my paper aside, recognising the signs of boredom; obliging. "Why wasn't I, then?"

"Oh," she waved a slender hand vaguely, "that idiot Dr Morgan, mistimed it all."

I knew my cues, knew too the following lines she'd speak. "And so I was born in a nursing home in Hampstead?"

"In the nick of time," she said swiftly. "Just made it. Otherwise you'd have been born in a taxi. God! You gave me a hard time, I can tell you."

I picked up my paper again and started to read.

She sighed deeply. "Is this all you do up here in the evenings?"

"Well, it's not bad, Ma. Music, reading, peace."

"Too bloody peaceful," she said. "I might just as well have stayed at home."

Writing this, reading it back, sounds cruel. It is not meant to be, and she didn't, I knew, mean exactly what she said. But she *was* bored. All life that was not before "an audience" was boring. That was the nub of the matter, and it never altered.

If I write here at length about my parents it is for one perfectly simple reason. I am half-and-half of each of them. I have inherited many of their faults and some of their virtues, naturally. To know the parents is to know, in part, the child. I recognise in myself today my father's stubbornness, his persistence, even his deep shyness and reticence. I also recognise, sadly, his particular form of selfishness, if you like, and the bitter depressions which, inherited by him from the aftermath of his frightful war, he handed down to me. Diluted, to be sure, but still very much there, and often a handicap. However, I trust that I have inherited his strange sense of order, for that he also had, and could not have existed without it: neither could I.

From my mother comes my easy boredom, my anxiety, some of the restlessness, all of the Theatre. I inherited her love for the theatre but never her passion or longing for an audience. I never even considered them, to be honest. Merely acknowledging that they were as much a part of the profession as the proscenium arch or the curtain. Of course I *knew* that one had to play to an audience: but as far as I was concerned they were just people who filled up the empty seats beyond my world. And the fewer there were of them the better I liked it: a sentiment which went entirely unshared by my companions, needless to say.

So there I was: the extravert and introvert mixed. The half-and-half. Clearly I was in the wrong job.

But it never occurred to me. I wanted to go into the theatre as a matter of course. It was as simple, as familiar, as unsurprising as breathing or walking. But I never, at any time, wanted the fame and adulation which is expected as a kind of essential in this career, I just wanted to act. I didn't much mind what, but to be there, to *do* it: the infinite excitement of representing someone else was overpowering, otherwise it was a stubborn, but passionless, love affair.

And then I discovered the cinema. Or it discovered me, to be truthful, and I was off. I loved, and I still do, the sheer mechanics of the cinema. Of working in a team, of learning from a team, of having, at the moment of greatest impact, no audience save the technicians who are assisting you towards that moment. They were, and always have been, the only audience I ever wanted, apart from the camera.

Forwood once said, "You know, I think that he really would like to make four films a year which no one would ever come to see." He was right. And often they didn't.

Of course, I had overlooked the fact that the cinema is money, and people have to come, otherwise no more cinema. So we had the audience all over again. But this was a subtly different one. I didn't have to witness their approval or disapproval: didn't have to hear the matinee tea-trays drop, the chocolates rustle, the drunk whistle from a box. I could be miles away while they were eating their peanuts and popcorn; I had done my work months before on a darkened set with my mates.

However, there were the dreadful premieres to which, while I was under contract, I was forced to submit myself. In agony I would go, in agony I would sit among them, in agony, but smiling (of course), I would leave. A dog returning to its vomit. A remark which once I made to my bosses with very unfortunate results. Of all the things I think I most detest about acting is the fact that one has to witness the spectacle of oneself doing it.

Now, of course, with television, it is harder than ever to avoid: but I do. I never watch a film of mine on what is called the Box: sometimes I have a look for ten minutes to see if the "print" is all right, what the colour is like, if my work has become mannered (it often has) or whether I am doing too much with too little (constantly). But never for longer. What was, was. It's over and done, and I have no residual sentiments whatsoever for the quacking little figure on the screen.

The only times I have ever enjoyed seeing anything I was in have been in a private projection room, with the director and the team, and a packet of cigarettes. That was peak-time. And, as far as I was concerned, the finish. The job is over, done and put together, good, bad, or indifferent. But done with as much honour as possible. It was only then that one realised that the whole thing was geared towards that invisible, for most of the time, looming bulk. My mother's deepest pleasure: the audience.

I had been working away all this time in a Factory-Fantasyland, absurdly overlooking the people for which this particular product was being produced. I suppose I really thought that it was only being done for me. Naturally, I learned otherwise.

★   ★   ★

Normally I detest September and dread October. I hate the slow decay, the fall of the leaf, the withering, the russet colours beloved by so many. I hate Michaelmas daisies, dahlias, and the mournfully urgent chiselling of the blackbird, the scent of bonfires and "the days drawing in".

But it seemed to me, on that brilliant September morning, that all these horrors might not occur here in Provence. Perhaps it wouldn't be autumn at all down here? Perhaps everything would sort-of just melt away, leaving no untidy traces of death behind to cart to towering rubbish heaps: but there was, even I had to admit, a certain charm in the turning of the grapes on the vine, and the soft yellowing of the leaves through which the still-hot sun filtered on to the lunch-table.

My father was wandering up the hill, hip-high in amber grasses and alien corn, the dog snuffling and routing in the track, like a pig snuffling truffles. I poured a cold beer.

"Golly! Just what I need. Gets jolly hot clambering up this hill." He settled at the table, foam round his lips. "Dog found a badger's sett right down at the bottom; you know you've got one, don't you?"

"Yes. Someone inside it too. Fresh droppings and a rabbit skin the other day."

"Got to watch Labo. He was very excited, they could give him a hell of a fight, he wouldn't stand much of a chance with that wonky leg of his."

"Four steel pins in it. Cost me a fortune, rotten animal."

" 'Course," said my father, wiping his mouth. "He's really a slum dog, isn't he? Not his kind of smells up here. Rather be in the gutters somewhere. You know, by the way, I have a feeling that under all this brush and stuff you've got a lot of old walls. He put up a fat green lizard down there and I poked about, and I think those big boulders are really tumbled walls. You'll have a hell of a job with them, won't you?"

"No. It stays as it is. Wild, savage, I'm doing nothing. Maybe sheep one day."

"But what *are* you going to do? I mean now that you've decided to chuck the cinema bit for a time? You can't just sit on your bottom."

"Don't see why not."

"You'd go mad. You've led a terrifically active life ever since the war, and even including the war; you can't just suddenly stop. Terribly bad for you. Bad for the system."

"Well, I told you in Rome: I might have a go at a book. Childhood."

"Oh well, that. Hmmm. I think you ought to have a look where I was this morning. I have a very shrewd feeling that this land was terraced once: and they are all there still. Splendid exercise for you, bringing it back to shape."

"All I'm going to do is dig over the old *potager*, grow a few vegetables, if the land will cope, some flowers for picking, and stick a few tubs and pots about. Pot gardening, I'm really not into archaeology and all that. If there are walls there they can stay. It's been abandoned for nearly thirty years!"

"What about my seeds then? The Canterbury bells, and so on; a few lupins. I do think you'd find it pretty boring up here after a while with nothing to do."

"Lots of natural springs about."

"I know. Soaked my good shoes." He peered at his feet.

"I might make a pond, have a few goldfish. Your feet really wet?"

"No. Ruined my shoes but not wet really. It was a little puddle, looking for the wretched lizard. What's that delicious smell coming from the kitchen?"

"Antonia's doing something heavily Spanish with rice and eggs. Garlic, I'd say."

"Yum yum," said my father. "Margaret," he said, as my mother came on to the terrace and took her place at the table. "He's just said he's going to do nothing here. Just sit on his backside. You have a word with him: he ought to start a garden, try and reclaim the land. He can't just do nothing, don't you agree?"

"Who could ever make a garden out of this wilderness?" she said sensibly. "You haven't the very least idea how hard it is."

"All I want to do now," I said, "is nothing at all for a while. And I'm not going to start a whole new deal digging up old walls. I haven't the money for one thing."

Forwood arrived with the wine. "Four francs fifty in the village, Ulric. I don't know if it's drinkable."

"Anything is drinkable in this lovely place."

"I think it's tragic," said my mother.

"What's tragic?" I said. You could never be absolutely certain which way she'd gone off on her own, or to where.

"Giving it all up. The theatre first, now the cinema. Tragic."

"It's not for ever, darling. A year or two or so. I want a rest, sort things out."

"I'd never have done such a thing. If I'd had your chances, my God! Just letting it all go and sitting up on this hill. Such a tragic waste."

"It's a very pretty hill, and I've worked very hard for a long time: now I'm just going to wait until I'm ready again. If ever. I'm doing it my way now."

My mother picked up her wine glass and made way for Eduardo who arrived with a large dish of saffron rice with eggs sitting in nests of home-made tomato sauce.

"Don't touch, Madame," he said. "Is very 'ot."

"So arrogant," said my mother sadly.

"Who is?" said my father, trying his wine. "Not bad, this. A bit sharp, but perfectly all right."

"He is. Your son. Arrogant."

"Hardly surprising, with his blood," said my father and winked at me.

"We're not an arrogant lot, are we?" I said, thinking of his humility and extreme good manners, his dislike of ostentation, travelling only ever third class, visiting his tailor once every five years, shopping for himself at Marks and Spencer. There was nothing arrogant about him, quite the reverse indeed. My mother might be a little more so: but in an "actressy" way. She was not naturally arrogant at all.

I started serving lunch.

"No, not us, I suppose," said my father. "It probably missed us, your mother and I, but perhaps you have got a bit of it. No bad thing, properly used."

"But where from, if not from you two?"

"Well," said my father, cutting himself a slice of bread, "your mother has the blood of the Buccleuchs on one side, and I've handed you down a bit of. . . ."

"Oh Ulric!" cried my mother. "It was all so long ago."

"Still blood. Wrong side of the blankets, of course," he said with a wide grin. "Very good blankets, but still the wrong side."

"But when, who, why did you never tell me this before?"

"No point really."

"The wine's gone to his head," said my mother.

"Oh come on, Pa! Tell me more."

He shook his head, grinning cheerfully. "No, no; no more. All done. That's it. You don't need to know anything else. Enough is enough. Maybe mother's right. The wine's gone to my head." But he was smiling. "I say," he said. "This is jolly good grub. Antonia really does cook marvellously."

We ate for a little in silence, looking out across the rough land, down into the valley, across to the smudged ridge of the mountains.

"Anyway: whatever you say. I think it's tragic. Just tragic."

"Oh, Mother! Do shut up."

"I will *not* shut up! I'm never allowed an opinion of my own. Can't even open my mouth. Tragic, that's what it is. It breaks my heart."

"Look, darling: I've only been here a month. I'm a new boy at school. Maybe I'll hate it and go belting back. I don't know. But I'm going to give it a damned good try."

"Well, I suppose you know what you're doing," said my mother, with a heavy sigh which clearly indicated her own opinion. "It's beautiful, absolutely beautiful, but it's a long way away, you'll be forgotten. I mean, after all, when did the telephone last ring? Tell me that? Not since Daddy and I arrived over a week ago. Silence. I'd go mad! They'll forget, you see. But you must do as you want."

"And so I shall."

"Arrogant," said my mother sweetly.

★   ★   ★

They left a couple of days later, brown, smiling, well: a little picnic of cold chicken and a bottle of a "not too bad Beaujolais" in a basket, and as I watched the train pulling out of the station at Cannes in the evening light I felt a deep surge of regret. Having them to the house had, to me, been vitally important. I wanted them to be the first to stay there, and they had. I wanted the "feel" of them about the place, the smell of his pipe tobacco in the long room, the sound of her busy feet clacking along the boards of the corridor, the sense of permanence they could bring, and did.

Like every other person I had forgotten, or chose not to remember, that mortal permanence is illusory. And that there is no such thing as "forever". Forever is just a measured length of time.

# 4

ON the morning after my parents' departure, Forwood drove Antonia and Eduardo down to the airport for their journey to Spain. They left with the bleak faces of people who are worried.

I was alone, suddenly, in my new, echoing, house. Not a tap dripped, no sound of gentle singing from the wash-house, no breath of wind. The vine hung still. No one slammed a door, rattled china, trod upon the stairs: the dog lay stretched as for dead in the shade.

It was a pause. Quite a long pause. Which, I confess, I had really not expected.

After the weeks of bustle and hustle, hanging things, un-wrapping things, arranging things with other people about me, after the months of work "inventing" Von Aschenbach, alone, so to speak, in the centre of a devoted team like a Queen Ant, of the years, in fact, of work, three or four films per year, more than twenty years of continual motion; after all that, here I was alone. And still. Sitting in the long arched room like someone who had missed the last train in a midnight station.

It was an oddly uncomfortable feeling. Rather as if one had suddenly slammed on the brakes in a speeding locomotive.

I had crashed to a stop.

To be sure, there had been a Past. There would be, I felt uneasily certain, a future, but at this present moment, momen-tum had ceased. I was an unwound clock. Timeless, silent, limbo.

I had wandered about the empty house, feeling an intruder, shy, in my own domain, of being caught peering into rooms which I knew, already, well.

Antonia and Eduardo's was stripped. Bare almost, as if they had never been. Would they, I wondered with anxiety, ever come back? Perhaps not. I'd be left on my own with only school French to help me.

Except Forwood, who had guided my career and work since 1939 and had volunteered, as his son Gareth was now a grown man of twenty-six and carving a way through his own particular theatre jungle, to join me in my exile. What else, he had reasoned, was there for him left to do? There was always the possibility that I *might* work one day again, and in any case I would need his help still, because every deed, clause and statement was firmly in his hands and head: he could also drive a car and I could not. He was in all degrees essential.

Perhaps, I thought, as I came down the stairs into the long room, my mother was right. It *was* too far away. "Out of sight, out of mind". I'd be forgotten. And it was quite true that, during their stay with me, the telephone had never rung. Not even a wrong number. Perhaps it never would again?

My fault. My decision.

The dog got up, shook himself into a scatter of legs and tail, stretched, yawned, curled round, lay down, slept.

Of course, if I was really desperate (was I?) I only had to pick up the crouching black telephone and speak to someone. About anything. Hear a voice. But my French, and spelling-out the London Telephone Exchanges phonetically, as one had to do then, was daunting indeed. Fremantle, Frobisher, Primrose were all so long, and the operators grew impatient and usually cut me off.

I should take my father's advice and go down to the bottom of the land and see just exactly how much brush and rubbish there was to clear away: perhaps have a look at the boulders which, he had assured me, were parts of long-fallen walls. This was the life, the life-site, the existence I had chosen: high time to get my backside out of the chair on which I now sat staring at the telephone, and go, in solitude and peace, to examine exactly what I had bought.

But if I *did*, supposing the telephone should ring? And I not be there to answer it?

"So what?" I said aloud to the empty room, alarming myself. "If it did ring and you were at the bottom of the hill you'd never know. So what would it matter?"

"Well. I don't know. They might be calling from the airport . . . flights to Spain cancelled, you know."

"Bunk. Excuses. Just admit you're in a funk."

"Not really."

"You don't think that this room will ever have people in it, do you? You think that you have severed all your ties, cut adrift, are floating into limbo."

"Well, that's all right. It takes time. People will come, of course they will."

"Certain?"

"No, not *certain*. But they will. It's early days. I mean, I have never really been absolutely on my own for years and years, it takes a bit of adjusting to. In all the other houses there was always someone around somewhere. Cleaning silver, ironing, watching TV, mowing lawns, peeling potatoes, that sort of thing: there was always a sort of 'life' about, a pulse beating."

"You said that you wanted solitude, now you have it."

"Yes."

"You so hated the telephone in England that you took it off the hook."

"I know."

"And now you are sitting here willing the thing to ring."

"I'm not. Absolutely not. I'm *glad* I'm here. This is what I wanted. I'm not going back on my word."

"What you *are* doing, mate, is talking to yourself. First signs of melancholia or advanced senility, something. I'd get your ass out of this chair and go up to the kitchen and wash the breakfast cups, clean a lettuce for lunch, start to function as you should. Away with self-pity."

Talking aloud to myself! Crikey! I rose from the chair in which I was slumped, my mood having slipped into total inertia and creeping depression, and made for the slate stairs and the kitchen.

A housewife. I'd become a bloody housewife, that's all. By my own choice.

The telephone rang.

An Olympic spring across the polished room, cracking my shin against a table, hobbling in agony to reach the thing before it rang off, catching it just, I imagined, in time.

Joyful voices! Old chums of many years suddenly in Nice, travelling home to Uzès in the Gard. Could I give them a bed by any chance, just for a night or two? Wings to my heels, cracked shin forgotten, lark-gay, stripping down Antonia's beds, throwing on clean sheets, scurrying about; a happy lunatic.

Of course people would come to the long room!

Of course I wouldn't be forgotten!

The telephone *would* ring.

It already had.

I put out fresh towels, blew away a thin drift of Antonia's talcum powder on the dressing-table, and started to sing. Very loudly. My sense of order had returned.

★    ★    ★

Thus, Daphne and Xan Fielding were the very first of the old crowd of steady chums from the past to come to the house and start the slow, subtle application of a patina of life on it.

There was laughter; discussion and argument, long conversations round a log fire in the late evenings, for it had already become cool once the sun plummeted behind the hump of Le Bois de Marbrier, and long lazy relaxed picnic meals round the tin table on the terrace in the heat of the day, or the cool of the early mornings, when the dew sparkled the spiders' webs in the long grass and butterflies, peacocks, red admirals, swallowtails, attracted by the nectar of the ripening grapes, flopped from cluster to cluster under the rustling canopy of leaves.

I knew, of course, that the house must have witnessed many lives in the centuries in which it had been built. Quarrels and arguments, laughter and deaths, births and toil. During the war it had sheltered, because of its isolated position, groups of frightened Jewish children collected from all over, who had rested up within its thick walls and then been smuggled, in the night, down to the sea where silent fishing boats bore them away to the Spanish coast: their names, some of them, still scribbled in pencil on the woodshed walls. The house had been filled with life: but since my arrival everything seemed, indeed had been, swept away, cleared and whitewashed, literally, and the old ghosts had fled. It was essential that a new force came in among the long beams and tiled floors. For the moment, spruce, clear, glowing, it was also to some degree sterile and without memories. They had to be re-started: no easy thing to do, and not one done immediately. One could not impose memories instantly, as one had imposed "age" on new plaster, they must develop. And the arrival of Daphne and Xan was just the start, the placing of a second layer upon the memory, already, of my parents' presence which had raised the curtain on my new beginning.

In the extreme pleasure of their company, with the pre-

1. ". . .I'd sit there on long summer evenings under the trees. . ."
The pond in its second year. May 1972.

2. At the tin table. My parents on their first visit to the house. September 1970.

3. 'La Malcontenta'. My mother by Hookway Cowles. 1923.
". . .I wasn't bad-looking, was I? Really not so bad.
I made the best of myself. Your old Ma."

occupation of meals to plan, washing-up, laying the tin table, cutting wood for the occasional fire in the evening, clambering together over my rough acres which, Daphne said, reminded her "quite amazingly of Crete" and on which Xan suggested that I had a herd of goats as soon as possible, who would deal with the thyme, the tussocks and the springing brambles, in all this I had completely forgotten the hunch-backed telephone until one afternoon, as we sat lethargically over the debris of a late luncheon planning how best to make wasp-traps, it rang. Shattering peace with an urgent bell.

Robin Fox, my agent, but more than that, a greatly valued friend, had fallen gravely ill just before I started work on the film in Venice. Months of uncertain news, of despair, rising hope, fearful operations and all the rest of the hideous things which accompany a desperate illness, followed.

He and his wife Angela had shared many holidays with me in various places from Padua to Rome to Hollywood and the awful Blue Room at Villa Fratelli, and when it was discovered that he was ill, we had made one of those rather wistful plans that when he was better (and we were all perfectly certain that such a thing was possible) he would come down to the new house high in the hills and convalesce in the calm and the peace, and above all, the purity of the mountain air. We called it "The Plot".

If, sometimes, I had an uneasy feeling that this "plot" was really no more than a ploy to keep his morale from crumbling during the interminable months of his illness, I let that feeling evaporate immediately at the sound of Angela's voice on the telephone. High, clear, confident, happy even. Robin was in good shape, the doctors had sent him off, recommended strongly that he should take his long-promised trip to the South and convalescence. They were, could I believe it?, presently in Paris and would take the Blue Train that night and be at Cannes early next morning. Was it too short notice? Had we all got settled in? Had we a bed? Wasn't it simply marvellous?

It was. It was simply marvellous news, and I quickly explained my situation, but that I'd go immediately up to a very decent little inn five minutes away and get them a room until Daphne and Xan left, in a day or so I guessed, and then the house would be theirs. The long-hoped-for "plot" was now, obviously, not a possibility but a fact. A day indeed for

55

rejoicing, I thought, as we drove down to Cannes the next morning in the early sunlight.

But early rejoicing is nearly always a mistake: the Blue Train, when we got to the station, was seven hours late. And any kind of rejoicing which one whipped up again, seven hours later, was quickly shattered into fragmented distress at the sight of Robin lowering himself very slowly from his carriage, a gaunt, ashen, aged man, stooped now and only able to shuffle towards one, a desperate attempt at a smile of welcome on his stretched lips, eyes blazing in a once-familiar face now the texture and colour of crushed parchment. Angela, leading him carefully, had mustered a brilliant smile and, braver than the brave, embraced me closely, explaining that Robin had had food poisoning all night, from something he'd eaten at dinner, and that they hadn't had a wink of sleep, added to which the train was so appallingly late, just their luck, but here they were now and wasn't it marvellous?

Well.

No question of a bed in "the decent little inn". As soon as we got to the house Daphne and I re-made my bed, and chucked some sheets on Gareth's bed in the little room next door. I would sleep downstairs on one of the sofas. The house, as once I had hoped and once I had almost doubted it would ever be, was full again: but not perhaps in quite the way that I had planned. But then, as one knows, the best-laid schemes . . .

Robin, a man of very firm decisions, of courage and, like my father to some extent, stubborn to a degree, insisted that he be shown round the house before he would even hear our imploring suggestions that a fresh bed awaited him. Leaning heavily on Forwood's arm, he shuffled from room to room breathlessly, but with intense interest, recognising, with delight, pictures and furniture which he had known in very different surroundings; amazed at the panoramic view before him of valley and distant mountains, and generally expressing himself delighted with everything, he finally insisted on a cold beer: and got it. He swore he felt better already, just being where he was, and breathing the purity of the air. After his beer he allowed himself to be taken up to bed, assuring us all that after a good night's sleep, etcetera, etcetera.

But it was not a good night's sleep which Robin enjoyed in my small bedroom. Very early the next morning I found Angela in her dressing-gown, wandering about in the black pit distractedly looking for a tea pot, a kettle, a cup. He had been desperately ill all night and most of the time delirious. Did I know of a nice little Frog doctor locally, because his temperature was still well above the hundred mark.

There was no French doctor that I knew—we hadn't got that far in the settling process—but Forwood picked a name in the directory which had an address the closest to us and, by the grace of God, the doctor was there, would come to us immediately, and knew the house from the past.

Xan who was, thankfully, bi-lingual, said that he would do the translating, since not one of the assembled group could speak much more than menu French which would be of little use to a medical man. Tactfully he explained that he would have to know the medical background, so that he could give the doctor a clear idea of what treatment was needed.

Angela was sitting at the head of the tin table, the sunlight easing in and out of the thick vine above. She pushed her tea-cup from her slowly and, as it were, laid her cards completely on the table.

Robin had cancer, and one lung had been removed; he was here because his doctors knew that there was nothing more they could do: this he did not know. He had so longed to make the trip that they were convinced it was wiser that he make the appalling journey than lie in his bed without hope, for even in the very blackest hours there could, couldn't there?, be a tiny spark of hope? It was, she suggested, for that spark of hope that they had come. A spark which Dr Poteau, brisk, efficient, sympathetic and comforting, swiftly extinguished for me as I walked him back to his car later.

Only months, he said. And outlined his plan of campaign to get the temperature down. He handed me a sheaf, it seemed, of prescriptions, said he'd arrange for the local nurse to come in immediately, and always twice a day for injections, warned me that none of us must smoke in Robin's presence, have a cold or a cough. He even arranged, with the care and immediate understanding which he possesses, that his laundry woman would take in the bedding, because we would certainly have to change all the linen twice, if not three times, a day, and I didn't really look as if I could cope with that too. Had I ever washed a double-bed sheet? he asked, and laughed when I said no. I watched his car bump slowly down the track.

Well: I had wanted people to come to the house, I had

wanted a "pulse" to beat, wanted the house to be a house again, to have the patina of life and of memories. And here they were, just beginning to impose themselves. It was idiotic that I hadn't quite taken into account that this could start with something so brutally distressing.

But then, I hadn't taken a lot of things into account. Life was all learning and burning one's fingers: grief was an unavoidable ingredient of the patina I sought, why did I think otherwise?

★   ★   ★

In the days which followed, Angela and I divided the chores between us, Forwood did the marketing, and a cheerful, very efficient, nurse arrived every morning and evening. We whipped off sodden sheets, remade beds; Robin's temperature started to drop, and one morning, bright-eyed and determined, he demanded a glass of champagne. He was on the mend. So far as any mending could be done.

Daphne and Xan had driven off home, tactfully, and Eduardo telephoned from a distant part of Spain to say that Antonia was all right: there was nothing at all wrong, no need to worry, but she was weak and tired and they would stay away for a bit; if that was all right with me? It was fine with me. I told him I'd call when they should return.

As September started to ease towards October, as the sun sank earlier each evening, the dew became thicker every morning, the days still blazed; and Robin gained strength. Sometimes he was well enough to come down and eat on the terrace, even though walking was a hazard because he kept falling over, which, in a man of some height, elegance and enormous pride, was wounding to see, though we all laughed as we hurried to help him up. But the days became happier, Angela braver. There were times now when it felt almost like the past, when we had sat together so often in England or in Italy, discussing, arguing, reading bits to each other from newspapers or books, listening to music, being together. All perfectly all right. A time switch. Each evening, about six o'clock, Angela went to her room to "preen a bit" as she called it, and would shortly re-appear fresh, crisp, groomed; pearls, a different dress, a cloud of scent about her. Immensely encouraging, and a swift reminder to oneself to change from the mucky garb of the day. It is something I have always admired tremendously in women, the extraordinary ability, which some possess, of being able to illuminate a room, lift morale, turn the edge of evening into an event, by nothing more, it would seem, than the changing of a skirt, a cotton dress, a quick brushing of the hair, a touch of scent, a stroke of lipstick all within, apparently, moments. Angela did this supremely well, charging the evenings with a brisk normality in which we all could function.

And then the mistral arrived.

I have lived here long enough now to know the warning signs: then I was quite unaware that there were any. I don't really think that I ever knew what a mistral was, except that it was a wind and blew sand into your eyes on the beach and sent the sea roaring. But just a wind, that's all.

The sudden appearance one morning of a shoal of slender cigar-shaped clouds drifting across the intensity of the late September sky gave me no cause for alarm. I accepted them as amusing and unusual and recommended everyone to come and admire them. We stood, that day, Robin supported by Angela, and watched with pleasure as the little silver zeppelins idled above us towards the sea. To us it was all a part of being "abroad", and "abroad" had a different sort of cloud; it also had a very different sort of wind, as we were shortly to discover.

First a zephyr. Nothing more. A breath which rustled suggestively, uneasily, in the vine and then went scurrying across the land whispering among the trees, swaying them, scattering fallen leaves across the terrace, sweeping dust into suddenly spiralling, eye-stinging, eddies. Then, gaining strength, it took off, and wrestled, tossing the trees like feather dusters, racing through the big oaks high behind the house with such force that they beat and swung, twisting, lurching, writhing, like a host of crazed Rackham witches, howling and rending.

Deck-chairs clattered, bowled over and over into the toss-ing scrubland, dustbins spun through the air and were lost to sight, shutters slammed, wrenched open, slammed again: dust and sticks, small branches, scatterings of grapes beat all about us until, unable to stand upright, we managed to drag Robin, and indeed ourselves, into the house.

Standing in bewildered disarray, the dog cowering in a far

corner, I saw a large potted fern, recently bought, career past the open door and explode into smithereens as it crashed into the side of the stone laundry-tanks, the water in which foamed and boiled like small Atlantics. It was all very impressive. I wondered how many tiles there would be left on the roof as they clattered down to shatter on the stones below. Not many, was the obvious answer to that. The roaring and screaming was such that we had to shout to be heard, and I then remembered the elderly builder who had told me that when the mistral came it would hit the house dead centre. He was absolutely right.

The only one of us who really enjoyed it all was Robin: he begged to be helped out again, notwithstanding shards of singing tile whipping about like shrapnel, and hung on to the orange tree by the door with both arms round its straining trunk, his head thrown back, eyes closed, mouth wide, gulping in the roaring air as it buffeted and bullied him, and far across the valley, high up on the mountains ahead, clear in the wind-washed air, I saw smoke.

At first I thought that perhaps it was scudding cloud, but in a second I knew that it was smoke streaming away in the wind towards the sea, for at its base, in the brilliance of the scoured morning light, there was a sudden leap of vermilion light.

The fires had started.

By nightfall more than half the long mountain range before us was alight. Acres and acres of pine and scrub, of mimosa and oak, blazed. Silently we watched the sudden shafts of yellow fire streak upwards when a great tree caught and burned, or the sudden bursts of billowing smoke from a house. And then we waited, dry-mouthed, for the explosion we knew must follow as the gas-tanks burst asunder, barrelling tumbling flames high into the crimson sky.

By morning the fires had reached almost to the sea, and they burned unabated for three days, until suddenly the wind dropped, trailed lazily off to Africa, and left the devastated land smoking in great clouds which curled silently into the high copper sky from a ten-mile ridge of black dust and cinders; the once pure air acrid with ash and the scent of burnt wood and earth.

Aware of Dr Poteau's strict advice, we had, on the first night, arranged that if by chance the wind should change and blow towards us from the fires, we would get Robin down to the coast by ambulance. But the wind stayed on its course and never veered. For days the mountains were blotted out in the thick haze of dust and ash, and the sun smouldered wanly in the sky like an umber disc.

And then, after all that, I caught a cold. Nothing much; a cold. A head cold. But enough to alert us to fear. It was time for Robin to leave.

"You know," he said on the morning he was flying to London, "I'm going because I *want* to go, not because of the fire and the smoke, or because of your cold; not for those reasons." He was sitting in a big armchair in the long room, a beer in his hand, which he could hardly hold but which he steadied from time to time with the other. "I want to go because I'm not going to die in your house."

"You're not going to die anyway."

"I'm not frightened of that. Bloody angry at fifty-six, but not frightened. But I'm not going to die here, in your new house, and leave you that memory, you're starting a new life. You aren't going to start it with a death."

At the airport, Angela pushed him through the barrier at International in a wheel-chair, he raised a hand, blew a kiss to the dog.

I never saw him again.

★ ★ ★

With the return of Eduardo and Antonia, relieved but 'flu-ridden though they were, a semblance of order returned to the dishevelled house, and I had the time, at last, to explore the land to which I had paid scant attention, apart from over-romantic delight. The fact that I actually owned twelve acres of France had seemed quite enough for me; what I did not know was anything about those acres in detail. So I set off. At close quarters, climbing and struggling through the wilderness, it was not greatly encouraging, and my father's ominous suggestion that the boulders were parts of long-fallen walls proved to be dismayingly correct.

The springs with which I had been so enchanted, the boggy areas of green watercress and rushes, the tiny rivulets which sparkled in the sun as they meandered down the hill among the myrtle, camphor and broom bushes were not, alas, quite what they seemed. So, call for expert advice.

A pleasant young man with thick-lensed spectacles, a box of many-coloured dyes in the back of his car, and heavy-duty wellingtons on his feet, arrived from the Water Department and, splashing about with the glee of a child in the soggy land, finally pronounced that it was flooded.

I suppose that I must have looked to him like a ventriloquist's doll, mouth agape, eyes glassy. For he explained, carefully and with infinite patience, that the many delicious springs and rivulets were not the result of Nature but were leaks from the reservoir buried deep in the hill above me, and that it was perfectly clear to him that my olives, to vulgarise Stevie Smith's immortal line, were not waving in the wind, but drowning. All four hundred of them. Their roots, he said gently, were deep in water and had been, by the apparent state of the land, for many years.

Gaining encouragement from my wooden-faced expression, he led me eagerly to the splendid stone beehive of a well which stood among the fig trees. Peering into the dark depths he assured me, with delight, that the water was doubtless polluted from the seepage of the septic tanks of the two houses on the top of the hill. To prove his point, and perhaps to try and alter my rigid expression of shock, he produced a phial of red dye from a pocket and dribbled it into my crystal well-water which immediately marbled into virulent shades of bile yellow.

His satisfaction was tremendous; his smile so warm and pleased that I shut my mouth abruptly, only to open it again when he asked, with enormous solicitude, if any of us had drunk from the well?

Fortunately, we hadn't.

"The solution?" he asked with a merry laugh. "You must sue the Water Board for gross damage to agriculture." Olives, he reminded me, were an extremely valuable crop. *Voilà*! Sue.

As my French was restricted to saying "Good morning", "Good-bye" and "Thank you", I didn't really see that I should get far in legal terms. In any case, I had been in France for barely nine weeks . . . it seemed a bit cavalier to start sueing people right, left and centre, let alone the mighty force of the Cannes Water Board.

The only other alternative, he suggested, ploshing happily along with me through the bogs, was to drain the land thoroughly. There was no point, it seemed to me, in having four hundred slowly drowning olive trees. Everywhere I looked I received silent reproof. I would be crippled with shame at my neglect for the rest of time. We would drain the land.

So one day a caravan of assorted trucks, camionettes, cement mixers, jeeps and dusty cars of various makes, came crunching up the track. A small crane swung enormous concrete pipes high above one's head and stacked them roughly against the shaking trees. They were wide enough to crawl through and could have dealt, easily, I was certain, with the entire sewage output of Paris.

Men arrived among this agglomeration, speaking many varieties of languages: some French, some Italian, some Spanish and Portuguese, others Arab. The once-calm oasis, where my badgers shuffled through the evening dusk, where my pheasants stalked with jewelled crowns, now rang to the urgent cries of many nations, the clang and crash of metal, the grind and squeal of gears. It all looked remarkably like a lift-off at Cape Canaveral: with more hysteria.

The star performer, like all true stars, arrived a little later and immediately dominated the scene. A huge, shuddering, orange dragon, groaning, howling, screeching, bowed its jointed neck and, with shining pointed teeth, ripped the soil of centuries asunder, tossing boulders, scrub and small trees about in wanton fury, biting deep into my limestone shale and dust, gorging itself into insensibility by the lunch-break, which thankfully arrived at twelve noon precisely. When a great silence fell. The men went off to the village to feed, the machines lay still in the sun, stinking of hot oil and metal.

I wandered alone among the drowning olives wondering how on earth I should ever be able to afford all this activity, quickly realising that to worry now was far too late, for the land was gashed and riven, criss-crossed with deep trenches which only needed yards of barbed wire to give a very good impression of a 1914–18 battlefield painted by Paul Nash or Orpen.

*　　*　　*

In a small dell, near the house, there was a little pool, inhabited by mosquitoes, and this I had long ago decided would be the basis of a pond; for water is an essential part of living to my scenic life. And so I had started to enlarge the area, digging away silt and sludge so that the water, which clearly was from a *real* spring and not one of the dreadful leaks from above, would fill out and make a fitting habitat for golden orfe, even carp, a waterlily or two and perhaps yellow flags. I'd sit there in the long summer evenings under the trees, maybe plant a willow even, and contemplate the book which I could feel stirring somewhere in my head.

My dell-digging, or pond-digging, kept me occupied during the roar and crash of the activity all about me, and I laboured contentedly. The pool area grew daily wider, I dredged up bucket after bucket of silt and muck, and was constantly happy to see the water run clear, until one day I noticed a small twist of paper swirl past my legs. It was nothing more than a scrap, possibly thrown there by one of the Arabs who, instead of going to the village for their mid-day meal, lay in Biblical scatters together under the trees and ate informal picnics. A couple of days later, knee deep in my pond, horror struck me at the sight of another fragment of swirling paper which, this time, it was not possible to pretend had come from any Arab picnic. It was instantly recognisable as a shred of flower-patterned lavatory paper. I knew it extremely well.

The bespectacled gentleman with his box of dyes was summoned. Eagerly he scattered his phial over my future carp-pond, triumphantly he cried, "*voilà!*" as it marbled from red to odious yellow, anxiously he inquired if I had at any time taken this water to my lips. Head bowed, I admitted that I had.

We clambered up the muddy bank together and he hurried off with more phials of dye and rods and poles while I swallowed a quarter of a glass of neat brandy. Two hours later he found the leak with the triumph and awe of Lord Carnarvon at the tomb of Tutankhamen.

The run-off pipe from my own septic tank was broken. My pond was the site.

I decided to pack everything "romantic" away, for the time being, and having been assured that I would not get typhoid, or worse, by Dr Poteau, packed my bags and left for London where I was to give a lecture at the National Film Theatre. Then, with my sister's invaluable help (women are so much less cowardly than men when it comes to fighting for their rights), I would go to the furniture depository where some of my goods still stood, uncared for and dusty, and demand some kind of justice for the destruction of all my Meissen birds and the rest of the things which had arrived that August morning in the container vans.

Elizabeth behaved splendidly: she went to war without quarter. In great dismay a huddle of the Company heard her out: grovelled with apologies which my sister turned aside as easily as if they had been scatters of confetti, and forced them to admit that "Our Mr Fellows" had been "very unwell at the time of the move."

"He wasn't 'unwell'," said my sister. "He was *drunk*! I saw him drinking almost all day long out of the bottles on my brother's table in the drawing-room. He was just swigging it down. Sherry, whisky, cognac, even vodka on top! He could hardly stand by five in the evening. I mean, let us be *quite* honest, you only had to look at his face to know he'd been boozing for *years*."

They paid up a very modest sum of money eventually, not enough by a long chalk to mend the Meissen, but just enough to prove their error and concede, very uncomfortably, that their Mr Fellows *did* have a "weakness", but would I please not mention this problem to any newspapers: it would prove to be greatly embarrassing to the firm. They willingly agreed to transport all the remainder of my possessions, which were surplus to my needs in France, to anyone I cared to name within the United Kingdom. The only person I could think of immediately was Lally, who lived in a tied cottage in Essex and who might be happy to have some extra cupboards, lamps and things.

She was. Or would have been. However, her cottage must have been very modest, not to say small, for none of the stuff would fit. So the firm had a wasted journey, which pleased me greatly, and they had to hump the lot back to London.

★　　★　　★

More years ago than I care to remember now, Capucine and I sat in brilliant sunshine on the terrace of a small restaurant near La Napoule eating oysters with a bottle of champagne, and rosemary-grilled *rouget* netted from the sea below us. It was two days before Christmas and our inordinate delight in each other, as well as the brilliance of the morning and a plump mimosa bush singing with bees, has stayed in my mind always.

I have forgotten, to be sure, many of the things which followed in the years to come, but never that moment: and it fixed in my mind forever the fact that Christmas on the Riviera would always be as warm, as golden and as pleasurable as it was on that long-lost day.

But not so. The first Christmas on the hill was as brutal as it was unexpected. Two days before Christmas, Gareth Forwood (he had just arrived to join the "family" for the celebration; if that's what it can be called) and I crunched over thin ice-fringed puddles, stamped frozen feet, crouched against the knifing wind which swung down from the hills, and in a grey light, as cheerless and bitter as remotest Sweden, went to admire the four big cypress trees which had recently been planted above the house. They had transformed the place splendidly from a Provençal kind of *Wuthering Heights* to a well-framed, friendly and welcoming abode. It was also, the local dustman who lived below told me, essential to have them. They kept off the Evil Eye, assured fecundity, and Faith, Hope and Charity.

I had planted the four, and they had cost a great deal of money; the eldest and tallest having reached the age of thirty years, the other three a more modest twenty. I was learning, very quickly, instant gardening. At a price.

Earlier in the morning in Rue d'Antibes in Cannes where we had gone to do the shopping, the first snowflakes fell and all the shopkeepers came running into the street in amazed delight at the sight, cupping them in their hands before they reached the pavements. It obviously gave them the greatest pleasure: it depressed me beyond words.

I hate Christmas. I hate its false good humour, its gluttony and greed, the idiot cries of "Peace on Earth" and all the rest of it. In actual fact the French manage it a great deal better than most people, and it is for them a holy occasion as well as a gathering of the family. I do my level best always to ignore it: beyond the obligatory gifts to local tradesmen and the reluctant sending of a few cards to people "abroad".

But this year, because it was my first in the house and Antonia and Eduardo's last, for they were leaving for Spain and retirement on New Year's Day, I decided that we'd have the wretched turkey, which pleased Antonia, but no decoration of the place with holly and mistletoe; to her chagrin. The turkey would be my sole contribution to that hypocritical day.

Antonia, naturally, was surprised at my apparent meanness, but on the night, sitting at the head of the long walnut table, elegant in black velvet and a rope of pearls, with a couple of goodish bottles of wine and the candles burning steady in the warmth, she enjoyed herself as we all waited on her, perhaps inelegantly, but with affection. And then we all shared the washing-up and went down to the big fire in the long room.

Sitting in the light of the fire, listening to Mozart, a cognac at hand, the dogs snoring, we sat in peaceful comfort together, relaxed, warm, replete. What more, I wondered, could one wish?

Of course, it is possible that Labo, the Roman slum dog who had chosen me to be his lifetime companion, much against my will and better judgement initially, might well have wished that Forwood had stayed his hand when he had purchased an eight-week-old Boxer bitch to be company for him when I was away, as I often was in these early months, in London or Rome.

Days before a departure, without a word being said, a suitcase being handled, a drawer opened, Labo would know what was afoot and begin shaking from head to tail wretchedly, trailing one from room to room, afraid to leave one's side for fear that one would leave his. It was a very distressing business: something had to be done, and Forwood had done it.

She had come from a very chic pet shop in Cannes a few weeks before: no puppy bought in a chic Cannes pet shop, just before Christmas, can be a good buy. And she wasn't.

She arrived with a smudged-brown bunface, enormous pads, no pedigree of any sort, worms, and rickets from gross underfeeding. Labo found her instantly disagreeable, thieving, greedy, and over-demanding of our affections. He resented her bitterly: but she stayed; we called her Daisy, and here she lay, bloated with turkey pickings, velvet face crushed deep into Antonia's indulgent and caressing hands. With the music, perhaps also the wine and the cognac, I looked about me in the warm glow with deeply satisfied pleasure. Taking stock.

At least from where I sat it didn't look too bad to me. We had made it into this new life, and somehow I had the impression that things were going to be all right: the house was a real house after all. Not just an empty Set.

My father had always believed that Christmas, rather than New Year, was the time to do a little stock-taking; it was the time for looking back and checking up on your life's balance. He would sometimes alarm unprepared guests at his, or my, Christmas table, when he stood to propose his annual toast, "To absent friends". In some strange way he would charge it with a sense of finality. Instead of thinking of people one loved who might presently be in Kenya or California or merely London, S.W.3, one had a distinct impression, for some reason, of Kensal Green or, anyway, of cemeteries. Many a gay and laughing heart was chilled by this toast offered across the remains of the pudding and exploded cracker-papers, and it was often followed by a sudden and intense series of worried silences, bowed heads, and murmurs of assent.

A very cathedral-like atmosphere indeed: which didn't go at all well with the paper hats and champagne. However, it lasted but a moment, and Lally always said that it was "just his little way". He was reminding us all that there was a bit more to it than just a feast of food and wine and high spirits. A gentle warning perhaps, that we had, according to our ages, spent time. . . .

Taking stock, as I now was doing, adding everything up in the last months, the extreme pleasures, the sadness, the shock surprises, the destruction of goods and chattels, of broken drains and lost electricity, of ruined wells and carp-ponds fed by a shattered septic tank, of too much money spent from too little an allowance, of rats in the roof, the terrible fires of September, and many more things besides. It might have seemed to be quite a lot for so short a time: but the happiness I now felt, induced by wine or Mozart or just the sense of ease and order at last, didn't seem to me to be too bad a total for such a sum.

And the fears that I had secretly entertained, at first, that I had made a frightful error, that I would be indeed forgotten, friendless, left a recluse five hundred metres up in a foreign land, had been unfounded. The reverse had been true, and even the hunch-backed telephone which once so unnerved me had grudgingly come to life, becoming, in time, almost as irritating as its predecessors in England. But it brought great consolations, not the least of them being the husky, impatient, for he hated telephones as much as I, voice of Visconti.

" 'Appy. Very 'appy," he had said one day in October. "I have seen the first rough assembly of the film, and it is not so bad: not so bad at all."

"Thank God for that!"

"Not God! Thank me," he said. "We have no music yet, but otherwise we have a film. You will come soon to Roma please, to see it, for I must take it to terrible Los Angeles to show the Americans. Like a poor student. Dio! They say to me, 'Sure, sure, Signore Visconti, *maybe* you have a fine film, but will they understand it in Kansas City?' What a remark. Bogarde! Where is this terrible place of which they are so afraid?"

"The Middle-West, I think."

"Of China, is it? Pouff . . . they behave 'orrible to me as always. *Merde* to Kansas City! You will come soon?"

"After Christmas, Luchino, I have to see my dentist."

"*Dentist*! You have so little finesse: no polish. You understand what I say? When I ask you to come to see *my* work you speak of a *dentist*! Dio mio . . ."

"As soon as possible, I promise."

"You have the toothache, this is it?"

"Yes."

"With so little sensitivity how can you know? Eyee . . . I must be patient: so all Roma must be patient until this dentist has done his work. Ecco! For your teeth we wait. We must. Ciao, Bogarde."

Remembering this in the firelit room, I laughed suddenly at the pleasure of recollection. Daisy farted. We all laughed and carried her out to the terrace. Heavy snow was falling. We looked at each other in astonishment.

A very strange five months.

## 5

THE rough-cut, or rough-assembly of a film is just exactly that: rough.

It is inevitably a depressing affair to the uninitiated, and very often to those who are not. In general it looks like a bad set of home movies. Scenes are stuck together in sequence, so that a "shape" is apparent, but there is no grading of light, of sound, of colour. There is no music track, there are no credits; not a single thing which looks, or feels, like cinema.

It is a scratchy, jerky business, best observed only by those with the strongest hearts and expert knowledge. Which is why many directors, rightly, refuse to let their actors see them. Actors, in general, have a great deal of ego. A bad rough-cut (and most of them are) is enough to send them wandering to the nearest river bank or whimpering round town that the film is "frightful!" What they actually mean is that they were unsatisfied with their own presentation, profile, or perform-ance.

The film, which is all-important, is forgotten.

The self-appointed intellectual film critics, and there are quite a number of these today, would probably sit through the whole business enthralled that they were in the know, as it were, and would certainly dub the result with their most often used words of approval: "gritty" and "grainy".

And in this I could not fault them.

That's how I first saw "Death in Venice" at three o'clock one afternoon in a cold projection theatre in Cinecittà Studios, Visconti sitting in a canvas chair surrounded by various members of his family, or such members as he deemed fit to witness the unveiling of his work, plus a few select members of the troupe.

There was a discreet flurry of princesses, a contessa or two, three or four actors who were *not* in the film but whom he had honoured because he knew that their sycophancy would be useful to him beyond the confines of the Studio. Men like Visconti always keep a little squadron of "favoured" people, the pilot fishes round the whale. He knew he could count on them to talk, in the most favourable way, about the film from Milan, Rome and Naples, to Paris and London if need be. They never failed him. If they did, their fate was a slow death from social, and theatrical, suffocation.

I can't remember, today, just exactly how I felt that afternoon when the last image flickered through the projectors. Numb; I do remember. That the film had a great, and curious, power, that my own performance depressed me deeply, that it was very beautiful to watch. Not more than that.

However, Forwood correctly said that I was too close to the subject to be objective or dispassionate, and that on this occasion it was wiser to behave politely and say as little as one possibly could.

Which wasn't, after all, very difficult. I had nothing to say.

Visconti, a cigarette stuck permanently between his fine strong fingers, received the homage of his Court with Pope-like dignity, moving his head in a gentle nod here, bowing there, waving a vague cigaretted hand at a shadowed figure, and greeting me, eventually, with two paternal pats on the hand.

"Ah! Bogarde. Va bene? No toothache today? And not tomorrow! For tomorrow we must re-voice some lines. You noticed? A motorcycle in the gardens, and those damned motor boats on the canal, but it is very little. Just words here and there: so no toothache tomorrow, eh?"

"No toothache tomorrow, Luchino."

As I turned to leave he suddenly halted me with my name.

"Bogarde!"

I stopped at the door.

"Bene?" he asked quietly.

"Bene," I said. "Molto bene."

His eyes were grey, clear, direct. Very still. Making me an accomplice.

"Grazie!" he said quietly, and then turned to someone who had come to kneel at his side with a favour to ask, or a compliment to pay.

Leaving the Studios, my heart lifted a little: I knew that he was pleased with the work we had done, even if I was not particularly certain, or pleased, about my own contribution. And there was further confirmation of his pleasure later when we were all bidden to supper with him at Gigi Fazzi. A certain sign of his confidence and content.

In Forwood's diary for that afternoon, he has written of the film, "tremendously impressive".

That same evening I wrote a letter from the Hassler Hotel to an American woman in New England:

*"He [Visconti] gave us a splendid supper later at Gigi Fazzi, the latest 'in' restaurant. A lot of noise, clattering of knives and forks, bowls of fettuccine, red wine flowing, a great deal of chattering and laughter. Why is it, do you suppose, that the Italians have fifty words to every one of ours? I could never learn to speak it, which annoyed V. very much.*

*"Anyway: it's all done now, and I am writing this in a rush so that I can get it off to you before I leave for work in the morning.*

*"I think that I have possibly failed in the film: a good 'try', but I don't think that I have quite done it. My fault: not V.'s by any means. He says that he is very happy with my work, but I wonder? I have a nagging doubt. Sad. But I suppose that it had to happen one day. I have had a very good innings: it is just possible that I attempted too much this time. Oh well. What is it you say in your country? 'That's the way the cookie crumbles?' Anyway: I did it. And I tried like hell."*

★    ★    ★

In time the film was finally finished. Scored, dubbed and all the rest of it, and Visconti, who had amazingly managed to keep it to himself and his technicians and not show it to the American Money, as he called them, was finally forced to go to "terrible Los Angeles" and show them what they had, in part, paid for.

It was a "Full House" I was told, and when the lights went up in the Los Angeles projection room, there was not a sound, and no one moved. Visconti said that this encouraged him enormously: obviously they had been caught up in the great emotional finale of the film.

Not at all. Apparently they were stunned into horrified silence.

No one spoke. Some cleared their throats uneasily, one lit a cigar. A group of slumped nylon-suited men stared dully at the blank screen.

Feeling perhaps that someone ought to say something, anything, a nervous man in glasses, got to his feet.

"Well: I think the music is great. Just great. It's a terrific theme. Terrific! Who was it did your score, Signore Visconti?"

Grateful that anyone had shown the remotest interest in his film, Visconti said that the music had been written by Gustav Mahler.

"Just great!" said the nervous man. "I think we should sign him."

Much later, safely back in Rome, we laughed. But no one laughed that day; least of all Visconti.

It was finally decided that the film was "un-American", and the subject matter very dangerous. It would never be a commercial project, and sure as eggs were eggs no one in Kansas City would know what the hell it was all about. It was even suggested, with some tact but not much, that if the film were ever to be distributed in America it could be banned on the grounds of obscenity.

Visconti and Bob Edwards, his Associate Producer, came back to Europe with the film, so to speak, under their arms. In a state of great depression.

I, of course, was blithely unaware of all this, paddling about on the edge of my new pond, which I had got the orange-dragon to scoop out during all the drainage business. Life on the hill was calm and serene, ordered. A pleasant elderly couple, Henri and Marie, had arrived to take over from the departed Eduardo and Antonia, and I spent most of my time either in the pond, arranging rocks about in "romantic" Salvatore Rosa cliffs and cascades, or hacking out the neglected *potager* so that a modest rose garden could be started. I was quite unaware that probable disaster was winging its way across the Atlantic.

The sun shone, the skies were clear, mine at any rate, and I was delightedly easing into my period of retreat with a smug pleasure and a varied set of garden tools.

In Rome the situation was quite different: Visconti remained at loggerheads with the Americans, refusing their suggested "cuts" and even, it was rumoured, a new, and happy, ending.

"How," Visconti had cried in despair, "can I give Thomas Mann a happy ending? It is what he wrote, it is his conception, it is the story, it is sacrosanct!"

Although, at first, I was out of this struggle, Bob Edwards began to keep me in constant touch by telephone, and each week seemed to bring more evidence of a total deadlock. It appeared perfectly clear to us that the American Money wanted the film "killed": this is something which has happened often before. I am told a "loss" is often set against taxation.

However, Visconti threatened to make "a great scandal in all the world papers if such a thing should happen" each time anyone in Los Angeles even reached for a telephone.

One evening Edwards called from Rome.

"Someone, how is it? John Julius Nor-wich? He's a lord or something, you know him? Well: he's started some fund to try and save Venice from sinking. It's called 'Venice in Peril' and he wants to have the film to run as a Charity First Night in London, very expensive seats, and the Queen has agreed to attend and has said that she will bring both her children. How about that!"

"When?"

"Soon as we can get things fixed up. We're working on March 1st, her first free night."

The excellent John Julius Norwich, it would seem, had perhaps saved "Death in Venice". It would remain to be seen if his valiant efforts could save Venice itself.

The Queen, anyway, had graciously accepted, at pretty short notice, and, as Visconti said to Los Angeles, "If you say it is 'off', that you will not show it, then *you* will tell the Queen of England. Not I. I do not. *Never.*"

We were "on".

On January 19th I was telephoned from London to be told that "we want you here about February 24th for pre-publicity on the movie. It opens March 1st, a Monday, so we want to try and get the week-end journals."

I said that I was not at all certain that I would be there.

"But you *have* to be there!" said an exasperated male voice.

"Listen! I don't *have* to do a goddamned thing. I did the film. That's enough."

Hearing, once again, the familiar, chivvying voice of the commercial cinema, knowing a little, but enough, of what Visconti and Edwards had had to deal with in "terrible Los Angeles", I regrettably allowed anger to overrule good manners: it was an intrusion, that voice, into the calm, orderly, very satisfying form of life which I had elected to live.

Of course, I knew perfectly well that nothing on earth would make me betray Visconti in any way whatsoever. I'd support him through whatever hells were ahead, but I would never again allow myself to be *ordered* to do anything by the cinema. I had had years and years of it. Enough was enough. As far as I was concerned it was all over, for the time being. I'd only ever return on my terms. Never on theirs.

"We'll get back to you," said the exasperated voice a little more calmly.

"I'll get back to you," I said. "If I have reason to," and hung up.

I felt amazingly refreshed! Golly! When the worm turns. . . .

I found Forwood digging away in the *potager*; sacks of peat and manure all about.

"It's definite, I gather. March 1st in London. Some Royal Charity thing."

"Well: that's something. What did you say?"

"That I'd consider it."

"Did you now. Well . . ." he thrust a spade into the earth. "You'd better have a look at your old dinner jacket."

"Why?"

"Moths."

"The hell with it. There's plenty of time."

The next evening Joseph Losey telephoned from London to say that Robin had died.

\*  \*  \*

More than a year before all this, an advertisement had been placed in the papers in Stockholm, Oslo and Helsinki as well as Copenhagen, to the effect that a youth, aged between thirteen and fourteen, was being sought by Visconti to play an important role in his forthcoming film, "Death in Venice". The role of Tadzio.

Wrapped in furs, scarves, and wearing a huge fur hat with ear-flaps, he set off into the snowy wilderness of Scandinavia like a very chic Eskimo. He thought to be away at least a month. As it happened, the very first boy brought to his hotel in Stockholm by a hopeful grandmother was, in his opinion, the one and only person to play Tadzio. Nevertheless, he was honour-bound to follow on with the tour so as not to disappoint the hundreds of anxious parents who dragged their children to the interviews in the hopes of instant fame.

However, he was certain of his choice, but went on with the tour anyway, though he saw no one who could even equal the boy, and on March 1st, 1970, Edwards telephoned in great excitement to say that Visconti had found his Tadzio and was starting the negotiations.

Exactly one year later, to the day, I stood in line with the boy awaiting the arrival of the Queen under an "EXIT" sign in the Warner Cinema, London.

In physical respects Björn Andresen was the perfect Tadzio. He had an almost mystic beauty. On the other hand he had a healthy appetite for bubble gum, rock and roll, fast motor-bikes and the darting-eyed girls whom he met, tightly jeaned, ruby of lips, playing the pin-tables in the local hotel bar on the Lido.

The last thing that Björn ever wanted, I am certain, was to be in movies.

What he did want was a Honda. The biggest and most powerful ever made. He spoke almost fluent English, but in that curious mutilated manner used by American disc jockeys. Which was perfectly reasonable, as he spent most of his time listening to the American Forces Network.

Thus, almost every other word was punctuated with "Hey!" or "I dig!" or "crazy", or most often, "man!".

Fortunately, as Visconti said dryly, he would never be required to open his mouth as Tadzio, so that the "enigmatic, mystic, illusion" which he appeared to have could be pre-served. It was absolutely essential that it was; which was why he was never allowed to go into the sun, kick a football about with his companions, swim in the polluted sea, or do anything which might have given him the smallest degree of pleasure.

He suffered it all splendidly, even the governess, sent by the Swedish Government, with whom he had to spend any time that he was not required on Set working. The only time he had to himself was at week-ends, if we didn't work, when he went off to the pin-tables in the little bars along the Lido.

On many a Monday morning he arrived for work with eyes hooped in mourning, and a pallor which was neither enig-matic nor mystic but almost close to death with exhaustion.

"When did you get to bed, Björn?"

"Heck, man, I didn't go to bed, we danced and danced. It was groovy, man."

"Well, get into make-up, for the love of God."

And he'd go like a lamb to the slaughter. And fall asleep within ten seconds of his backside hitting the chair.

However, his manners were at all times impeccable, he was never late, and never once was he not ready for a "scene". He was unafraid of Visconti, even in a rage, and perhaps the only fault he really had was that of chewing away constantly at slabs of black bubble gum which he would blow into prodigious bubbles until they exploded all over his face; or yours if you were close enough.

We were not what you could call a rich company. By that I mean no one had vast film-star trailers with showers and TV: no one even *had* a trailer. We made up, and got dressed, in whatever school room, church, deserted palazzo, or cellar was nearest to the location we were using in the city. Sometimes we even did it all in small, noisy bars, dodging frantic waiters, deafened by shouts, and the hissing of the Espresso machines.

One night, early on in the production, we were all gathered together in a dank, abandoned chapel. Björn and I were dressed and ready (it didn't take either of us long). All round people were being laced into desperately tight corsets, having their hair teased, curled, waved and pinned up (Visconti insisted, rightly, that hair was living and he would never allow anyone to wear a wig: dead hair, he said, *was* dead; and that was that), while others were being painted and powdered. A little removed from us, as she almost always seemed to be in some curious way, Silvana Mangano sat in a chair doing a crossword. Her hair and make-up finished, but not yet in her costume. She wore a pair of slacks and a fur coat; quiet and contained.

"You know, man?" Björn was twisting his sailor cap thoughtfully in his hands. "You know, she is just so beautiful. Don't you think so?"

"Yes, I do. The funny thing is, she doesn't. She thinks that she is plain."

"You kid me! She thinks that? I think she is the most beautiful woman I have ever seen in my life, man."

"Why don't you tell her? Or have you?"

"Tell her! Crazy, man, crazy."

"I think that she is too. Why don't we go and tell her?"

He looked at me with astonishment. "Tell her. She'd think we were nuts."

"No she wouldn't. If you really feel that about her, that she is so beautiful, then I think it is your duty to tell her so. It's a very great compliment from a young man: I'll come with you."

"You would?"

"Sure. We'll both go across and kneel . . ."

"Kneel!" He looked horrified, twisted his cap round and round. "Kneel, man!"

"You can't make a statement of that kind to a woman if she is sitting and you are towering over her, and so we kneel."

Which we did, one on either side of her chair. Silvana looked up without surprise.

"We are probably interrupting you . . ." She waved my remark away lightly. "But Björn has something which he wants to say to you."

He was kneeling upright in his blue sailor suit, a tumble of fair hair round his shoulders, cap in his hand.

"I think that you are the most beautiful woman I have ever seen in all my life," he said, and looked across at me.

"And I agree," I said.

Silvana didn't move; a very small, warm smile. Then she put out her hand and touched his cheek.

"Thank you, Björn. You know you are kneeling in your new uniform?"

"I know."

"Thank you," she said gently. "You are both mad. But thank you, thank you, really."

Back in our chairs across the dingy chapel, Björn pushed his hair from his forehead. "I think she liked that, she had tears," he said. "That was a very nice thing to do, man."

★   ★   ★

Three or four evenings later, crossing the Piazza San Marco on the way to yet another make-up room, Björn came belting up behind me, scattering pigeons and some Japanese tourists with their cameras.

"Hey, man, I just read it."

"You just read what?"

He fell into step beside me. "The book. This film, I read it."

"The book! Now look, for God's sake, you're not *supposed* to read it. It's strictly forbidden, no script, no book. You do just what Visconti tells you and no more."

"I know that, man, but it's so crazy. Someone left a paperback in one of the rooms so I read it."

"So you read it. And so what?"

"Hell, man, now I know who I *am*," he said. "I'm the Angel of Death, right?"

"In one," I said.

*   *   *

So there we stood in the presentation line one year later. I was at one end, beside Visconti; at the other, the American Money and their frilly wives; somewhere in the centre, Björn and Silvana.

The Queen, followed by Princess Anne dressed in orange furnishing-fabric and ear-phones, came slowly along. I think that she murmured something to the Americans (they did, after all, speak a form of English) but I am not certain that she said a word to anyone else. They were all Italians, so she nodded and smiled and came to Visconti, at whom she looked rather fixedly for some moments as if he were a cenotaph; wordless. She reached me and commented on how long the film had taken to make, and then wandered off with her daughter and a small posy to the auditorium.

It was over. Visconti watched her go with a sad smile.

"*Maladroit*," he murmured, and shrugged.

It is tremendously sad that a Royal Occasion of this kind is inevitably plunged into a doomed kind of silence. No one laughs, dares to speak, cough even. No one can possibly enjoy it, most particularly the Queen herself who, as I know, is much more fun than the glumness of these occasions would lead one to suppose.

However, there it was. We were enormously grateful for her patronage; it would have been *extremely* pleasing had one of us been able to tell her.

The audience, too, is affected, and sits as lead: not daring to laugh, applaud, or even speak above a church whisper. So it is impossible to judge how anything is received. At the end we all rose as the Royal Party trailed up the centre aisle, and it was only when they had left the auditorium that people came alive and I found myself grabbed in a tight fist-hold by Moura Budberg, ebony cane in one hand, me clutched in the other, a flowing grey dress. Her eyes twinkling with mischief.

"Hello, my darling," she said in her whispering Russian voice. "It is marvellous, *very* marvellous, but it is *not* Mann!"

The reception was held at Burlington House, but by the time I had got there with my small party of five, the place was jammed, and all I could see was what appeared to be the entire audience, and it had been a very heavy turn out, crammed round small tables in candlelight. A harassed man at the door said it was full, so we all started down the elegant staircase again to try and eat elsewhere.

Leaning over the slender banister, one of the American Money, who looked like a bar tender in his evening dress, was talking to some of his associates. They were clearly worried.

"We open in Rome, Thursday—you be there?" he called as I was halfway down the stairs.

I said that I really didn't know at the moment.

In actual fact I knew very well indeed: it was just that no one had asked me to attend. Rome, when all was said and done, was Visconti's territory. No one was about to muddy his pitch there. He was to have it all to himself. And he did.

"Well, we'll talk about that tomorrow morning maybe," said the American Money, busy biting the side of his thumb with ill-suppressed anxiety. "You know," he said, turning to his companions on the stairs, "what I can't understand is how the Queen of England could bring her daughter to see a movie about an old man chasing a kid's ass. . . ."

Outside in the courtyard snow was falling. We drove back in silence to the Connaught where, although it was long past dinner- or supper-time, the night porter, oh, blessed man!, made us pots of black coffee and two piled dishes of ham sandwiches which the six of us, for I had collected another lost soul unable to force her way into the candle-lit glory of the reception supper, ate with a couple of bottles of Krug, shoes and jackets cast aside, sitting on the floor of my sitting-room before a glowing fire.

We all agreed that by far the most moving, and regal, moment of the whole evening had been when John Julius's mother, Lady Diana Cooper, had made a deep, and graceful curtsey in the presence of her monarch.

Twenty-four hours later I was once more back at home on the hill.

The next day the film had its premiere in Rome to tremendous enthusiasm while I was busy on my hands and knees sealing the tiled floor of the long room with a fifty-fifty mixture of linseed oil and turpentine.

And the morning after that the household awoke to an astonishing sight. Eight inches of snow; an unfamiliar, unwanted, cold white world, in which the lanes were blocked by drifts, the olives were bowed with the excessive weight, and the cypress trees had turned into mutilated bottle brushes.

This was not at all what I had expected; but nothing that had happened to me since I had arrived in France was quite what I had expected. Crunching up through falling snow to the village with baskets and boots, I knew that if I had determined on a sense of order in life, as I had, there were to be a great many unexpected factors which would arrive to dismay me; but not to defeat me.

★　★　★

Fine words, those. But I was to be severely tried.

After the worst snow and ice seen for seventy, some said one hundred years, in the area, there had, one presumed, to be a thaw at some time.

And it came; warm winds blew in from Africa, the leadened sky swirled about and ran clear, the snow and the ice dissolved as one watched, and the land was left a ravaged, beaten, mire.

The damage was quickly revealed. And it was devastating. The orange trees had all been burnt away by ice, the great lemon tree, proud beside the house for more than fifty years by the size of its girth and height, stood dead in a tatter of frozen leaves and spiked twigs. Roses, so expensively bought, so carefully planted, were slimy and brown as a bar of chewing tobacco. Nothing which had impudently budded was spared. The ice had thawed, re-frozen, thawed again. The land was a sodden ruin, and the olives, whose slow death by drowning I had tried so hard to arrest, would take another four or five years before showing the signs of another death; the withering of their leaves. Fortunately for me. For if I had been aware of that at the time, as well as all the other disasters which stood wretchedly before me, I think I might have, possibly, slung the whole business in and gone off to the tropics.

But I didn't know. So it was a matter of starting again from scratch, something I have never found impossible to do: merely exhausting. Not daunting. So back to work again. The *potager*, in a short time, was re-planted, dead trees cut down, grass seed in quantities sown anywhere and everywhere, beds re-dug, and a fair semblance of order brought back to the land torn by drainage-trenches, trucks and bulldozers.

And then, quite suddenly, as happens in this oddest of climates, it was Spring. Almost overnight the whole area was clothed in tender green and starred about with a million wild anemones: hazed here and there with long drifts of grape hyacinths and violets, and a willow which I had planted by the pond hung golden in the still air; broom and bramble were in bud, and I bought a small plastic bag of goldfish from the local Monoprix and set them free to swim among my Salvator Rosa rocks, and awoke one brilliant morning to find that I had reached my half-century.

I was fifty.

I was not particularly surprised by this event: after all I had been expecting it for a number of years. Now that the moment had arrived it didn't seem to me that any fearful metamorphosis had taken place overnight. My hair had not instantly gone white: I was still able to hold my razor unassisted, the lines and bags scattered about my face had been with me for some time now, and were familiar: and even though the face which peered back at me from the steam-misted mirror was, without any doubt, that of a middle-aged man, the innermost heart, I knew, was still unnervingly that of a mildly retarded sixteen-year-old.

So much for being fifty.

Forwood called up from the terrace. "Marie says it's mince, sprouts and mashed for lunch. Or would you rather go out somewhere? You won't be fifty again."

So to the Colombe d'Or, lunch in the sun under the budding fig tree with Vivienne and Paddy Glenavy (Patrick Campbell), the former a very old friend from the early Ealing Studios days and now happily rediscovered as a close neighbour, Simone Signoret and Yves Montand and, later, James Baldwin who very sensibly suggested champagne for such a rare occasion.

A perfectly balanced table, a perfectly pleasant way of easing into one's second half. No standards had been lowered.

★　★　★

With the Cannes Film Festival only a few weeks away, I found myself in a curious situation.

From amongst the wealth of films being shown, "Death in Venice" had been selected as the official Italian entry, and Joseph Losey's "The Go-Between" as the British one.

I was inadvertently in competition with the director who had, perhaps, had the most effect on my cinema career. We had attended Festivals together with our joint works in past years. But this time we would be rivals; a fact which neither of us took very seriously and which amused us in a wry sort of way. After all, the cinema was supposed to be international, so whether I was in an Italian movie or a British one didn't make much difference really. And anything and everything in the cinema was "up for grabs", as they say: which eased my tremor of conscience. I had, I must confess, a very small, never expressed, hope that I might perhaps "grab" a bit of something for myself this time. As usual, rumours had started wheeling about the Croisette like swifts on a summer evening, and one which came to my ears, and gave me a feeling of keen pleasure, was that I was "definitely" up for the prize of Best Actor.

But this kind of thing happens every year at Cannes and no one really takes any notice; in any case I never win prizes. I'm not the sort that does.

However, it was a warming, if suppressed, idea.

Squashed, rather than suppressed, almost as soon as it had started to wander about in my subconscious, by a long, apologetic letter from Visconti saying that the film as the official Italian entry *had* to be shown in Italian. That is, dubbed. A rule of the Festival (now conveniently set aside during the last year or two) stated that any player who was dubbed in a film was not eligible to qualify for an award.

This was a rule with which I absolutely agreed: a dubbed performance is not a performance at all. An actor's voice is, in my opinion, more than seventy per cent of his work.

However, we had made the film originally in English, and although I had hardly ever opened my mouth during the thing, I had made a very careful effort to speak what words I had in English but with the cadence and nuance of German. The construction of each sentence was precisely planned, and I had followed Thomas Mann extremely closely. The thought of that dry, unsentimental prose being dubbed into Italian, which is a lyrical language at best and romantic at worst, depressed me very much.

Visconti agreed sadly the next day when I managed to get him on the telephone.

"It is tragic! I agreed to come to Cannes for the Festival with a copy of the film in the English tongue. *All* was arranged. All. We would have the subtitles in French. Va bene . . . I insisted on this out of respect for you, Bogarde! I want your voice to be heard in Cannes, in our film. All went so well . . . I controlled with Pasquale de Santis [who had photographed the film] every single frame so that it would be perfect: we made two copies. Ayee! Much work, you understand."

"But what happened?"

"I have enemies, Bogarde. There was a protest made to the Italian Ministry that the film was Italian and must be submitted in its own tongue."

"But we made it in English!"

"When I made *my* protest I was warned not to show the film in English because I would risk something worse. We could be banned!"

"Oh really. . . ."

"Sì, really. Now I must start all over again to do another two copies in Italian. So you will be speaking in Italian but not with your voice! What can I do? I can not revolt against a silly law and possibly risk something far worse. . . ."

"Who are these enemies? You know them, of course?"

His voice was as dry and black as charcoal.

"I know. Certo, I know. So alas. . . ."

So alas I was out of the running for an award, which angered me far less than the idea of all my careful preparation and "German" of the text being sung by some Italian tenor. My anger stayed at a high point for a day or so, and then dispersed into a vague sense of disappointment. There was no point in whining on.

One thing cheered me considerably. Now that I had been eliminated from the competition, I was on neutral ground as far as Visconti and Losey were concerned. I could cheer them both on to the winning of the coveted Palme d'Or. For Best Film.

The American Money hit the roof with fury at the Italians' decision, and a terrible battle raged between Rome and Los Angeles: the Italians said that they were "desolate" but the film *was* Italian, and must be dubbed; the American Money protested that it was made in English and must *not* be dubbed. Then the Italians brought up the heavy weapons and warned those concerned to keep out of the argument and stop resisting.

There was a slightly uncomfortable feeling of politics about, especially when it was very tactfully leaked from some quarter that "the film was scheduled to win in any case".

All very Italian.

But, to give them their due, the American Money fought on bitterly, and finally a compromise was reached. The film would be shown in English, as shot, to the Press, but the Gala Performance in the evening would be in Italian.

Under these circumstances, I agreed, therefore, to attend the Press showing, but not the Gala.

No one attempted to dissuade me. Everyone was very pleased with the turn of events and, after all, there could only be one loser, the actor.

At the same time that this unseemly business was taking place, another event, far more important than this, was also going on. The waiters and waitresses, indeed all the hotel staff, from top to bottom, decided to go on strike indefinitely, so that the chances of a Festival being held grew daily more and more remote. However, in the end someone gave in to someone else, as usual, and the strike was called off just in time.

Unfortunately, the rain was not.

It was the wettest Festival for years, bitterly cold, drenching, grey. Flags and bunting hung limp among the banners, the gutters raced with muddy water, and those who went to the movies did so in plastic macs and huddled under umbrellas. We might just as well have been in Manchester.

But on the day of our Press Show, God, as Lally sometimes said, leant out of Heaven, and cleared things up. The rain stopped, the sun came out, and when we reached the Palais des Festivals, Björn, myself and Visconti, the day was bright and there appeared, at first glance, to be a major revolution beginning on the steps of the building.

The place was jammed with a seething mob of jeans-clad youth, intent on forcing the doors in spite of the "Complet" signs displayed everywhere.

The auditorium was packed to the roof. People sat in the

aisles, on the stage, stood five deep at the back of the circle: the Press were outnumbered by hundreds. The majority of the audience was young. A very different kind from the one in London which, doomed by the presence of Royalty, and consisting in any case of elderly Diplomatic Corps, Social Figures, or just people whom John Julius had forced to part with a hefty bit of money to help save Venice, had offered no warmth and almost no signs of life.

This was very different: there was a surging atmosphere of excitement. The feeling that an "event" was about to take place. I felt that if they hated it they could very easily throw rocks or bottles at the screen. It was not to be a passive crowd, and some of them had fought, and queued, for hours to secure a place.

Sitting between Visconti and Björn, I wondered if they would think that it *was* too slow: the music too obscure? Or, remembering the remark made by the American Money on the landing at Burlington House, perhaps they would send the whole thing up and laugh at the old man who was chasing. . . .

But I put that thought aside quickly. It even distressed me to remember it. I sat back as the house-lights started to dim and a sudden hush fell over the packed place. They sat there in absolute silence: no one moved, coughed, crackled paper, turned a head. There was an incredible feeling of intense concentration until, at one specific moment, halfway through, when Von Aschenbach makes a silent decision to return from the railway station to his hotel on the Lido and confront his future, no matter what, the entire theatre exploded with a tremendous roar of spontaneous delight, and a thundering of applause and cheering which drowned the sound track and astonished the three of us by its force. It must have lasted only a few moments, though it seemed at the time, far longer, and then almost as suddenly as it had arrived it faded into intense silence once again. Somewhere I heard a girl sobbing.

I turned to Visconti and in a low whisper, much moved by what had happened, for I had never witnessed such a moment in a cinema before, nor since, I said, "Luchino! I think we have won!" He turned his grey-cropped head briefly towards me, eyebrows arched in shaggy reproof. "Certo!" he said, implying that I had been an idiot not to have realised that from the start.

4. Charlotte and Jean-Michel Jarre.
New Year's Day 1980

5. With Capucine.
May 1982.

6. Editing the typescript of this book with Norah Smallwood. May 1982.

7. Tony Forwood with his grandson Thomas. Summer 1978.

8. Natalie Wood. April 198⟨

We walked through a dense crowd of cheering people to the obligatory Press Reception. Visconti moved slowly, enjoying every second, one hand raised to the left, then to the right, a Benediction, or a monarch on a walkabout. Björn and I trailed him, pleased and relieved, moved by the hands which thrust to take ours, by the cries of "Thank you!", the gentle thumps and pats as we moved among them, and by the flowers, some in battered bunches, others just single blooms, which were pressed upon us.

The news had spread all over Cannes. We were a triumph, and the world loved us.

Except for one important member of the official jury, who had *loathed* us, and let it be known in every bar or restaurant that he managed to visit in the course of his onerous duties.

Unfortunate. However, that didn't prevent the crowds from gathering for the Gala that evening, and the reaction in the theatre, for an "Italian dub" was every bit as exciting as the morning one.

I didn't know about all that, because I had gone up to the Colombe d'Or to dine with Losey and his wife, Patricia. Joe was uneasy and depressed about his own film, due to be shown in two days' time, and felt that it had no chance of winning, mainly because of our overwhelming success, but I did my best to lift his morale by reminding him of the chattering jury member who had spread his gospel of hate far and wide. There was no certainty, yet, that we had won. And that cheered him up for a time.

People started to telephone through from Cannes to tell me how the film had been received, and couldn't I be persuaded to come down, just to the reception?

I apologised politely and explained that, at the moment, I was extremely busy trying to encourage the Competition.

★ ★ ★

And the Competition won.

Just before noon on the day of the Awards the news leaked out, whereupon Visconti quietly packed all his Vuitton luggage, checked out of his hotel, and went to the airport where he sat on his suitcases awaiting the next flight to Rome. Consternation reigned; officials flew about in harassed flocks, traced him and begged him to return, they had a special prize for him, and he must, they implored, be there to accept it. He sat as still as a block of granite; considering this.

Then reluctantly agreed. On condition that the prize was awarded at the very end of the evening, *after* the Palme d'Or.

I can't remember now what the prize was actually for: twenty-five years of the Cannes Festival, or his contribution over the years to the cinema. However, in the packed theatre that night no one seemed to care what it was for, just as long as he got it, and when the Best Film was announced, and Losey walked rather uncomfortably on to the stage, he was booed just as much as he was cheered. But the announcement that Visconti had won a "special" prize brought the whole house to its feet, cheering and applauding.

He strode on to the stage, accepted, with the greatest grace, his award from Romy Schneider, bowed briefly to the cheering crowd, and left. He did not stand, as all the other winners chose to do, in a self-conscious line, embarrassedly holding their scrolls and scarlet boxes.

After the awards, the final film is run: usually pretty boring. And that year it was no exception, but Visconti insisted that we all sit through it as a mark of respect to the director. Fortunately I wasn't near him and managed to slip out and have a meal at the Blue Bar next door, returning only in time for the last few moments. Losey, we discovered, had taken his prize and left for his hotel, leaving the field wide open to Visconti, who took it . . . marching down the great staircase to thundering cheers and flashing cameras, clearly the winner: not only of the evening, but of the whole Festival. Romy and I followed him down, I holding his Burberry, she the prize, so that his hands were free to acknowledge his triumph with gentle gestures all about. It was the greatest fun. A perfect example of "winner takes all".

Afterwards an enormous supper party was given to end the Festival. The only person not present was Joe who had gone earlier without any farewell.

"He is not here, your Losey?" asked Visconti.

"No. He went home."

"He has *la grippe*, perhaps?"

"Perhaps . . ."

"Poor man."

"And this is the finish now, isn't it? Cinderella time?"

"I do not follow you, Bogarde."

"I heard midnight striking. The Ball is over."

"Oh no! Not over. Now we just begin. In Tokyo, in New York even, in Cape Town, in London, Rome and Paris . . . all over the world they will see our work. It is not yet finished! You must be pleased to go back to your shepherd's house with poor Poverino [Labo], it is as you wanted."

"And you?"

"I? I start with Proust. Maybe three years' work, you know. It is complicato."

"I may never see you again after tonight."

He drew on his cigarette in its paper holder. "Is possible. Sì."

"I mean . . . well, it's all breaking up, and you'll go and I'll go, and we may not ever come together again. Do you see?"

"Sì, sì. I see." He stubbed his cigarette into a saucer.

"I feel rather bereft," I said.

Visconti had no time for sentimentality: he was also curiously shy. Suddenly he got up, gathered his Italian clan around him, bowed over hands here and there, and started moving towards the big hall.

This is how it all ends, I thought. I was *very* sentimental: even if he wasn't. I remembered, sitting among the debris of the supper table, the long, long haul we had come together since the day, years ago it seemed now, that he had arrived at my villa in Rome for lunch and, after an enormous helping of Antonia's trifle, which he liked more than anything, he had pushed a wrapped packet across the table towards me. "A present," he had said. "Not for anything . . . but perhaps for the pudding Inglese, certo . . . for that."

It had been a paperback copy of *Death in Venice*.

Finale now, in a dispersing, laughing, supper party crowd at the Carlton.

He had almost reached the doors when he turned suddenly, looking about him with those steady grey eyes, bright beneath shaggy brows, and saw me.

"Bogarde!" He raised his hand and I went across to him. "You have a dentist in Roma, you tell me?"

"Yes."

"So. You telephone me one day, eh?" He patted my shoulder, turned into his group, turned back once more, waved, and was gone.

## 6

ILLITERATE 1. Unable to read or write. 2. Violating accepted standards in reading and writing. *Collins' Dictionary*.

I cannot, in all truth, be accused of the first, although I am well aware that I am guilty of the second part of the definition. This stems, of course, from an almost total lack of education.

My father's desperate efforts to try and alter this sorry situation were to no avail, as I have explained. I resisted placidly, peacefully and stubbornly all attempts at learning. Tutors were engaged; hopelessly shrugged shoulders, and left; I achieved the supreme accolade of determined non-education once by being rewarded with two marks out of a possible one hundred in Maths. It was pointless trying to explain to me, as a great many people did, that a sound knowledge of Algebra, Geometry, or Mathematics would assist me in the acquisition of a logical mind.

As far as I was concerned I had no need of a logical mind. I was absolutely certain that I already possessed one: so why waste time?

I made a strenuous effort to try and do my best only in those lessons which would cause me the least stress or strain. And there weren't many such.

Strangely enough, reading was one thing which I found fascinatingly simple and exciting to do, even though I could neither spell correctly nor punctuate; but that didn't bother me. I just ploughed on, only reading those books which were not "difficult" or "dull" or "dense" (favourite words of mine at that time). Perhaps this was inherited from my mother who was, what she was pleased to call, an avid reader, devouring like a python anything set in her path by Michael Arlen, Ethel Mannin, Daphne du Maurier or Mary Webb etc.

And I swallowed them too. Whole.

These were splendidly easy books: and although my despairing father offered me the chances of reading Trollope, Collins, Thackeray, Hardy and Dickens, I scented the dust upon their pages and turned instead to the bright, well-spaced, simple, cheap romances best digested with a box of chocolates at one's side. Which is exactly what my mother did, most afternoons, lying in elegant splendour on her day-bed. Chewing and reading.

The result of all this was that I left school at sixteen, stuffed to the gills with Romance and Fuller's chocolate (metaphorically speaking), and lacking in almost any other kind of education whatsoever.

The main thing, as far as I was concerned, was that I could *read*. And reading was, in itself, Education. It was all that I could possibly need to assure me of a safe future in the profession which I had chosen, long ago, to follow. The theatre. This was, perhaps, my first major failure in assessment.

The theatre was the one place where the reading of cheap, bright novels would *not* be quite enough. There was, I found out quickly, more to it all than that. Shakespeare, Shaw, Wilde, Congreve, Ibsen, Tchekov . . . oh! how appallingly difficult they were after the delights of *Rebecca*! With what relief I turned to Dodie Smith and Merton Hodge, with whom I felt far more comfortable.

I learned my Shakespeare (I realised wistfully that I had to if I was to follow in his profession) in much the same way as I had learned to take syrup of figs—by holding my nose, swallowing it all down, and then sweetening the dose with something by Agatha Christie, perhaps, or Dornford Yates: they caused me very little pain or trouble and wrote convenient, easily digested English, requiring no kind of dictionary at the side to aid me.

In time I spouted Shakespeare like a spiggot, without having much idea of what he was saying: from the Plays to the Sonnets; and about the only thing I wrestled from Wilde was his encouraging remark that, "The stage is the refuge of the too charming." With which I heartily agreed.

Shaw left me glazed of eye: Ibsen and Tchekov were the Dead Sea Scrolls. However, Wilde's pleasing remark lent me encouragement, and leaning heavily on what I interpreted as his version of "charm", I trod blithely into my theatre life unaware that I had the education of a mole and the assurance of Mont Blanc. I also had an unshakable belief, at that time, that I was God's gift to the theatre, so there was absolutely nothing for me to worry about at all.

It was exceedingly fortunate that after two short years of this tiresome behaviour I found myself in an ill-fitting battle-dress trying, with no success whatsoever, to come to terms with the absurd mysteries of the Morse Code in the Royal Corps of Signals.

However, I was not in the least bit cast down: it was not my fault that some idiot in Whitehall, or wherever it was, had sent me, of all people, to learn how to send the S.O.S.

They had picked the wrong man for the job: and that was their bad luck. Not mine. I muddled about generally: worked hard at the standard things which one was required to do, like throwing grenades, or forming fours, and polishing fire buckets, and discovered, with mild interest, that I was a deadly shot on the rifle range. I also turned out the very best kit inspection it was possible to see, arranged, within the very strict limits of regulations, with the precision and elegance of the fish counter at Harrods.

I was still, however, not doing very much to become a Signalman. That was quite beyond me; and bored me witless, even though, somewhere in the darker recesses of my mind, I knew that my life might one day depend on it.

There were, on the other hand, some extraordinary compensations in this idiotic, to me at any rate, army life.

Even though the days were crammed with the trivia, effort and exhaustion of training, there were long, wearying Sunday afternoons when Church Parade was over, and the interminable evenings of boredom once one had polished one's brasses and boots for Morning Parade.

I had brought with me, at my father's suggestions, a couple of books which would be my constant companions in these slack moments. For he had told me that, although much of his own war had been fright, a great deal more of it was lethal boredom. So I took, predictably, the *Oxford Book of Modern Verse* and a pocket edition of Shakespeare (to keep in touch, as it were), only to discover, in a relatively short time, that they became as heavy and dull as the majority of my hut mates. There was a limit to my patience with the "hey-nonny-no's" and James Elroy Flecker and company.

And then, one evening, wandering about the hut begging a book which I could *read*, I found, to my amazed surprise, Auden.

I found Isherwood too: then Evelyn Waugh, Cyril Connolly, Emily Brontë, and even managed, with one finger pressed hard to every line, the negativity of Ivy Compton-Burnett. There was Hemingway for the first time, and the rustic joys of John Surtees. I went through a catholic library with the voracity of a silver-fish.

Not all my hut mates were leaden and dull, lying on their bunks reading what my father always called "housemaid's trash", or smoking lethargically like a host of opium eaters, occasionally scratching some unwashed portion of their bodies and farting genially. Some, and they were the ones who loaned me these wondrous volumes, actually read books.

A small reading group had been started in the dingy NAAFI, and we would sit around our two tables drinking thin beer or thinner cocoa just before Lights Out, discussing, arguing, even reading selected passages aloud (I rather fancied myself at this part, naturally), debating and questioning.

But I sat, for the most part, in silence: an unusual habit for me, for I knew only too well that I was woefully behind in this "school", and that I had a great deal on which to catch up. I had a lot to learn, and, quite suddenly, I wanted to: so I stayed silent and listened.

I had realised, just in the nick of time, what I had so carelessly left aside; and although I had been a bit slow in starting the race, at least I was now among the runners.

If it had seemed to me that learning in civilian life was a chore and to be avoided at almost all costs (for my life had seemed to be so splendidly simple without it), I was now discovering that it mattered a great deal in the army. I was much surprised.

I had quietly become aware, for example, that my hut mates who lay about reading papers or just scratching, staring blankly into space and smoking, were, for the most part, not much good at anything else. They could argue indeed: and did almost constantly, about their "rights" and what they would do when they got back to Civvy Street, but all of their arguments amounted to little sense and no awareness of life at all. They were the untrained minds.

Stupid on the rifle range, lethal chucking their grenades at Practice, clumbering about like heifers on the parade ground, brilliant at avoiding duties, and useful, "nifty" one of them called it, with motor transport, they slouched through their lives complaining and protesting.

It was from their numbers, I had the wit to notice, that hastily assembled squads were issued with khaki shorts, pith helmets and a pass for embarkation leave: after which they were dispatched to Alexandria, Calcutta, and Bombay grumbling bitterly.

The reading group members were not.

This culling of the untrained minds alerted me, almost too late, but in time, to become aware of my own need for survival. Trying to keep up with the people I had selected to assist me was extremely hard with almost no educational background, but I struggled on determinedly. Often I fell. I wallowed and splashed about in ignorance, floundered and became lost a good deal of the time; but I was never afraid to ask questions, to seek help, to admit defeat, even to invite ridicule. Which never came.

The assistance I received in return for this humility and determination was constant, for the people who knew what *I* wanted to know were delighted to share their knowledge, patiently, calmly, cheerfully, setting me out on my rather rutted track, helping me to pick up the scattered pieces of my knowledge like so many fallen packets; they were clearly glad that I was trying to learn, and rewarded me handsomely.

Of course I knew very well that starting my Prep School education at the age of nineteen in a gloomy NAAFI was, facing things absolutely squarely, leaving things a trifle late; to say the least. Almost an afterthought indeed; but I threw whatever pride I might have had to the winds and got on with things.

I knew that there wasn't much chance, really, of repairing all the holes which negligence had made in the fabric of my life: I also knew that I would never quite recapture the squandered years. There could be, at this late stage of the game, no possibility of my weaving a good thick blanket to hide the tears and rents: all I could hope for now, and I was well aware of the fact, was some kind of rough and ready patchwork quilt which might, with any luck, help to distract a really discerning eye away from my grosser intellectual faults, and help to cloak the draughty holes which I could not hope now to fill, late starter that I was, but which I would continue to try to patch continuously.

A patchwork quilt, however, needs a good needlewoman. Which I was not.

And how could I know, at nineteen, with a long war ahead of me, that there were two such women, many miles apart, and many years away, who were old hands at "patching", and who would come to my assistance quite unexpectedly?

★   ★   ★

In 1967, Mrs X, sitting under a hair dryer in her local Beauty Parlour in a small American town, idled through the pages of a cheap woman's magazine.

It was not her kind of reading matter at all, and she was just about to set it aside when a photograph of an unknown man standing on a daisied lawn before a house, stayed her astonished hand.

It was a fortunate moment: for it was to make a difference to her life and have a profound effect on mine.

I was the stranger in the photograph, and the house belonged to me. But it had once belonged to her, many years before. She knew every tile, timber and brick. It was the house in which she had spent the happiest years of her life and she had not set eyes on it, until that moment, since September 1939 when she and her husband, as Americans, had to leave England at the outbreak of the war.

She left the Beauty Parlour with the magazine; and having read the sorry little article which accompanied the photographic spread, she wrote to me, enclosing a small, sepia snapshot of the house as it had been when she had first found it, uncared for, crumbling, overgrown with nettles, in 1929.

It was a hesitant letter. She hoped that I would forgive a total stranger for making such an unwarranted intrusion, but the coincidence was so odd, and she wondered if the house had changed a great deal in the years . . .?

It is not unusual for a film star to receive letters from total strangers: it is, in fact, the norm. My letters are usually replied to by a secretary and only very rarely by myself. And I do not write a second time.

But in this particular instance it seemed that we were not total strangers, for we both shared the common love for one particular house, and we both knew it intimately.

So I wrote back. And started a correspondence which was to last, unbroken, for five years, until her death in 1972.

At first I wrote formally about the changes in the house and the gardens over the years: I drew a map, in red ink, to show her where new tree plantings had taken place, or where paths now went, and where doors had been blocked up or windows re-opened, for there had been other tenants before me and since her.

March 18, '67. DB to Mrs X:
"... *mucking about below the wall where you said your pond had been. Ain't no pond there now, not even a shallow dip, I dug around and all I could find were a few bits of broken flower pot, some pebbles and two shards of blue-glazed terracotta. Anything you recognise? The big ash went years ago, there is a sort of Humpty Dumpty kind of depression . . . covered in thick meadow grass . . .*"

April 5th, '67. DB to Mrs X:
"... *I am very well aware that my syntax is 'all to hell' . . . so is my spelling and punctuation . . . relics of a mis-spent youth . . . Alicebright Lane was called after one Alice Bright . . . Gipsy girl who sold wild daffodils outside the pubs and was found 'drowned' in a horse trough in 1888. Want any more?*"

To begin with, our letters were formal in address, Dear Mrs, Dear Mr, but in a very short time these were dispensed with and we wrote to each other without any form of address. The letters became "essays" rather than mere letters, and we had so much to say to each other, it seemed, that I started writing more than spasmodically, but at least once or twice a week; and she wrote to me every single day.

Gradually it emerged, though she never at any time *said* so, that she was alone, and that she was ill. The illness, I deduced for myself, was possibly grave, and the essays, letters, what you will, became a "steadier" for her and gave her strength when,
"... *the pain gets really intolerable, which it does from time to time, but I get tremendous comfort from re-reading your letters and (I suppose I'm hinting?) when I get a new one . . .*"

Sometimes, due to pressure of my work, I was not able to write letters, and so I sent postcards. From 1968 onwards I sent one every day. Sometimes these postcards got "bunched up" in various sorting offices for some unknown reasons and, when released, seemed to "*fly about my head like huge flocks of birds*", which is why she called them "starlings".

At her death, five years of letters and "starlings" were returned to me from America, according to the instructions which she left in her will. They were all neatly filed in paper folders. Some, for her own fun, she had "corrected" in pencil, altering my spelling, correcting punctuation. The last item in the file for 1972 is a postcard (starling) of the local village church here. To my bitter regret I wrote:

21st April, '72
*"Up to the eyes with work. Don't give a damn to whom you leave my ruddy letters, Yale, Harvard or the British Museum, or try St. Pancras! Do as you like, if it makes you feel better, I really don't care. Will write when I'm sorted out."*
It, like all the others, was carefully dated in her fine handwriting with its arrival, and filed. She died that night, suddenly and alone.

I never met her. I never saw her. We never even spoke to each other. I had no idea of her age.

Late in our correspondence she once wrote:
*". . . I did fall desperately in love when I was twelve. With the most stunning steward on the 'Lusitania' . . ."*
But I wonder?

All I know for certain is that she wrote like a joyous girl: and gave me five years of extraordinary pleasure and "learning".

In all that time I can't remember that we ever asked each other a personal or direct question; we both knew that we were "the people of the letters" and left it at that. Gradually, like a puzzle taking shape, I learned that she had one child who was in Holy Orders, and a husband, whom she greatly loved once, in a nursing home, who was to die during our relationship, causing her bitter distress, for even though the marriage had fallen into decay and desolation, it had once been glowing and glorious. More than that I did not know, nor presumed to ask. That neither of us presumed upon the other was, I am certain, the core of our friendship.

And, after all, it is not an unusual one, two people meeting through letters: there have been many others like it before. But it is a once only business. It can *never* be repeated.

As far as I know, this correspondence was kept a complete secret from most of her friends, and she had a great many, except for three or four to whom she confessed, with some guilt lest they should laugh. Which, thankfully, they did not.

97

The only person who was privy to the whole thing was her devoted, and adored, Polish maid, Anna, who couldn't really be prevented from seeing the long air-mail envelopes, which arrived so frequently, or the starlings, which she had to gather up and carry to her lady, as she called her. In time, Anna became bold enough to signal the arrival of these envelopes by placing a single red rose in a fluted vase on her mistress's miserly (because of a stringent diet) breakfast tray.

One red rose meant a letter. No rose, no letter.

April 2nd, '69. Mrs X to D.B.:

". . . *got myself downstairs unaided, big deal! Awake from three am with the most hellish 'jangles', so found it an effort. Depression maybe; no rose on my tray. I guess I am a spoiled woman. Somewhere Anna was singing and came into the 'salon' bearing a great jar of the first forsythia, just beginning to break bud. 'You got forsythia!' she said. 'I didn't get a rose,' I said in my self-pitying voice (which you are spared!) 'Why don't you take a look at the electric light fittings in the kitchen?' she said.*

"*There, sellotaped to the wires, three glorious, beautiful letters! Red, white, and blue, strung like bunting: all from you. I was as 'high as the Flag on the Fourth of July', truly. Anna's delight at MY delight made us both laugh and the 'jangles' faded. She is SUCH a clever one . . .*"

As far as I know, other than these few, no one else ever knew, although she was to have some narrow escapes: after all, it is perfectly reasonable for a young boy or young girl to write to his or her favourite film star, or pop singer, but it could not be considered at all fitting behaviour, or even balanced behaviour, in a patrician lady associated closely with an extremely respected American University in a small town.

The least said about writing to film stars the better; especially as she had never really seen one outside the pages of her newspapers where, she said, they

"*seem a bit 'flashy' really, fighting waiters and getting drunk on Chat Shows on the Television . . . but I have never seen EITHER, so can't really judge. You SEEM all right . . . but in general they appear to me to be very shallow people, most often poorly bred so that sudden fame and riches must be desperately hard for them to deal with: so of course they don't. Oh! Lord! I am sounding DREADFULLY pompous, and you ARE a Fillum Star! I keep on forgetting . . .*"

In all the years, all I ever really knew of her background was that she had a British-French passport, was possibly Viennese, had travelled widely, and was now doing a job at the University which was

"... well, you know: literature, books, research, cataloguing, writing. All that kind of thing. I'm, I suppose, a Book-Worm, deadly dull truthfully ..."

She lived in an old-for-America house on a quiet street in a pleasant garden (about which she knew a very great deal), surrounded by a picket fence; and her "salon", as it amused her to call it, was

"... stuffed with books and papers everywhere and has a pot-bellied window which sticks out over the street. Pretty ugly, but ugly-pretty, if you know what I mean ..."

All this was shaded by a huge white chestnut tree of great age, and a high bush of lilac.

The "salon" seemed mainly to consist of writers, students, Deans and their wives and people from the University who "come at all hours to pick my poor addled brains". In spite of almost constant pain, she was seldom able to say "No" to any request for help from some unhappy student, a poet with pentameter problems, or a Dean's wife going through the change of life. She took all that came her way because she dreaded so

"... the haul up stairs after they have all gone, my room so softly reflected in my beautiful Vauxhall glass mirror, the awful loneliness, and fear of pain coming on again and having to wait until the first light comes to start another day. The nights, even though I am now struggling with 'Meeting Mrs Jenkins' by Richard Burton (I see no reason for its publication. Do you?) seem terribly long ..."

But it's all gone now. The pot-bellied window, the giant chestnut, the lilac and the little "salon". It's all a parking lot. And she is dead.

★   ★   ★

She was the first of my two "needlewomen" and started in on the "patching" almost from the start, or at least as soon as the direct formalities of writing to a stranger were mutually dropped.

One can't be taught to write, any more than one can be taught to act or to paint or play a piano or any other musical instrument. All that can be done for potential students is to offer the basic rules, advise, suggest, counsel, encourage and correct. The rest is entirely up to them, and if they have a spark, an ember so to speak, they might get through the tremendous seas of chance.

But the spark is not always present; and no amount of encouragement will kindle a dead ember into a flame, and the flame into a fire.

Fortunately for me, Mrs X seemed to think that, from the letters which I sent her, I had some kind of ember worth the fanning, and fan away she did. My appalling punctuation at first amused her, as did my spelling:

"*I don't see why you SHOULDN'T spell 'cough' as 'koff' . . . it's perfectly reasonable but ugly . . .*"

I carried on, explaining that she was bloody lucky to get letters from an overworked, illiterate movie star in the first place, and she correctly countered that it just seemed a waste not to do it "properly". My punctuation was so negligible that I simply resorted to dots, which drove her frantic; but as the years went by I was amused to see that she resorted to the beastly things herself:

"*. . . they do save time, somehow. However, it is not 'literate' and that's what we should be trying to concentrate on . . .*"

Sometimes she would carefully correct an entire page of one of my letters, have it photocopied, and send it back for my thoughtful examination. And sometimes I tried, but the efforts made her laugh so much that she decided that the best way to try and penetrate my thick head was by reading. Books were sent. We spent a fortune on books which flew to and fro across the Atlantic.

She was wise enough to realise that I wrote as I wrote: straight off with no set of rules to bog me down, and she much preferred the "straight off" letters to the ones which I wrote with Fowler and the Oxford Dictionary. So I was let off the hook gleefully.

"*. . . do it all your way, I'm used to it now and would HATE the letters to be any other way, they are vivid, funny, alive. I see all you see, all you share with me, and that is more than enough for a grumpy University critter like me . . . it's no good stuffing you in a strait-jacket of correct literature-behaviour! I'd far rather you were able to wave your arms about, and shout freely. And that you certainly do!*"

The books were something else. We shared them constantly. I discovered that there were "gaps" in her knowledge, much to my open delight, and sent her books on people she had hardly, if ever, heard of, to my surprise, and on whom she feasted.

". . . *finished reading your Margot Asquith autobiography and diaries. How good of you to alert me! I was in at the birth of 'Puffin', and her theories of educating children. To confess to you the depth of my ignorance, I had suffered all these years under the illusion that she was of American birth! And used to cringe at some of the things she said and did as being vulgar Americanisms! . . ."*

". . . *the book on Rupert Brook (Michael Hastings) saddened me. You are of course, wise enough to know that one can thoroughly like a book, and yet be critical. It struck me as really 'mordant' . . . almost a cruel piece of work. I'm all for 'debunking', but at the same time, I feel that we need myths. Ridiculous, isn't it?"*

"B---- *here today, barged in saying 'There'll be a long wait, the Library (University) hasn't even heard of it!' And his eyes popped when he saw your copy (Cynthia Asquith's Diaries) lying on the table. Of course if you WILL pay air mail postage, which is almost the amount of the book! But oh! I AM grateful . . ."*

And here they all stand, the letters of a long time ago, packed tightly into fat box files. Each in its original envelope, hundred upon hundred, all marked carefully in pencil with the exact date of delivery, some with scribbled pencil notes concerning the information they hold. Or questions to be asked next day. "*Malamud's 'The Fixer' offered as film. He refused.*" Or "*Arrives Plaza Hotel, NYC.*" Or "*Has he read Connolly's 'The Rock Pool'?*"

She, for her part, offered me writers I had never read, or set aside as "too difficult" in the past: T. S. Eliot, Ezra Pound, Albert Camus, Robert Graves, James Joyce, Faulkner, and, early in 1967, Thomas Mann for the very first time. She "introduced" me to a host of people I had little or no knowledge about: Zelda Fitzgerald, whom she had known; Gerald and Sara Murphy, who, many years later, were to "spike off", as it were, my second novel; Leonard Woolf, and Rilke, Theodore Roethke and so on. The "patching" was very subtly beginning. And I enjoyed it.

". . . *absolutely no need to thank me. You make me feel like some ageing spinster-teacher, like the one in 'The Corn is Green', and that isn't me at all. I have grown wondrous used to your intriguing spelling: at least it is real! Not like that idiot Dora Carrington whose spelling was pure affectation. I think everything she did was 'affected'. Except, perhaps, some of her painting . . . but your spelling is just downright 'iggorance' Sir! . . ."*

Needless to say, after a while, we both cheated on the strict set of rules I had insisted upon, and which she had accepted (a bit reluctantly at first) that we should never meet or speak, but must remain only correspondents. I had had too many unpleasing encounters, in the past, with elderly ladies who wrote packages of junk and would, as often as not, arrive unannounced and unwanted at my house in their best C & A hats and coats with, for the sake of appearances, some autograph book to sign. So I took particular care.

But eventually she managed to wheedle me into sending, against my better judgement, a portrait-still so that she could *"take it into hospital when I go, next month"*. It was a rough picture taken off-set, not a glossy, retouched thing, and of course she didn't take it to hospital at all. She framed it in a neat shagreen frame and foolishly stood it on a small table by her chair in her "salon" hiding it, she swore, every time an unexpected visitor arrived, under a book of Klee's works. It gave her, she said, *"a terrific sense of danger . . . very stimulating"*. I accepted this "cheating" because, after all, she could see me, if she had so wished, on someone's television, and I was, even in America, often to be found in illustrated magazines, and if she enjoyed the vicarious thrill of hiding a picture under a book, that was entirely her business.

In any case, I really couldn't take a hard line: I, faced with a telephone in my suite in a New York hotel, and a little advanced in my wine, pressed the buttons on the machine which I knew would ring a bell in the salon with its pot-belly. It did. And the moment I heard the receiver lifted, I hung up; my hands shaking with treachery.

*   *   *

If I take up five or six of my returned letters, spread them like a fan or a hand of cards, they appear to be just what they are. Envelopes. They have no life, only the postmarks hint of something more. Budapest, Rome, Crowborough, Paris, New York, Lewes, Port Antonio, Sidi Bou Said, Venice . . . it is impossible to believe that once their contents gave immeasurable happiness, or that they even assisted to sustain a failing spirit, or gave me incalculable pleasure.

What on earth do they contain, these spread envelopes, and the hundreds of others stuffed into the files before me? What did I write about over all those years to divert her and, I always hoped, to amuse her?

They seem to me now more like journals than essays or letters, and that is what they eventually became, four to eight pages of close typing. (I never, or seldom, wrote in hand because mine is illegible.)

I wrote of every day and that day's events, detailed accounts of every conversation which might amuse her, and thus the voices of my parents, or Losey, Visconti, Resnais or Cukor and so many others, spring vividly from the paper, even now, so many years later. There was never any reason, when I started to write my autobiography, to invent conversations; they are all here, in the letters, verbatim, at least as far as I could recall them three or so hours later, or perhaps next day.

But more than conversations, I wrote the most minute details of sights, sounds, of smells, and texture, light and colour, so that sitting alone in her salon or, as was so often the case latterly, lying alone in a hospital bed, she could share my world, and escape, if only metaphorically, for a time the sterility, the fear, the meandering odour of ether and polish.

It was her unyielding determination that I should write. And this was my homework and practice. She bullied and cajoled; I crumpled and gave in. Willingly. Looking at these bunches before me, I do rather wonder how on earth I managed to put out so much energy on top of the work which I was then doing for the cinema. But somehow I managed, because her daily letter became of paramount importance to me, because I knew, in some strange way, that I *had* to write, that I wanted to do so above all else, and the most important thing was that I had a recipient.

I could not have written all those hundreds and hundreds of pages without that: it would have seemed absolutely pointless to me, and my inherent laziness would have taken over. But I was kept alert, even though my emotions had been all but drained from me after a difficult, or even an easy, day of shooting. But I went on, because I knew that what I wrote was important. To one person.

And that person was my "patcher", leading me on with

tacit encouragement, fanning my vanity at the same time as she was pushing me towards taking the halting steps of a writer. *"Write anything that comes into your head,"* she once said, *"but write!"*

Before a particularly unpleasant operation on what remained of her poor mutilated body which we called the "Banjo Belly" because of the amount of stitches an earlier operation had necessitated, she wrote:

*"Oh! Poor Banjo Belly . . . how I twang! And I can't scratch, sit up, can do nothing but lie here staring at this particularly uninspiring shiny-green paint on the ceiling, or scribble as I am now, notebook above head. Oh! Do send me something again soon, it seems days since your last letter. A delicious, idiotic, 'puff'? Don't worry about spelling and so on, but don't make me laugh too much for fear I bust all these stitches and have to go through the dreadful cobbling business again. They have removed my poor little Contemplating Navel . . . somehow they seemed to take a tuck here and there. I am bereft. Write ANYTHING. About the vegetable garden NOW. This instant. Write about every stone, every shoot, every precious clod of English earth. Are there, oh COULD there be? any stray relics somewhere of my cherished Parma violets in the cold-frames which you recently discovered behind the 'sagging greenhouse'. No. Too long ago now . . ."*

And I wrote. And wrote.

Holding hands for comfort, really.

There came a time, as there had to come, when I decided to leave England for good and, therefore, the house which had been our common bond and which we had both, in different ways, loved so much. I wrote to break the news as gently as I possibly could, and my letter provoked a response which had nothing whatsoever to do with patching or learning or even teaching.

*"Coup de grace . . ."* she wrote, *"if you leave the house. The little fringes of my heart that have never hurt when the whole heart ached, now feel pain at the very thought of the house without you.*

*But c'est la vie . . . and it helps me not to care very much whether the surgeon's knife slips tomorrow or not: except that you do, I think, make it feel as though our silly literary 'amour' could still go on, even without the common bond. But please don't cast me off with the house . . ."*

It is, alas, not possible to regulate the arrival of a letter, and this of mine, breaking such saddening news, had reached her at a cruelly inopportune time. A risk taken in correspondence liaisons.

My arrival in Rome, to live, provided more "stuff" for letters, and although the house was never forgotten, we moved on into other things and the balance was kept, although now, of course, it was difficult to find books in English and we had to make do with those we already had.

I had never lived in a rented house in a foreign country before, never "lived" abroad, never had had so little to occupy my days. Trips to the supermarkets and the street markets were tremendous treats, but they didn't exactly fill the day. And my days had hitherto always been filled. From five a.m., when I was called, to eight or nine in the evening when I would return home. Time started to lie heavy on my hands and I hated it. Never social as a person, I shunned invitations and turned to the rented, very uncared-for garden of Villa Fratelli, and dug about, planted annuals (for I had only a year's lease and wasn't there for permanence), got happily stupid on the Frascati wine, of which I drank far too much, and often found myself drifting about oblivious to the world, filled with wine, in my swimming-pool at seven in the evening.

A correction had to be made. My sense of order had completely vanished.

★   ★   ★

"*I am amazed,*" she wrote one day, "*that you actually SAW Virginia Woolf! And to think that you thought her a witch. Poor creature, so maligned, I feel, by Holroyd . . . but what can the truth be? And this person 'Lally' is absolutely irresistible . . . did she let you both play with those village louts, what are their names? Reg and Perce . . . and marvellous Mrs Fluke! You made me laugh out loud about her. And I assure you, sir, I don't do that often! almost not ever!*"

I found a clue.

Rather than clattering my trolley through SuperRomano in search of the day's shopping, or drifting, slightly drunkenly, in the warm shallows of my pool, I decided I'd rough something out for her: a longer kind of journal about childhood. At least it might keep me sober: which would be a very good thing indeed. Sudden idleness had almost brought me to a full-stop. My initiative had dried up entirely. Incentive had been dissolved by the sun and wine.

I set up the typewriter, bought a stack of paper, and started.

Heading the blank piece of paper (which in those days seemed to be friendly and inviting, but today fills me with dread and anxiety that it will remain in that condition, blank) with a rough and ready title, I started off on *The Canary Cage*. My intention, apart from trying to return to a strict life-routine and remain sober, was to amuse her, to write a story which would be far away from the cold sterility of a hospital room, and from the almost unbearable waiting for what she called, *"their dreaded prognosis"*.

It was a tough start, but gradually some kind of form emerged, not easily, with effort. For a time it seemed that I had swung an arc lamp on to a long-forgotten part of my life which lay discarded in the dark. My youth. A life so completely different from the one I now lived in a rented house on a Roman hill where once Constantine had pitched his camp on the eve of the battle of Milvio. It took me all of a week; a bit longer to correct, re-write, and make a fair copy which I could send her. And then I had to wait for the verdict. Drinking Frascati cheerfully, without guilt, because, I felt, I had done something.

The verdict, when it came, was daunting:

*". . . the first pages are okay-ish. I mean I see what you want; to recapture Time Lost. But it doesn't start to 'grab' until you write from the point of view of the child. That's good. That's nice stuff. But it has a patronising air about it when you merely write as you. Get back to the child's mind. Write from his point of view. Be twelve again! Bet you can . . ."*

But I felt that I couldn't. "FORCE memory!" she counselled. But memory was dimmed by years of a war, the cinema, the struggle to survive, to create; childhood could not be forced back upwards from the darkness into which it had been thrust; but I struggled on bleakly trying to find the childmind, to "be twelve again". It was, I felt truthfully, hopeless.

I wrote one day:

*"Alas! The years of innocence have sped away. Elizabeth and I, in those days, had never heard of cancer, a race was something which you ran, and either lost or won, communists were people who lived quite near China, and we didn't know where THAT was exactly. A Golliwog was a black doll in a striped weskit and*

*fuzzy hair which you took up to bed as a comfort against the dark.*

*But we knew about Ouzles and Thrushes, and the difference between them, about cuckoo-spit and cowslips: roach and perch, about emptying what was politely known as 'the night soil' or making ginger beer, and saw Virginia Woolf wandering along the banks of the Ouse and quite convinced ourselves that she was a real witch . . . and . . . and . . . oh hell! It's ALL GONE.*

*If only we could have that innocence back again . . ."*

She replied, in an unsteady hand on a piece of paper torn, I imagine, from an old exercise book:

*"Lovely letter of the 5th has just arrived. Clever you! Hand a bit shaky from the 'shot' they give you to steady your nerves before the Op. Idiots! I'll be going in soon, but before I do, I must say something important to you.*

*That Innocence of which you speak. You CAN have it back.*

*Write it for me. Please?"*

I did. They were eventually the first three chapters of my first book, but by that time, as she had once warned me that she might, she had "slipped away", and another needlewoman had come along to assist me with my patching.

But that is still a long way ahead.

## 7

There was a Rover, badly parked, outside the village shop. On the back window-ledge, a set of Travel Scrabble, a dusty *Daily Telegraph*, a battered box of Kleenex. Spoor of the middle Middle-Class Briton abroad.

Inside, the shop was empty; except for Madame Raybaud who owned it, and two young women with a small boy. One woman in a crumpled Laura Ashley garment with puff-sleeves; the other, with the generous buttocks of a dray horse, was in shorts and a brief cotton halter, hair cut in a fringe, glasses, and flip-flop sandals. She was poking about among the bottles in the mineral-water section.

"Nothing here that *I* recognise as lemonade. Something called 'Pschitt'! Too funny; *really*, the French! Would Coca-Cola do?" she shouted. "It's in litre bottles."

The Laura Ashley one was down at the vegetable section thumping melons as if they had once betrayed her. "Oh, get anything! And tomato juice for Giles' Bloody M . . ."

The small boy picked up a tin of peas and rolled it the length of the shop. It clattered to a stop at the check-out desk. Madame Raybaud looked down impassively, hands folded.

"Jason! I'll give you the hiding of your life! Put it back at once and do up your fly-buttons."

The fat girl wandered slowly past me scanning the shelves murmuring, "Tomato juice . . . tomato juice . . . tomato juice . . ." like a whispered snatch of forgotten catechism: she saw me; wandered on uncertainly; stopped as if struck by an axe. Then she turned and hurried back to the vegetables, great breasts bouncing.

"It's *him*!" she said loudly.

"It's who?" said the Laura Ashley one.

For a moment there was a gobbling sound of smothered conversation, they both turned round and looked at me with distrust and hostility.

"Jason! Stop playing with yourself. I've told you before; you'll get stuck like it."

"*Much* older than he looks on the screen, don't you think?" said the fat girl.

"Never watch him," said the Laura Ashley, sorting angrily through the leeks. "He's balding anyway." There was a glint of triumph in her voice.

"And skinny," said the fat girl, rattling the bottles in her basket. "I do think it is quite extraordinary to come out dressed like that to do the shopping. I mean, *anyone* can see him. Filthy jeans . . ."

"No pride," said the Laura Ashley woman. "I imagine they just go native when they live down here. Give up . . . these melons are like rocks and the leeks are limp."

"The Saxbys say he's frightfully stuck up."

"Stuck together, more like it."

"Well, poor thing. I've got the tomato juice; four tins enough? And the Coca-Cola, although I don't suppose it's the real thing: you know, English. Probably made here. French yuk. He's buying cheese now! Do we need cheese?"

The Laura Ashley girl suddenly reached out and caught the small boy a swift, stinging blow on the side of his head; he opened his mouth to scream, saw her hand raised in threat, closed it again sharply and pulled a row of tins off the lower shelves.

"I'll *kill* that child! What's got into you? You've been the very devil ever since we left Dover!" She shook him roughly, dropped her shopping list. "Tins everywhere. Put them all back just as you found them, or else . . ."

"Jennifer! He's tired that's all. We all are," said the fat girl.

At the check-out I paid my bill, asked for a loaf and a copy of *Nice Matin*.

Madame Raybaud smiled.

"Anglais?" she murmured.

"Oui. Anglais."

"Ahha."

"He's paying his bill," said the fat girl brightly, her voice carrying the entire length of the shop as, indeed, it had all the time. "Bought bread. Do *we* need bread? Or would Ryvita do? I can't remember if we have bread left from yesterday. I mean, he's so much smaller than he looks on the screen, don't you think? So disappointing."

"Oh! For God's sake shut up, Barbara!" said the Ashley girl

angrily. "Do shut up, and don't stare at him all the time. You know they *love* it!"

*　*　*

When Clair Loschetter had told me, at the very beginning, that the village was "quite by-passed, it is almost undiscovered, you could say," she was, to all intents and purposes, perfectly correct. It was well away from the main road, stood high on its hill, surrounded by acres of olive groves and terraces of orange trees, and looked down across the plain and the woods to the sea and the sprawl of Sodom and Gomorrah which edged it in the far distance.

But what Clair didn't know, or perhaps chose not to tell me, was that the local name was La Colline Anglaise. The English Hill.

It was littered with them, and many of them had found it long before Clair or I had ever set foot in the area, when the land, so far from the sea and "quite by-passed", was a cheap place to retire to; and retire to it they had, in droves. To my consternation, my determined attempt to seek anonymity after years of living in a metaphorical goldfish bowl had failed, for here I was: surrounded by the voices of Tunbridge Wells, Godalming and Gerrards Cross, with a few Dutch, Americans and Germans thrown in for good measure.

They walked their "doggies" every morning through the lanes, sought their day old *Telegraphs* and *Daily Mails* in the paper shop, lived in Walt-Disney-Provençal cottages in desperately cultivated gardens, threw noisy cocktail parties almost every Friday evening ("Our turn *next* week, remember, Phyllis!") and "barked" (there is no other word for it) at each other in the local shops and called the French "They" and "Them". Good-naturedly. Perfectly pleasant people.

I had obviously made another error in calculation. It vexed me greatly to think that I had hauled myself and my shattered possessions almost a thousand miles in a desperate search for privacy and peace, spent a small fortune on a half-ruined house, and had found myself almost full circle again: back where I had started. The Home Counties. In France.

However, my French neighbour assured me that things were far worse up in the Dordogne where practically every village, he said sadly, was a British Fort; and I did have a good deal of land about me for protection, and La Colline Anglaise was on the other side of our hill. So . . .

As long as I was careful I need not, I felt sure, become involved. For I had never played whist or bridge, been to a wine and cheese party, or run a stall for any charity. (To my shame.) I saw no reason why I should do so now: even if asked. Which was most unlikely, because although the English abroad can often seem noisy and sometimes appear to be overwhelmingly patronising and arrogant, they are, in fact, extremely shy and on occasions perfectly polite, but their peculiar class system (usually self-invented) would preclude them from dealing with "Film People", who are unclassifiable, except as extroverts, and in consequence alarming.

The Working, or Labouring, Class and the Aristocratic Top have no such fears. They know precisely where they belong and are therefore quite secure: but the Middle Classes are not absolutely certain *what* they are, and for that reason anything which might unsettle them to any degree is best left alone for fear it could bring them all tumbling down from the comfortable, if uneasy, position in which they exist.

They distrust, intensely, anything which is different; and actors, painters, writers, even musicians, are of course different and to be approached with caution. Hence the reaction in the village shop from Jennifer and Barbara: a scene which was repeated a good number of times until I managed to rearrange my marketing hours, and although I became, in the end, perfectly used to the performance, it always saddened me, and made me feel like Dr Stiffkey sitting in his barrel on Blackpool Pier.

M. Marc, my local mason, came one morning to continue some job he was doing in the house. He was in a depressed mood, disinclined to talk: unusual in him, for he normally chattered like a magpie. This morning he did not. Fearing that perhaps his wife, who did my laundry, or one of his children was ill, I asked him if all was well at home.

He suddenly pulled off his cap and threw it on a table. "It's finished!" he said, and his eyes were strangely bright.

"What is finished?"

"You didn't hear the radio last night?"

"No."

He brushed his eyes roughly with his sleeve. "She's *dead*! Josephine is *dead*! *Malheur*! The light has gone out, there is no more light!'' He pulled on his cap and went about his business without another word.

Josephine Baker had died during the second performance of her new show in Paris: France was distraught over the death of an artist. And no one more so than M. Marc.

I wondered ruefully if it could have happened under the same circumstances, in England. We do not, in the most general terms, rate the arts very highly: even though we have produced so many men and women of unique brilliance in all its fields. For the average Briton, Sport is God. Art is pretty cissy. In Latin countries sport is equally revered: but an artist, be he painter, musician, dancer, writer, singer or actor, is treated with equal esteem and affection as is his sporting counterpart. Sometimes more. After all, they are all a part of the same game. Achievement. And no one chucks bottles at the referee.

★   ★   ★

In my first year in France I had not made up my mind, absolutely, to settle there. I had some vague idea, unexpressed clearly even to myself, that I might make it my base and wander, as a free spirit, from place to place, perhaps even take a small flat in Rome, a city which I loved.

But the tremendous amount of money, which I could not afford, and which I had spent on the restoration of the house, the clearing of the land and pruning of the drowning olive trees (they cost nearly five pounds a tree to save: and with 400 I had to do them in modest groups of ten or twelve when I could afford it) put any ideas of that nature, or little flats in Rome, however humble, right out of my head. I'd have to stay put. There wasn't anything spare for wandering abroad.

It was the habit that if you resided in France you could only stay unregistered for a period of three months. Now it is six. Some foreigners found it desirable, and easy, to slip across a neighbouring border, Italy or even Switzerland, for a day or so at the end of their three months, get their passports stamped on re-entry, and start another period of residence.

But once I had made up my mind to live for good in France, and not wander about, I found the uncertainty, and my sense of order, such as it was, would not permit me to join this country dance. I knew that I could not jig about to Italy or

Switzerland every three months because the house, which contained all that I owned, would never really seem to be mine. Also I'd probably forget when my time was up. It seemed far too temporary a life and I wanted, above all things, to be settled. To this end, every three months (I marked the date on the kitchen calendar) I would go up to the Mairie in the village and sit in the ante-room on a bentwood chair with a clutch of foreign immigrants, mostly Arab, Spanish or Portuguese, and await my turn to go into the inner sanctum, where the Deputy Mayor sat at a cluttered desk, chain-smoking, and writing down, in immaculate copperplate, all one's particulars, which didn't amount to much anyway, on a small piece of grey paper which was one's permit to live in his country for another three months free of complications. It seemed, to me, easier, and pleasanter, than fleeing to a border like a fugitive. But in time the three-monthly haul up to the Mairie became a bit of a chore. I was more certain of my feelings now, less anxious to trail about, and wanted roots. So I decided to stay in France legally and for as long as they would allow me.

I had got fed up with the lurking sense of impermanence, I knew that I was fairly well known in the village and the neighbouring town and that, if anyone asked, it would be absurd to say that I didn't live in my house all the year round, winter and summer: I was too familiar locally for any kind of deceptions, however modest.

Another thing which forced this slightly dramatic decision was the almost constant inference in the British press that I was doing something illegal anyway. If a photograph was published of me in the cheaper papers the caption often contained a reference to the fact that I was a Tax Dodger, in much the same way that they might have said I was a member of the Great Train Robbery gang. I resented the implication bitterly.

★   ★   ★

The British Consul in Nice was a pleasant, florid man in a crumpled blue pin-striped suit and a service tie. About the walls of his fairly gloomy office above a shop and opposite a bar in a side street hung photographic relics of his more adventurous youth.

Motor torpedo boats, or something of that sort, cutting through rough seas, the flag streaming. They were framed in too-thin passe-partout and hung haphazardly on the butter-yellow walls.

He politely offered me the chair standing before his barren desk (or perhaps it was just tidy), listened carefully to what I had to say about becoming a resident, played thoughtfully with a ruler, lips pursed like a child at the breast.

"You're *quite* sure, are you?" he said uncertainly.

"Quite. So I wondered if perhaps you could recommend a local lawyer, I don't think that it is anything my London man can handle, I mean, he doesn't live here . . ."

"Quite." He shrugged his shoulders once or twice before speaking again, eyes still on his ruler. "Local?" he said finally. "You did say local? Not easy. No. Not easy. Lawyers, I mean: it's a bit difficult."

"Are there any British ones then? There must be a pretty large British population here in Nice: all those retired nannies and so on."

He looked at me balefully. "*Nannies?*"

"Well, retired people living here. There are masses where I am."

He cleared his throat uncomfortably, looked vaguely round his collection of motor boats. "Couple of fellows here who are all right. British, I mean."

"Could you perhaps recommend one to me?"

He looked at me for a moment, reached out and tore a sheet from a small, virginal memo pad, scribbled two names.

"And these are all right? They know all the rules and regulations? I mean, I *don't*. Haven't an idea, so I don't want to put a foot wrong, and I need the advice."

He picked up his ruler. "They're all right. Use one of them myself, s'matter of fact."

"Ah! Could you tell me which one? I mean of the two? If *you* use him he's very likely the best bet."

"Can't tell you that. Sorry. Find out for yourself. Not my business." He dismissed me by opening a drawer under his desk and taking out a thin file which he rustled importantly.

I had obviously made a grave diplomatic blunder. I left with some relief. A couple of weeks later I filed my papers at the Mairie in the village requesting permission to become a Foreign Resident of the Alpes Maritimes. Six months later I got it.

*　*　*

The first two years at the house passed pleasantly enough; and slowly. Time didn't race away as it seems to now, when every second day is suddenly Saturday again. There was a great deal to be done on the land; and bit by bit a garden, of sorts, was wrenched from the shale and rock. Bales of peat, and tons of earth were brought in by truck, trees planted, the terrace made comfortable with chairs under the vine, and all the other terraces, once a wilderness of tussocky grass and bramble, were brought under control and mowed as smooth as they could be got.

I had inherited, from one of the early labouring teams, a lunatic Arab who spoke no known language, anyway to me, couldn't use a machine or sow a nasturtium, but was strong enough to lift rocks. He started off by re-building all the fallen walls, and erected a high stone pillar at the entrance to the track which he decorated with broken bits of red glass from some-one's rear-light, and crowned, majestically, with a metal sign bearing the word "Fiat" in gleaming letters. I managed to get this off before the cement set. Much to his sorrow. But between us, Forwood, Aziz, and myself working almost non-stop, the place suddenly began to emerge from its years of neglect; and in the second spring the scent of wallflowers and stocks reminded me that it was about time that my parents came back: to look and exclaim in pleasure. And, I hoped, to praise: for a great deal had been done since their last visit.

"Well," my father sounded uncertain on the telephone, "you've rather sprung it on us . . . but you *always* do that, I suppose. I'll have to ask Mother. She's not been too well, filthy cold all winter, and that fall shook her up a bit. It's all the train and the boat business. Rather tiring, you know, at our age."

"You'll fly out. Much easier, far more comfortable, and quicker, too."

It wasn't.

London airport was in chaos as usual, it was Easter, or just about to be, the plane was an hour late, and they had had a bumpy trip.

However, here they were on the terrace, a little wobbly from the journey, a little amazed by being here, surprised at and praising, as I hoped, the changes which had taken place since their last visit two years before.

They looked a little frail. I noticed that my father's hands were not perfectly steady, but put this down to the exhausting journey they had made, and my mother walked much more slowly, taking her time to cross the polished tiles. "Still no carpets . . ." she murmured. But they both looked incredibly young, and she, trim and beautifully made up, a long ritual which took her a lot of time each morning, still had hardly one grey hair in her head, and moved her ringed hands graphically and vividly: an actress's hands, of which she was justly proud.

Sitting there in the warm March sun they were a splendidly handsome couple, and I felt an enormous lift of pleasure at their presence.

★　★　★

I opened a bottle of Krug: the cork popped, and flew upwards into the budding vine.

"Champagne!" said my father. "I thought you were bust?"

"The last of the Christmas stock. I am bust."

"Well, not for me. You don't mind, do you? I'd rather have a glass of beer."

"It's a celebration," I said.

My mother took her glass eagerly. "Just what I needed. The people in that airport! Really. It's steerage, all pushing and shoving. I could have died!"

My father opened his beer carefully, poured it so that the foam lay lightly on the top. "Don't want to waste a drop. What's the celebration? Oh yes, you mean us?"

"And today I'm fifty-one. My birthday."

My mother, who had almost finished her wine, set the glass on the table. "I forgot! *Many* happy returns, darling. God! Fancy me forgetting that!"

"You've come a long way. Plenty of other things to remember, and anyway fifty-one isn't such a big deal."

"Fifty-one," she said, and drained the glass, holding it out for re-filling. "My God! You gave me a time! Nearly eight pounds you were: I told you, didn't I, that you were conceived in Paris? This is going to kill you . . ."

"Now, Margaret," said my father. "We've been into all that."

"Oh, I know! I know! But he was, and I wanted you to be born in France. Did you know *that*?"

I nodded obediently. The story was starting. I took up the bottle.

"But it was all mistimed or something, wasn't it?"

"*I* didn't mistime a thing. That idiot Dr . . . whatever his name was . . . Mortimer . . . or something." I poured her another, modest flute of Krug.

"Dr Morgan," said my father quietly, scraping the bowl of his pipe with the blade of his penknife.

"Morgan. That's who it was. No: *I* didn't make a mistake. He did. Idiot. I could have wept."

"Well, it doesn't matter much really, does it?" I said.

"It did to me. Terribly. I was furious. Some awful nursing home in Hampstead."

"But here I am! In France anyway, just as you wanted."

I was keeping my patience because, although the stories were as familiar as my two hands, to lose patience, and I did quite often when they started, would have been insufferable at such a moment.

"Many happy returns," said my father, putting his penknife away and taking up his beer. "I must say, you look very well. I suppose it's all this air, the sun and the light. . . ."

"Hard work, digging and mowing. Hay-cutting, I mean, it's hardly mowing. I'll show you the machine later on, it's enormous."

My mother drained her glass and handed it to me. "I'd like some more, while you're on your feet. My tiredness is going. Oh those people!" I poured her wine carefully.

"Ma, you'll get tiddly."

"Who cares?" she said. "My dear! My wallflowers aren't even in bud yet, just look at yours! And the camellia . . . oh, this is heaven," she said, raising her face to the late March sun.

I caught my father's eye: he was smiling lightly, but there was a shadow of concern on his face. He winked at me, sipped his beer.

"Now then. Where's this doss house you're going to put us in? Not far, you said?"

"At the end of the road, it's very clean, comfortable . . . you've got the only self-contained suite. Won't have to go padding about corridors for a pee in the night."

"Should hope not," he said. "We'd lose your mother. No sense of direction. Remember the 'Queen Elizabeth'? We lost her for two hours . . . amazing woman."

"I remember that!" said my mother. "The *dear* 'Queen Elizabeth'. I met a charming woman in one of the corridors, a steward or something. From Ayrshire . . . I can't think why you were so worried. We had a wonderful talk, she was a dear soul."

A little later I took them up to the small hotel where they were to sleep and have breakfast and from which, each morning, I would go to collect them at about ten and drive them back after supper. It seemed a sensible arrangement, and they were delighted with their room which had a splendid view down the valley, and a comfortable, modern bathroom.

"Only one thing," said my father, vaguely picking the side of his nose, a sign that he had a slight doubt.

"What?"

"Well, these awful sausage things on the beds. I can't sleep with those, and I know Mother can't. Be a good boy and bring us up a couple of real pillows when you come to collect us, will you? About six o'clock, all right?"

"Yes. Unpack, have a bit of a rest and I'll bring you some proper pillows."

My mother was singing in the bathroom: water ran.

"She's happy now she's here," said my father. "Had a bit of a job to persuade her to come, mind you. Seems to be giving up a bit. Everything is too much trouble; she is very emotional, you know. Your birthday and all that sort of thing. A long time, fifty-one years; and she's getting a bit shaky, won't walk much." He folded his tobacco pouch, put it in his pocket. "Fortunately I can get about, do the shopping and so on. She's not keen now . . . cooking and that sort of thing." He leant across and touched my arm, "So, be a good chap and don't snap at her, it's difficult sometimes, but it makes her so miserable."

"I *don't* snap, Pa!"

"Oh yes you do! When she starts her 'stories', I know." He was smiling.

"Well, we have heard them since birth, almost. I don't mean to snap."

"Be patient then, perhaps I mean that? Let her have her say, she loves it. She won't read now, you know? I read to her; she likes that. I think."

"Why won't she read?"

"Oh, can't be bothered. Loses her glasses. Concentration a

9. With Charlotte Rampling in "The Night Porter". 1973.

10. As 'Max'. "The Night Porter". Rome 1973.

11. Liliana Cavani at the London Press Reception for "The Night Porter". 1974.

bit fragile. She is seventy-three, you know. Got to remember that, amazing, she looks so much younger but . . ." He sat on the edge of the bed, thumped it. The springs twanged. "I think we'll be very comfortable here. With proper pillows, of course! Do you know? I spied a nice little bar when we came in? Might have a little drink before you collect us. I'm going to be eighty in June, you realise? So I feel a bit of self-indulgence is in order."

At six o'clock Forwood drove me up to the hotel with a pair of pillows and a bunch of extra coat-hangers. The hotel seemed deserted. I went through into the small lobby and saw my mother lying at the foot of the stairs, an anxious group of people in holiday clothes standing round her, my father, with a waxen face trying to help her to sit, but as he touched her she screamed out, "Don't! Don't! Oh don't, please!"

I pushed through the crowd; someone murmured that the steps were always dangerous. I knelt beside her, she lay on one side, a tumbled ruin of black lace and Chanel beads, her earrings had fallen off and her face was chalk white, eyes blazing with pain, her shoulder pressed high against her ear.

"The steps. I fell on the steps," she said.

Somehow we got her into the car and drove, at snail's pace, because every rut and stone caused her to cry out in agony, to the house where a horrified Henri and Marie helped us to get her into the long room where I gave her a treble brandy neat, and Forwood called Dr Poteau.

"Double fracture or dislocation," he said swiftly. "Look, the upper arm bone is almost pushed into her ear. Dislocation, I think; the bone is out of the socket." He started to dial an ambulance but I asked him if he had any morphia in his bag. He did and gave her an injection which would have calmed a raging bull.

There was no single ambulance in all the area, which could find the way to the house. The ultimate irony of my search for privacy, anonymity and peace. The only person who did know the way through the lanes was Maurice in the bar in the village who ran a taxi. He was free and on his way. Poteau called a clinic in Nice.

"Nice! Isn't there somewhere nearer? Nice is an hour away, and she's in terrible pain, and in a taxi . . ."

"It's the best place, St George's at Cimiez; they are waiting for her. You know," he looked at my mother who sat slumped against the whitewashed wall on a low stool, the nearest we could get her into the room, "it is grave. She may never use that arm again."

It was a kind of living nightmare, the journey to the clinic. Forwood, my father and I sat crushed in the back, my mother in the seat beside Maurice, her head lolling; silent, sedated.

When we got into Nice it was dark and no one knew where the clinic was. We drove about desperately, winding down windows, asking for directions. No one knew, or if they did were uncertain, and we ended up lurching along unlighted roads in the middle of unfinished building estates.

Eventually we found St George's, an enormous new building, white marble, plate glass, more like a very expensive hotel than a clinic, and three-and-a-half hours after her fall my unfortunate mother was in the gentle, competent, hands of hurrying nurses, being wheeled down to the X-ray Department. My father, Forwood and I followed, as useless and out of place as skiers in a ballroom. I suddenly realised that I hadn't even changed, and was still wearing old jeans and a T-shirt.

Dr Fallacci, a tall, quiet man, came out of the Radio Room, a dripping X-ray plate in his rubber-gloved fingers. The damage was grave. A severe dislocation, a fracture, an operation and the chance that, as Poteau had said, she would never again be able to use her left arm. Did we, he asked politely, wish to have her bandaged and strapped up so that she could be flown back to England for treatment? She would have to fly out the next day, not a second later.

I translated this to my father, who spoke almost no French and who was standing apart in a fringe of shadow in the long corridor. He was holding, cupped in one hand, my mother's rings which I had helped one of the nurses to remove, with some kind of lubricant. They clinked and winked in the light as he turned them.

"I don't want her moved again," he said. "Can they do it here?"

They could and they did, with the greatest care and skill, and Dr Fallacci found, to his obvious delight, that he was able to manipulate the bones back into place without using surgery, and that the chances of my mother regaining full use of the arm were very possible. But that was all to come later.

After we had left the clinic that night to drive back to the house, we were not certain of anything: a decision had been made, we'd have to wait until the next day for a verdict.

"She was incredibly brave," said Forwood suddenly. "Not a word of complaint, didn't cry once."

"She's very brave," said my father.

"But she did cry," I said. "One time only: when I had to remove her wedding ring. She wept then."

My father cleared his throat. "Got them here, in my pocket. Curious thing . . ." He patted his pocket vaguely: I heard the rings chink.

★　★　★

He was sitting on a fallen tree-trunk down beyond the cane-break: I could just see the top of his white head above the easel. Otherwise he was completely hidden by the canvas on which he was working. Daisy and Labo careened past him after some imaginary rabbit (they had long ago flushed them off the land, alas). He looked up as I came down through the tall grasses.

"You have come to tell me something dreatful," he said. He always pronounced the second "d" as "t" for some reason.

"No. Nothing dreadful. Just that lunch is in fifteen minutes and I called the clinic and Ma is in fine fettle and she can come out on Friday. Afternoon."

He made no reply for a moment, stroked away with his brush at the canvas. "She's all right, is she?"

"Sounded fine. She said she's been having a marvellous time with the nurses, telling them funny stories: in Glaswegian."

"Oh, she would," he said. "She's wonderfully good with people; what on earth they can possibly make of her Scots accent I don't know, but she loves a crowd."

"An audience?" I said.

"Yes. Very fond of audiences, your Ma. A performer, like you. She really comes to life with people to listen to her. She finds it pretty dull, you know, at home now." He mixed a little yellow paint with a swift movement, loaded his brush, applied it to the canvas. "These cane-things. More beige-green than yellow, wouldn't you say? I really shouldn't have married her."

It was very still: then Labo barked.

"Mother? Shouldn't have married her?"

"Been kinder, really. She's missed the theatre and all that hurly-burly her whole life. I'm afraid it was all my fault. But I was very much in love with her." He was painting with neat, tight strokes.

I moved round the easel, sat down on the trunk beside him. The dogs came lolloping up the hill, tongues hanging, foam flying.

'Silly dogs, then," he said. "You'll give yourselves heart attacks."

I looked up towards the house, Henri was turning the cushions on the terrace chairs, small clouds drifted towards the sea across the brilliant blue sky like fat cherubim.

"I don't think I ever knew two people who were more in love than you and Mother. I mean, that's what it seemed like. As children, Elizabeth and I were really pretty disgusted when you took each other's arms; touched. We called you the Lovers. Thought you were both terribly soppy."

He started to clean his brush carefully on a piece of cloth. "Oh, we managed. When you were young it wasn't so hard for her; lots of things going on, people about, she liked first nights at the theatre, going to stay at Hever, parties. People flattered her. She was very striking looking, I don't know how she managed to dress so well on the little I was able to give her: a wonderful mother to you and very loyal to me. I can't complain, she had the worst part of the bargain. Gave up such a lot, all her cronies. Theatre people; I didn't much like them, you know, I was happy pottering about, at the cottage; it was too lonely for her. She was bored most of the time away from London. No; she made the sacrifices, not I."

"What do you mean, though, that you 'managed'? It's not really so, is it?"

He placed the cleaned brush into his paint-box, started to screw on the lid of the turpentine bottle. "Yes it is. I was twenty-seven when we married: if I had had the money then that *you* had at that age, we would have been divorced in four months; but as it was, I didn't have the money; you know *The Times*? So we just muddled through."

Henri's voice called down thinly from the terrace. "Dix minutes, Messieurs!"

We collected the easel and the paint-box in silence; my father carried his wet canvas carefully up the hill behind me.

"You carry on," he said. "I'm not hurrying up this path: got a splendid thirst so I hope there is something very refreshing in the bar-cupboard. We've just got time, eh?"

"Yes. Yes, there is. All waiting for you," I said. There was absolutely nothing else that I could say.

★    ★    ★

We never spoke of it again: I think that I was too frightened to talk of it, to question the shattering confession which he had made so casually, so calmly, down by the cane-break.

It was obvious then, that after all he *had* realised the deep current of frustration which ran beneath my mother's otherwise cheerful and ordered surface; it was equally obvious from his confession that this frustration had caused desperate pain to them both. I had had no idea that there had ever been a case of "muddling through" in their lives which at least on the surface is all I suppose I ever took the trouble to see, and had seemed as stable and devoted as any marriage I had ever known.

But a tropical island, serene in a limpid sea, can suddenly explode into a Krakatoa; a stretch of golden sand, shimmering serenely in the sun, can pull you into its depths and drag you implacably to your death: without warning. Nothing, in short, is ever exactly what it seems. And a human relationship is perhaps the hardest to evaluate, and quite as treacherous as natural phenomena like sands and volcanoes, and causes just as much damage and pain. But, as I have said, things which distress me greatly and about which I can do nothing, I tend to smother into oblivion: and I did so that day. It was far too late, in all our lives, to make any changes or offer solutions, they could do no possible good. Habit had taken a tight hold; and habit, at least, can sometimes be comforting.

When my mother went into the clinic, I cleared everything from the little hotel with its three treacherous steps, and made my father comfortable in the little single bedroom at the house. For a week he broke all his habits and was content to potter about with his sketch-book and easel, read and listen to music in the evenings, or even, on occasions, help out with the garden work. He was perfectly happy. Indeed, he showed very little anxiety in my mother's situation, knowing, I suppose, that she was in good hands and well taken care of: he just enjoyed himself, by himself.

When I suggested that we would have to drive over to Nice and see her he was always agreeable, but not over so.

"Today? We must? Oh, very well, it's just that the light is perfect and I'm in the middle of a job. Might not quite recapture it if I let it go."

But we went, and he sat uncomfortably on a wooden chair while my mother, in a frail voice filled with pleasure, told us how superb the food was, that she had a "dear little half-bottle of wine" for each meal, and that the nurses were "out of this world" and loved her stories. She was rested, not in pain, and only resented the heavy plaster which covered her damaged arm and shoulder. Dr Fallacci came in each day to see her, she said, and he loved her stories too.

"You must be having a whale of a time," I said.

"Oh, I am! I am! I'm never allowed to open my mouth with you lot. I'm having a *wonderful* time."

But the time ended when we collected her, finally, and brought her back to the house and a local *Maison de Repos*, which was not, perhaps, the most cheerful of places, but in which she could be given the treatment which she still needed. My father, rather silently, moved in with her but spent all his days up at the house. She was in bed for two weeks, and only allowed out for a short time, as she became stronger, on condition that she went to bed every afternoon. It was not what you might call a riotous holiday for anyone: and she firmly refused to walk an inch, terrified that she'd fall again.

"She *could* walk perfectly well," said my father impatiently. "But the other night she said it was 'all coming true'."

"What is all coming true?" I asked.

"Oh, that damned woman at the Coxes' wedding, years ago in Brighton, don't you remember? She came up to your mother and said that she was a medium and that she could 'see' Mother's 'aura'. Apparently it was violet or purple or something, and the woman said that showed that Mother was a Tragedy Queen."

"Well, she is rather, isn't she?" I wasn't taking it very seriously, for his sake.

"She also said that she'd lose the use of her legs and they'd have to be cut off! I ask you! What a thing to tell anyone, and especially at a wedding. Of course Mother believes every word. So now she is convinced that she fell because she is losing the use of her legs. Honestly! That bloody woman.

They ought to lock up people like that, they cause so much damage. There's nothing wrong with her legs, we've had doctor after doctor, all say the same thing. Remember that doctor of yours in Rome when she couldn't walk?"

"Frank? Very well."

"Said all she needed was a good kick up the backside. Well. I wouldn't have used quite those words, but *he* did."

"She was furious. I remember."

"Still wouldn't walk, though: would she? Oh, women!"

On the morning that they were to leave, finally, for London, my mother was sitting out on the terrace, a huge Dior scarf slung round her shoulders, in her broad-brimmed hat, and the trim jersey suit in which she had arrived four weeks before.

"Do I look all right?" she said.

"Smashing. Very 'chic' indeed."

"My face all right?" She smiled up at me into the sun.

"Perfect. You are clever, once an actress, always an actress."

"To the death," she said. "A hell of a job putting on your make-up with only one hand. My eyelashes all right? Not smudged?"

"Immaculate. Where's Pa?"

"I don't know. Went off with the dogs somewhere. Go and find him, you know what Ulric's like, we'll miss the 'plane. He drives me mad."

"Hours for that. Don't worry."

He was up at the end of the Long Walk under the cherry trees, looking out across the valley to the sea and the mountains. I walked towards him slowly, not wanting to disturb him, but he turned and raised a hand.

"Ma's getting into a fret. Thought you'd gone off somewhere with the dogs."

"No. No, just having a look, that's all. Curious about Renoir, isn't it? Living in that house in the village, opposite the paper shop. And you didn't realise?"

"No, clever of you to spot the plaque-thing."

"1900 to 1903, wasn't it? I made a note somewhere. Is it time we were moving? We're all packed."

"In half an hour. Time for a little drink if you want one."

"Well, not a bad idea."

"Pa, no goodbyes at the airport, eh?"

"Lord, no!" He followed me down the grassy track to the house. "I've said all mine."

I turned in surprise. "Said them?"

"To this," he said, and nodded his head briefly towards the far mountains.

"Not goodbye! Au revoir, surely."

"No. I don't think we'll be back, you know. I'll never get your mother to move out here again. We're getting on a bit now, and I think that she feels, well, safer in her own house, she really doesn't enjoy travelling much, and this fall business. Rather put the lid on things, I'm afraid. Bit of bad luck, that."

"Well, next time she can stay with Elizabeth and George and you come out on your own, why not?"

"Oh no," he said, kicking a forgotten dog-ball into the grass. "I couldn't leave her. Anyway I've done a lot of work here this time, painting. I've got a mass of sketches, too, which I can work up, keep me busy all year. Oh, one thing you might do for me, that square in Le Rouret? Where they play *boules*, with all the plane trees round it?"

"Yes. What?"

"Could you send me a photograph of it? From the doorway of the bar? I never seemed to get the time to go there, so much here to paint. Will you?"

"Of course," I said and followed him down to the terrace.

★   ★   ★

At the airport I pushed her wheelchair to the barrier at International.

"Can't come any further. Pa will have to take over."

"Is this where we go?"

She looked splendidly defiant, the green silk scarf about her shoulders, concealing most of the plaster-cast and the empty jacket sleeve; the wide-brimmed hat.

"Someone will get you aboard, and Elizabeth and George are waiting at the other end: it'll be super. Home in a flash." I stooped to kiss her.

"Goodbye, my darling. Give my love to the dogs, it's been a *wonderful* holiday." The platitudes of farewell came easily to her lips.

My father was sorting his papers and passports.

"You won't need anything here, Pa, just the passports. Give Ma the boarding passes."

"No, no, now don't you start bullying me. I like to have them all together like this, you see?" His hands were shaking.

I kissed him briefly on both cheeks. "No goodbyes, remember?"

"No, off you go. We can manage now."

I left them and walked away into the middle of the mall. He pushed the chair through the swing barrier. A shimmer of green silk, the broad-brimmed hat, his Burberry; small tweed cap.

Angela and Robin at the same barrier.

Two men in blazers hurried through, laughing, "We've missed old Rodney . . ." Obliterating my parents.

I suddenly had a lump in my throat. Forwood said, "Well, that's that. I'm going up to the Post Office, coming?"

"No." My voice was unsteady. "See if there are any London papers. Meet you at the doors."

The paper-stall was small and crammed, a good place to hide in, to compose oneself. In the far corner among the children's books, my back to the shop, I felt safe enough to let the sudden, unbidden, tears well. Idiotic to blub at fifty-one. I thumbed through some coloured pages, they blurred: I blinked. They cleared.

"I think it *is* him," said a woman's voice.

"No. Couldn't be."

"I think so, saw him come in."

"Well, ask him then, silly! Don't stand there staring."

"No. *You* ask him. Anyway, he won't mind us staring. They love it, you know."

## 8

FORWOOD was showing, as usual, the greatest patience. "Now; look at it this way. You have twelve eggs and use eight for an omelette. Right? How many eggs have you left?"

Oh Lord! I thought. Here we go again. Arithmetic.

"Ummmm. Four?"

"Right. Splendid! You see you *can* be quite bright if you put your mind to it: now then, supposing that the one hen you own . . ."

"One only?"

"One. Supposing that hen is 'off lay', that no more eggs are coming your way after you have used the last of your four. What then?"

"There won't be any more eggs."

"Marvellous. You've got it."

"Well. I try. I'm not as daft as you seem to think sometimes: what's all this rubbish about eggs and hens; non-laying hens, I mean?"

"Money. It's rather where you are, I'm afraid, after two years of 'off-laying'; if you follow me?"

"Oh yes. Yes, I follow you. So what am I supposed to do about it?"

He closed his note-book, collected the stack of bills together, put the top on his fountain pen. "Start laying again," he said. "And soon. There are four eggs left."

"You mean I'm the bloody hen?"

"That's exactly what I mean. Looking at this pile of stuff here, it occurs to me that you will be in need of a big basket of eggs. And pretty soon. And as you are the only hen you've got, as far as I know, you'd better start laying."

In the two years since I had retreated, as opposed to retired as has so often been said, from the cinema after "Death in Venice", there really hadn't been much corn, so to speak, to induce a hen to lay anything. Scripts had come in fair quantity; and they stood stacked in a slithery pile down in the cellar, which seemed to me the best place for them.

Depressingly, the work which I had done in that last film

had resulted in my being firmly established, at least in the film-makers' minds, as an aging "oddity", apparently willing to play a wide range of schoolmasters with secret lusts for their pupils, either boys or girls (it didn't really matter) or priests in flowing robes creeping about the Gothic corridors of suspect public schools hearing appalling confessions in the confessionals. That sort of thing. The only other variation was the spy thriller, and there was a pile of those too, in which I was variously asked to play Philby, Burgess or Maclean.

Here and there, lying among the suitcases and wine bottles, you could perhaps lay hands on an "updated" version of, say, "Dr Jekyll and Mr Hyde" or a brand new version of "Rasputin, The Mad Monk". There was also quite a number of "Today Subjects" (as they were then called), which were concerned with "bent" policemen, or rapist photographers who liked schoolgirls; and so it went on.

So much for Thomas Mann, Visconti, and the work which we had shared together so lovingly. Apparently, all it had done was to prove, without any shadow of a doubt, that I was now "available for degenerate parts". A saddening, chastening blow.

So I had bunged them all down in the cellar and got on with pruning, planting, mowing and sowing where the air was fresh and, at least, clean.

To be fair, there had been one or two, in the welter of muck, which were of higher quality; and Losey had offered me a subject at which I baulked only because of its politics and its over-simplified script; my reaction alarmed him until another actor, far more bankable than I, accepted it happily. So that was all right. And there were one or two dull things with splendid players like Deborah Kerr, Joanne Woodward and Peter Ustinov or Topol, and one even with Elizabeth Taylor, indeed; but none of them could tempt me away from the bucolic life into which I had entered that hot August day two years before. I was perfectly happy; for the time being.

However, I could see Forwood's point of view. I had to.

More money, by far, had been spent on the house than one had ever envisaged at the start. Not just in the reconstruction, which was modest, but on all the unexpected things which had occurred to make life expensive. Re-wiring the whole place for a start didn't cost pennies; and then the water-pipes were discovered to be made not of iron but of black lace, which leaked lakes into the limestone and shale, but made little impression in the bathrooms or the kitchen. So they had to be relaid, miles of them; the olives had to be "pruned", the land drained, and so it went on.

Unfortunately, I had never been what is now known as a Superstar, a debased word coined, I think, in the 'seventies, and I had never, at any time, earned the kind of money they commanded; and got.

Fourteen years under contract to Rank, starting at a humble three thousand pounds a year and increasing, if they took up the yearly "option" on your talent, modestly every year, did not make me a millionaire: although it did allow me to live very comfortably, with care.

A pound was a pound in those days of the 'fifties and 'sixties: and when I was "loaned out" to other companies or even to Hollywood, Rank took a sharp share of the profits, and I got a pleasant percentage. However, I was not a greedy fellow. Until then I had never earned more than ten pounds a week, so I justly felt that as long as I could pay my way and save a bit for the old age which I hoped lay ahead, barring some unforeseen disaster, I was perfectly happy.

In any case, my total ignorance of money in any form prevented me from worrying, really. I never actually knew, to the figure, what I earned, was never permitted to have a cheque book, or sign cheques (for fear that I would hand them round like communion wafers) and almost never carried money in my pocket.

Sometimes, if I was unaccompanied at some event or even on a location, I was given a few pounds in order to buy cigarettes or a round of drinks, otherwise I never saw the stuff, and was happy in my ignorance.

The facts of life, that is to say money, which so bewildered me, were handled by Forwood and by the accountants and lawyers, trim in their black jackets and pin-striped pants, who saw to it that I was kept solvent, saved tax, and did not overspend. They were all good men and true, and I saw, and had, no reason to question them at any time.

The only things that I insisted upon were that I should never owe anyone a penny, not even the local greengrocer for a week, and that I need never take out a mortgage on, or for, anything. If that was needed then I went without. Debt had terrified me ever since the days when I had carted my money about with me in an old Oxo tin: I had always expected to go back to the beginning again, and start anew, and I was determined that when this happened I would be debtless. Bad enough to start off again, without owing money.

I think the only time I actually agreed to have anything on credit was for the television sets for the staff room: I was certain that such a vulgar "toy" did not merit a purchase, and it was only many years later, when I came to France, that I had to change my point of view and buy one in a desperate effort to silence an extremely talkative guest who, literally, never drew breath for a week. I thought that it might shut her up in the evenings. But alas! It was, of necessity, all in French which she could not understand, so she went on talking: and the television gathered dust.

It was also many years later that I was persuaded to work in a film, which the French so aptly called a "Khaki Melo", that is to say, a "War Film", which was as stuffed with Superstars as the proverbial pie is with plums. They were all perfectly pleasant young men, some of whom earned, for just fourteen days work, more than double the amount of money I had earned in fourteen years in forty-plus movies, with Rank. If I had earned, for just one film out of the many I had made, what these young men got for a two-week stint in this single Epic, I wouldn't have been faced with the idiotic "chicken and egg" analogy, and I could have secured the house and my old age, without worry.

But as it was, I hadn't got that sort of cash, had overspent at the beginning, and was now, it seemed, spending more on its maintenance and general upkeep. Quite simply, I hadn't got the wherewithal to do so.

So, in a very irritated way, I was forced to agree with myself that the glowing idea I had held of being able to do as I wished in security was all nonsense. I wasn't secure at all; and I'd have to go back to work again.

My ideals had been too high. And so, now, were prices in general.

But how many people ever realised that the vengeance of the Arabs would strike them to their very souls? I was not the only person who feverishly rustled about in the pages of a school atlas to find out exactly where these terrible new areas of danger really were. Most of them were unpronounceable; all of them inhospitable.

So I came to terms with things rapidly. The next reasonable script which arrived, if one ever should again, must be viewed with a little more care: unless it was about yet *another* demented priest or raving schoolmaster. Surely there *had* to be some kind of alternative?

Meanwhile all about me spring had made rapid advances towards summer. The skies had taken on a more intense blue, the grass was thick and green, and up on the Long Walk the cherry was exploding into blossom; and my pond, the pond which I had caused to be torn from the barren land where no pond had ever been before, was pulsing with life and mating-toads, who waltzed inelegantly together, stringing ropes of glossy black pearls among the budding water lilies. Creatures which had never existed on the hill arrived in quantities. Dragonflies of every shape and hue flicked and spun above the thrusting spears of water flags; wagtails, both the grey and the yellow, skipped and dipped from stone to stone. A fat, edible, frog quietly appeared and nestled himself into the sedge and water-mint on the island which I had built, by carting rocks down from the upper terraces, and the six goldfish, bought in a plastic bag from Monoprix, mated and now swept in brilliant shoals about the Salvator Rosa rocks (already, after only two years, romantically mossed) like the tails of comets. And the king of this man-made extravaganza was a large carp, brought in a bucket from the fishmonger in Grasse, nudging lazily in the mud, blowing little puffs about him, like an aging wrestler; his belly gleaming copper in the sun.

Of course I had altered the ecology. No question of that. But surely for the better? These creatures had never existed up here. Mint, brought by my father in his washbag, from Sussex, had never flourished in the dry shale, nor the high arum lilies which ringed the pond, or the bulrushes which had suddenly appeared, or the nettles, already starred with butterflies, or the whispering papyrus.

Of course it was for the better. And sitting under the giant olive tree on the bank, the early May sun hot on my back, my new water-world just below, I found it incredibly easy to set aside the nagging fear of a return to work. But it was, and now could only be, a "setting aside".

However, I felt calm and contented and considered myself to be exceptionally fortunate. Eggs or no eggs.

That kind of complacency usually meets with an unpleasant, sometimes even brutal, end. And mine did: in fact my rare moments of complacency always do; which is why I have moved through my life with more caution than most. I have never believed that anything I had could last; always aware that, at any moment, a door could be slammed in my face.

Six years of a fighting war, I suppose, had taught me that the only *certain* thing was the moment. Anything else you got was a bonus.

The postman came bumping up the track in his bright yellow van. We exchanged greetings, shook hands, admired the carp and agreed that, indeed, the day was brilliant. He handed me a small blue telegram, tipped his cap, accepted my coins for his trip up the long track, bumped away again, the dogs leaping and capering beside him to the gate.

It was a brief telegram, the postmistress's elegant handwriting spelling out a bleak message.

"Regret Inform You Mrs X Died Saturday Heart Attack".

I did not know the signature; but I heard the slamming of a door somewhere along the corridor of my life, and the day, and quite a number of days which followed, lost its brilliance.

★　★　★

There was no one now to write for: no one to save up the bits and pieces of the day, the scents or sights, the grabbed fragments of conversation overheard, or conversations held. And my life, for a time, seemed strangely empty. I had to keep reminding myself that there was now no recipient for the scraps I collected to write down, to amuse or deflect: it was no good seeing something and saying, as I had done so often in the past five years, "I must remember that. It'll make her laugh". Or, "*That's* the colour a poppy ought to be; just like that, the sun burning through the scarlet petals, translucent. How can I describe it?" None of that was needed now, so I got on with the ordinary work on the land and dug, hoed, mowed daily. And a poppy became just a poppy; not something worth the noting and the careful setting down.

If my days were fully occupied with the problems of weeds, peat, fertiliser, white fly and general garden chores, my evenings were free, for there now was no letter to be written, and it was on one of these evenings, I can't remember exactly when, that I aimlessly pressed a button on the despised television set hidden away in a bookshelf, and was instantly transported into magic. It was an Italian film with French sub-titles, and I had tuned in somewhere in the middle.

But I stayed, uncomprehending of the words, visually amazed. I had never seen colours used like this; nor a camera moved with such fluency and authority. I hadn't seen costumes of such style, brilliance and simplicity. It was as if a giant fresco by Caravaggio had come to instant life at the touch of my aimless finger.

All, I regret to say, that I could understand of the work was that it was the story of Galileo; and that is as much as I could follow. But of one thing I was absolutely certain: the storyteller was a master, and I waited for the final credits with impatience. None of which I recognised until the last one, which was that of the director: Liliana Cavani.

Somewhere, far away at the back of my cluttered mind, I knew that I had seen this name before, and that it was very likely lying down in the cellar among the pile of discarded scripts: which it was indeed. Thicker than the Bible, badly typed and appallingly translated into American-English, there it was among the others in the slithery pack: damp, crushed, the gold-embossed letters faded but still legible. "The Night Porter".

By Liliana Cavani.

Standing in the cellar among the fallen scripts, flipping through the limp pages in my hand, I remembered that I had originally refused the thing because it was, yet again, about another degenerate, this time an SS officer in a concentration camp. I remembered that I had only "skip" read it originally. Perhaps, now, I should give it a little more attention.

I re-read it that evening: the first part was fine, the middle a mess, the end a melodramatic mish-mash. Too many characters, too much dialogue, two stories jumbled up together where only one was necessary, but the point was that in the midst of this tumult of pages and words, buried like a nut in chocolate, there was a simple, moving, and exceptionally unusual story; and I liked it.

I telephoned Rome and spoke to Bob Edwards, Visconti's associate producer on "Death in Venice".

Yes, indeed, Cavani had made a film called "Galileo", and yes she had written a script called "The Night Porter" which he had submitted to me but which I had rejected. What could he do for me?

"Well: I've just re-read it, has she made it by this time?"

"No. She wrote it for you. Remember?"

"There's a hell of a lot wrong with it."

"She knows that."

"But there is a pretty good story somewhere way-down-there-at-the-bottom."

"Thanks. She knows that too."

"Is there a producer?"

"Yes. Me."

"Would you like to come down here and talk about it one day?"

"I would indeed. Do I tell Lilly?"

I hesitated. Eggs and chickens. What the hell. "Yes," I said. "Tell Miss Cavani."

"Fine. If you want any, well, you know, references about her, call Luchino."

"Visconti?"

"The same. She is one of his favoured few."

Visconti, who had faded into the distance since our last meeting in Cannes, had embarked on what he wrote of in a letter as "a small thing, about Ludwig of Bavaria. For [Helmut] Berger to play. But only a *little* film, nothing so much. While we work on the Proust."

But in time, as was so often the case with him, the "little thing" developed into a marathon and Proust was set aside. Indeed, strong rumour had it that Proust was no longer his, but Losey's, who had acquired the rights.

A telephone call, under these circumstances, must be handled with tact. He was, when I finally reached him at home one Sunday night, extremely affable and apparently pleased to hear me.

"And the Poverino? Poor creature, he is happy in France?"

"I think he prefers the gutters rather than the fields."

"Certo. He is a city dog. You deny him his heritage. For years and years they have scavenged the streets of Italy. You will see him, Bogarde, even on the walls of Pompeii, you know this?"

"I know this. Luchino, Liliana Cavani . . .?"

"Ah ha! So?"

"She has sent me a script."

"You like?"

"Some of it. But she is . . . Do you think she is good?"

"Very good. You speak of 'Portiere della Notte', eh?"

"Yes. She sent it ages ago and I said no. Now I've re-read it."

"And you must do it. It is very important to you."

"Thank you. I was just picking your brains really."

"Non capisco niente. But you must do it."

"They will come to see me, there are many things to discuss. How does your film go?"

"Ach, very fatiguing, you know. So many problems, actors, costumes. I smoke one hundred cigarettes a day, you know this?"

"Madness. And Proust?"

There was a slight pause as if, perhaps, he had taken a sip of water.

"Proust? What of Proust?"

"Will you do it after 'Ludwig'?"

"Certo, but there is a lot to do, adapting, this you know: the Americans have now agreed to finance Olivier for Charlus because he has been made a Lord. It is so crazy."

"I asked because there are rumours that Losey has acquired the rights. Did you know?"

The same pause again. When he spoke, his voice was gruff, impatient. "Rumours! All Rome is full of rumours. It could not be true what you say, it could not be. Losey would have told me of this. He is a gentleman, so. You will give my compliments to Poverino?"

I called Bob Edwards again and said that if Cavani could agree to some hefty cuts in both dialogue and characters and reduce the story to just the simple one, of two people, I would do it.

He said that Cavani had been told of all this and was busy re-writing: he said also that he was very happy about my decision, and that she would be too. I said that I was.

And part of me was; the other part, the idle non-laying hen was not, but the die had been cast. I cheered up remarkably quickly when I remembered that it was quite possible that they wouldn't be able to lick a complex script into shape. I could still back out if things did not work.

Forwood was busy staking some delphiniums which had got battered about in a mild mistral the evening before. The air was soft and warm, the first crickets were singing. Now that I had, for the moment, committed myself to a film again, my good humour began to fail me at the thought of having to leave the calm and beauty of this place for which I had worked.

But calm and beauty cost money.

I remember Vivienne Glenavy saying that every time her husband had to go to London to do one of his television shows he was in such despair at leaving that he would walk round his garden embracing every olive tree the evening before departure.

That's exactly how I should feel when, and if, the time came for me to leave. Except that Paddy had thirty olive trees: I, four hundred. I'd have to pick just one token tree. But, with any luck, it wouldn't be for ages yet: if ever.

"That's that," said Forwood, collecting a bundle of canes and twine. "You been on the telephone all this time?"

"To Rome. Edwards and then Visconti."

"I see. You've lost a case of Scotch and a case of vodka."

"How?"

"That's what it'll have cost. Probably more."

I followed him up to the house. "You needn't worry. I got your message loud and clear."

"Did you now?"

"Yes. I'm going to start 'laying' again, I'm sorry to say."

\* \* \*

An aimless finger had pressed the button on an almost forgotten television set and had ended two years of perfect, if unheeding, peace and happiness. The thoughtless gesture had done more than that: it had re-opened a door which I had most deliberately closed, and now the furies, even though pleasant ones, were a-snapping and tugging at my heels.

Edwards arrived on the terrace one day in early July and Forwood and he started to rough out a draft contract: no one was losing much time it seemed, and the next day I signed it. Now there really *was* no going back. I was in, unless perhaps the script would prove to be unmendable.

Which, as I well knew, was always possible. We would start

137

shooting in Rome and Vienna probably in January. It seemed comfortably far away.

Two days later, Yvonne Roux called from the Colombe d'Or to say that a distinguished French director called Henri Verneuil was staying there and wanted me to read a script. Could she give him my telephone number?

He arrived the next day, an energetic, bright-eyed, pipe-smoking gentleman who, once settled comfortably in a chair under the vine, outlined the whole of his considerably detailed script ("Le Serpent") which proved to be, yet again, another "spy story based on the truth", in which I would be required to play (as I had already guessed from the start of his monologue) Philby: or "a kind of Philby". He said that he had already signed Yul Brynner and Henry Fonda, and that everyone would be a star on this ambitious production.

The idea of working with Mr Fonda was, I had to admit, attractive. I would apparently have one "marvellous scene with him: the most important in the film". But they always are at the wooing stage of the game, so I didn't take much notice of that; however, the money for a mere fifteen days, five of them in Munich, the rest in Paris, was really quite interesting under the present circumstances. And so was Mr Fonda.

I agreed to read the script, and give a speedy decision. Satisfied, he left in a flurry of pipes and pouches, assuring me that I must realise that he was an Armenian and that in Armenia every village had its own story-teller who would sit cross-legged in the market-place weaving tales of magic and beauty to enthralled audiences: that is all he was, he said with humility. Just an Armenian story-teller in the market-place; and he climbed into his expensive car and drove away.

Watching him go down the track, with great prudence, I realised that my re-opening of a once-closed door had now thrust upon me many things which I had hoped would stay out of sight for a long time to come: like opening the door of an, almost, forgotten attic; all the junk and jumble of the cinema was falling about my ears once again. Two films now, not just one. Not my intention at all.

"It never rains but what it pours," Lally used to say, although it was obviously fate of some kind which had caused me to press the button on the TV set when an urgent replenishment of funds was so badly needed. Well. If I had to play yet another Mr Philby, or a degenerate officer in a concentration camp, then so be it: I would. I had no alternative, alas.

Summer had arrived with the cuckoo and the swallows, and the work on the land could not be neglected. Philbys or SS officers must be set aside for the moment, and the big chore, the mowing of the hay, had to be tackled without delay. One bright afternoon Forwood, thinking that his great rotary mower had jammed, stuck his hand under it to discover why: it hadn't, and sliced off the tops of his fingers.

Blood, bandages, Poteau.

Two days later the front page of the local paper carried a small story that Visconti had collapsed at dinner and been rushed to a clinic in a police car, as all Rome's ambulances were on strike. I tried to telephone to find out what had happened, but to get a call through to Rome, then or now, and to get any kind of response is as unlikely as meeting a pride of lions in Hyde Park.

However, the next evening Edwards got through to me: Visconti was in a clinic but it seemed at this stage of affairs just a matter of a complete fatigue, and he appeared to be in typical form, because, although it was being kept as secret as possible, some friend had managed to smuggle himself to the side of Visconti's bed, where he knelt in whispering hysterics.

"Oh God! Dear God! My brave Luchino, Luchino! Tell me, how are you?"

Visconti opened one slate-grey eye balefully.

"Better than you, my good friend," he said.

"Oh dear God! Dear Mary! I thought that you were dying."

"I shall know when my time comes," said Visconti. "It is not now and it will, in any case, not be before yours."

So, if the story were true, we had high hopes that it was simply a matter of exhaustion after the marathon work he had done on "Ludwig", "the little thing", as he had called it only a short time ago. However, I couldn't help remembering one hundred cigarettes a day . . .

Edwards said that he would shortly bring Cavani down to see me, so that we could discuss the many problems which "The Night Porter" posed. As she only spoke Italian, I was pretty certain that it would be a one-sided discussion, as all the Italian I could speak, put together, would hardly get me through a market, or even enable me to order a meal, with a very patient waiter, in a restaurant. There will be translators, said Edwards cheerfully.

I can't, at this moment, really remember what I expected Cavani to look like. Certainly, because I have a literal mind, I expected someone dark, vivid, passionate and, in all probability, extremely noisy: with a great many gold bracelets and the fierceness and aggression of an Italian woman driver.

I did not expect Caravaggio, of course; but neither did I expect the shy, slender, fair-haired young woman who arrived with Edwards one evening, and a hustle of people who had come to discuss business and help to translate for us both. Translation, as it happened, was not needed; because for some reason we immediately established a strange kind of inner bond, based on mutual respect for each other's work. And so, while the others sat out on the terrace with a bandaged Forwood discussing contracts, dates, money and all the ugly paraphernalia which goes with the making of a movie, she and I sat alone in the long room with a bottle of wine and no common tongue.

And got on exceedingly well: in a hideous tumult of French, Italian and English. No one else might have understood us, but we understood each other completely, and it was only after a very short time that I knew, without any reservations, that I had been right in my first assumption that here was a master, and I wanted to work with her.

However, I realised that I could easily be drowned in the torrents of Italian with which she flooded me, so I firmly made my own points as best I could.

I said that there was far too much political polemic in the story.

She nodded agreeably and said that she *liked* the political polemic.

I said they wouldn't stand for much of that in America or England, which, as the film was being made in English, would constitute her main market.

She nodded cheerfully and said they'd have to.

I suggested that under all the welter of polemic there was just a very simple, very moving story of two people, a man and a woman who had come together in Hell, had discovered an extraordinary love there in the mud and the filth of the camp, rather like a tiny flower thrusting through the brutality and degradation of a battlefield.

I was rather pleased with this analogy, and she smiled brightly and said that that was the original story anyway, and that it was true.

She had been making a documentary for Italian TV on prison camps in, I think, Dachau. Bad weather had forced work to a halt. Sitting under an umbrella in the mud she saw a smartly dressed woman walking through the drenching rain carrying a sheaf of red roses, and she watched as the woman searched among the sites of the long-demolished huts where the prisoners had been held. In time she found the place for which she was looking, the brick angle, flush to the ground, of the hut foundations, and knelt there placing the roses on the spot, and remained, head bowed, in the rain for a few moments, then rose and walked away. With Cavani in pursuit.

With a woman's innate curiosity, and a film-maker's eye for the bizarre and equally for this tragic fragment of life, she hurried after the woman, who had obviously come to mourn her family (dead), who had died in that terrible place.

There had been no family. She was not Jewish. She came back, she said, every year on the anniversary of her lover's death. He was a member of the SS, she a girl who had been imprisoned for holding Socialist beliefs, and having a well-known Socialist father. The hut foundations, where she had placed her roses, was the site of the one in which she had been imprisoned; the day was the anniversary of the day on which her lover had been executed by the liberating Americans. She lived now in America but came back every year on that day. It was perfectly simply told, and unemotional. She left in the rain leaving Cavani with a story which haunted her for months.

What, she thought, would have happened if the SS man had *not* been killed? Had escaped and gone to ground like so many of the others, and years later, in some unexpected place, at some unexpected time, the two had met again? What then? She wrote "The Night Porter".

But, I said, in the script the girl is definitely Jewish. In life this was not so. I was convinced that if we made the girl a Jewess, it would cause the bitterest offence in Jewish circles even to suggest that such a thing could possibly have happened.

But it did! Cavani said, thumping the table. A number of

141

women, of all faiths, had fallen strangely in love with their gaolers. She discovered this, to her consternation, interviewing survivors of a number of women's camps while she was gathering her information for the documentary.

And *that's* the story! I said, the lovers. Not the political polemic, which is distracting and swamps the simplicity of the story.

Cavani was cracking a walnut. It was politics, after all, she mumbled through a mouthful of nut, which had brought the two together in the first place, didn't I agree? She grinned happily.

I could not disagree.

But I begged her to cut as much as she could, remove a lot of extra, tiresome characters, and concentrate on the essence of the thing. The SS man and the girl, and that she must be, as she was in life, Aryan. She shrugged a couple of times, cracked another walnut, shovelled the shells into an ashtray and used her only English word, reluctantly.

"Okay," she said.

Cavani was young. Anyway, young enough to have missed the war about which she had known almost nothing, living in the safety and comfort of her family retreat in north Italy. There had always been butter on the table, she had never heard a bomb fall, the jug was always full of oil. Luxury; removal. She had only gradually become aware of the terrible things which she had been spared when she eventually went to university after everything was over; and the impact had been overwhelming. She began to make up for those protected years with a blinding dedication to the facts; none of which she was going to relinquish.

But she had, finally, said "Okay". I was greatly relieved.

The new script arrived in September. Pale blue. As slim, sleek, empty and dead as a gutted herring.

The rough, deeply felt, over-written script which I had retrieved from the cellar had been sent to the dry cleaners, and nothing remained of the fabric. I refused it, and said that we should continue working on the original; somehow we'd manage, although I was not at all sure how.

Meanwhile, the Armenian story-teller had sent his script. Highly polished, slick, fast-paced, unoriginal, it required me to do very little except stand about in a black raincoat looking enigmatic.

There were, however, two goodish scenes, one indeed with Mr Fonda, which didn't look as if it was going to tax either of us. But in the main it was, apart from the raincoat, what I call a "cardigan and knitted tie" part, and I had hardly to open my mouth. Which suited me perfectly well. And, aware of the situation in my egg basket, I accepted my "kind of Mr Philby" role; at least I had the necessary wardrobe.

So October found me sealed, literally, in a palatial suite in the Munich Hilton with unopenable windows looking out over the Englischer Garten, and with a spiral staircase leading up to a vast shelf on which stood what appeared to be the Bridal Bed. The central heating roared day and night.

No matter that each morning I awoke with a face like a boiled turbot; the whole thing was extremely luxurious, the work unexacting (Mr Brynner and Mr Fonda had not as yet joined our merry team) and it seemed to me a very good way of getting broken in again to playing for the cinema. I had been away for over two years, the longest I had ever been out of work, but it all came back smoothly, and five days later I was released from my chores in Munich and was free until work commenced again, for me anyway, in Paris on the giant set which M. Verneuil had erected. "An exact copy," he said proudly, "of CIA Headquarters in Virginia."

We left early one morning with Forwood at the wheel of his BMW just as the first frosts whitened the long alleys of the Englischer Garten. A few days before he had suggested that, on our journey back to France, we could perhaps make a small detour, of some two hundred kilometres, via Lake Como where the Visconti family had a country villa and where, at this moment, he was resting. It would be good manners, Forwood said, to do so.

I spent half a morning looking for some kind of gift to take, finally deciding on a large photographic book about Ludwig of Bavaria and his epoch. We arrived late in the afternoon at the splendid Hotel Villa d'Este, which I knew to be very near Visconti's villa, and which was "supervised" by my old school friend from Convent days in Hampstead, Giovanna Govoni Salvadore. I felt certain that she'd get us in to the hotel somehow. And she did.

"But you'll *never* get into the villa. It's right next door to us, adjoining our land, and no one is allowed," she said. "But try . . ."

I telephoned the villa. A sombre-voiced man took my name and address and hung up. Half an hour later a telephone call, and this time a pleasant English-speaking woman's voice asked me if I could, please, identify myself, because the message I had left was not very clear. Who was I? I explained briefly.

"Ah, sì, sì. Goodbye," she said, and rang off.

It was obviously not going to be easy; as Giovanna had said.

"Never mind. But I told you. He is guarded day and night and *no* one gets there. You come and have dinner tonight with Luca [her husband] and me. I'll show you what real Italian cooking should be. Not a pizza or a meat-ball in sight."

In the hotel bar, where Luca had opened a bottle of champagne to celebrate our reunion, for Giovanna and I had hardly met since she was thirteen and I sixteen, when my father and I had managed to push her aboard the last boat leaving from England for France in the war hysteria of 1938, I was summoned to the telephone.

Visconti would see me. For only ten minutes because he was very tired. If I came immediately.

I can't remember much of the journey in detail, which was anyway very short. Only impressions come to my mind today.

Two fine lodges, a great iron gate being dragged open, Albino Coco, Visconti's First Assistant Director, there to meet us. We embraced warmly: "For Papa you come?" he said, and immediately put a warning finger to his lips. I knew why. I had, years before, christened Visconti, strictly behind his back, "Papa," for he was the Father of his troupe and his actors. The troupe had been appalled at my levity, but in time they started to use the term, in hushed whispers, recognising it to be, as I meant it to be, a form of affectionate respect. But it was never, at any time, mentioned in his presence, and we took the greatest care to see that it never was. However, tonight the old word of endearment and respect had come from Albino's lips, not mine.

"He is okay, Albino?"

"Is okay, you see, but . . ." he shrugged and we moved into the drive.

At the side of both lodges, servants standing in formal rows, their white aprons and pinafores glowing in the flickering fire from giant torches which continued all the way up the drive, held by liveried men at regular intervals. As we reached the house, Albino ran ahead and we turned into a great courtyard to be greeted on the steps of the villa by the housekeeper, who conducted us to Visconti.

A footman opened double doors. A high, shadowed room, shabby English-grand, books everywhere, a blazing log fire, dogs sprawled, chintz chairs, a pile of *Country Life*s, a pleasant-looking woman in a worn armchair knitting: she smiled, nodded in greeting. Another, younger, in tweeds and cashmere sweater. On a small table, an abandoned game of Solitaire, and almost in the centre of the room, facing me as I entered, Visconti in a wheelchair, a tartan rug draped across his body.

"Ciao, Bogarde," he said quietly, and I crossed the room with my gift, and kissed him on the head, a thing I would never have dared do before. He was grey. Shrunken. Small. The Lion, the Bull, the Emperor, was now an aged man hunched in a chair, his one good arm lying idle across his tartan lap.

"I have brought you a present," I said.

He reached up slowly and took the book in his right hand. "Kind. Very kind," he said, and started tearing the coloured wrapping away like a child at a birthday. The paper fell in scraps at the foot of his chair. "Ah sì!" he grunted, holding the book close to his eyes. "I know this."

"You already *have* it! It's just come out this week in Munich!"

"I have it," he grunted again. "I have *everything* on Ludwig." He pushed open a few pages, set it aside. "You have come then from Munich?"

"This morning."

"You have a dentista also in Munich?" There was just a glinting light of amusement in his eyes.

"No dentist. A film."

"Is good, the film?"

"Just started. Fonda is in it."

"Ah sì. Is good, Fonda. And so you come here to see my photographs? Of 'Ludwig', is so?"

It wasn't, but it had to be so. Of all things I detest it is looking at books of other people's photographs.

"Forwood, you ring that little bell, we see the photographs. Very beautiful."

A footman in house livery arrived, took his orders, left through the great doors.

"And the Poverino? Tell me now." The tartan rug had slipped from his shoulders, his paralysed arm lay dead at his side. "You see this damned thing, eh?" He lifted it with his right hand. "Look. Is morto. Finito. I have to make exercises, but it will not work. Ah, ha! Finito, finito."

Two footmen arrived with stacks of enormous red leather-bound albums. My heart sank.

For two hours we sat and looked at the, admittedly, glorious photographs of "Ludwig". Visconti grew less and less tired, less and less morose, more and more eager, the fine right hand caressing the photographs, pointing out overlooked detail, turning pages, dragging his paralysed arm across the springing covers to hold them down. The two women were watchful, but seemed pleased.

"Visconti," I said at length, unable to face a sixth great album being placed upon my knees by a footman. "We'll have to leave soon."

"Why soon!" His voice was strong, the voice I once had known was there again.

"We've been here two hours. I have to dine at the Villa d'Este. You must dine too, it's almost nine-thirty."

"I eat late, you know," he said. "But if you go, you go. Very well, va bene."

He thanked me for the gift.

"You will come to Roma to see the first assembly, eh? Just a few people, private. Family only, you will come? And where is Charlotte [Rampling], someone tells me is married, is true, and a baby?"

"Yes, it's true."

"If you speak to her, tell her she must also come. I tell you when."

"I promise," I said and stooped and kissed his head. He took my hand in his strong right one and held it for a moment, the grey eyes like chipped flints under the bushy brows, smiling at my audacity, knowing it for the homage which it was.

"Ciao, Bogarde, ciao, Forwood. You will drive safe."

I turned briefly at the double doors and looked back. His head was lowered, chin to chest, the right hand possessively caressing the red leather binding of an album on his knees.

A week later, on the morning that I was setting off to Paris to join M. Verneuil on his vast set of CIA H.Q. in Virginia, I collected the mail from the tin box at the end of the track. I instantly recognised the handwriting on one small envelope, the sharp, staccato, and at the same time florid, handwriting of Visconti.

On a small piece of paper, probably from a message pad, he had written:

*13 Oct. 72*

> *Dear Bogarde,*
> *Thank you for coming so far out of your way to see me:*
> *now that I am no longer of any use to you.*
> *With very much love*

He had signed it simply: *Papa*.

★   ★   ★

The CIA set was splendid and extremely impressive. Mr Brynner was exuberantly polite, and spent a great deal of his time amusing the crew with funny faces and varied tricks; which delighted them.

Mr Fonda was polite too, and highly professional, sitting silently in his chair with the day's script in a tidy little plastic envelope on his knee. He spoke only the lines of his part: otherwise he was to all intents and purposes mute.

I sat about aimlessly in my tweed jacket and knitted tie and listened, which was all that was required of me, and spoke to no one because, quite frankly, no one spoke to me. It was with some relief that my second week was over and I headed back to the house in the South.

The vine was turning fast, the grapes hung heavy, the sun warm, and green and yellow mantis climbed anxiously away from the path of the mower as the last of the hay was cut before winter. I resented that I had to go once again to Paris to finish off my piece in "Le Serpent", but at the same time I was well aware that I had put a few more eggs into the basket and that there could be more to come in the New Year, because "The Night Porter", it appeared, was almost definite.

One evening in the Lancaster in Paris, Forwood had had a sudden brilliant idea that we should play Charlotte Rampling as the girl. I had met her first on "The Damned" some time before, and had been tremendously impressed by her work, and Visconti had said that one day, if she so wished it, she would be a star. He didn't make those remarks lightly. I knew, instinctively, that she was right for the girl.

I immediately telephoned Edwards, who was cautious but interested. So was Cavani. I had then called Charlotte in London and explained everything. Yes, she was interested; yes, she had a baby, but he wouldn't be a problem; and yes, she could be free to work in the early part of January. Was there a script?

"There is a script, it's a terrble mess, but I think you'll be able to see the nub of the story in the welter of polemic and junk, it's pretty marvellous. One snag though . . ."

Her voice was cool. "What's the snag?"

"It's to the knuckle. It's not MGM or anything. There's no money."

She laughed wearily. "There never is, love, is there?"

But she had accepted a few days later. We were ready to go. With the old, original, black script.

So that last evening, mowing among the crawling mantis, I felt cheerful about things: I had gone back to "laying", and although it hadn't exactly been the greatest joy, it hadn't been bad. I hadn't lost my touch, I thought; I'd done the best I could do with the material given me, and the future now held an exciting promise. I wanted to make "The Night Porter", I wanted to work with Cavani, and I wanted, above all things, to work with Rampling. I'd got all three amazingly.

On the Blue Train that night, going up to Paris, I started to cut away at the pages of the old black script from the cellar, and the more I reduced it the more sure I became that we had an extraordinary film to make. Always supposing that Cavani would agree to my ruthlessness. I consoled myself that she couldn't speak or read English and that Charlotte and I would blind her with our magic. I felt dangerously confident.

We arrived in Paris the next morning, got to the Lancaster and ordered a huge breakfast, and I started to shave, when the telephone rang.

Nine-fifteen on a Sunday morning? M. Verneuil checking me in, I supposed.

I heard Forwood in his room talking, heard him call me: I turned off taps and, razor in hand, went through the sitting-room to his room where he was sitting on the edge of the bed, his hand covering the mouthpiece of the receiver.

"What?"

"It's bad news, I'm afraid. Ulric's dead," he said.

# 9

My brother's voice was calm, firm.

"Heart attack about six-thirty this morning. Been trying to reach you."

"Train was late."

"We're all here. George and Elizabeth drove up right away. Cilla [his wife] and I got here about an hour ago."

"And Ma?"

"Marvellous. Wonderfully calm. Shock hasn't hit her yet."

"Of course."

"When can you get across?"

"When's the funeral?"

"Wednesday. We'll have to have an autopsy, just to be sure."

"Of course. I don't know *when* I can get across. We start work tomorrow, I'm in every damned scene."

The shaving soap was drying on my face, the tiny bubbles fizzing as they burst. I studied, with infinite care, every millimetre of the carpet between my feet, razor slack in my hand."

"Well, it would help to know."

"I'll call the film people today. But it's Sunday; they all go off to their little bungalows in Fontainebleau."

Fortunately, M. Verneuil hadn't. He was, he said kindly, deeply sad, such a thing to happen! But of course I knew that tomorrow was the start of the big week with Henry Fonda and I was in every shot? Saturday was a day of rest. Sunday the last shooting day, my scene with Fonda; I knew that, of course? If I could get there *and back* on the Saturday. . . . Otherwise. He was desolate, but of course the film . . .

My brother's voice was still calm and firm, and very reasonable. He knew, because he worked for television, that nothing short of a national disaster, and a big one at that, could possibly alter the "schedule". Personal affairs had no part in our job.

"Well, we'll try for Saturday. It's the gravediggers. Over-

12. Ellen Burstyn, Sir John Gielgud at Ambazac, between shots on "Providence". June 1976.

13. Alain Resnais, the poet-director, at work on me in Limoges for "Providence". 1976.

14. My first-ever signing session. Hatchards, Piccadilly. March 1977. Forwood, Norah Smallwood, my sister Elizabeth, behind me.

time, that sort of thing. I'll try for Saturday and you call if anything alters."

"Nothing will. They have to get rid of Fonda by the end of the week. He costs."

"Of course."

"Saturday then?" said Elizabeth.

"Soon as I can, night ferry on Friday, be with you about ten. I can't make it before."

"I know. Typical, isn't it? You go back to work after two whole years and the first week, Daddy . . ."

"Typical," I said.

It was a grey, bitter Sunday in Paris. The Grands Boulevards deserted. A cat perhaps; a huddled figure with the morning paper, a sharp wind whipping the last November leaves, bowling them across the cobbles.

The whole length of the Champs Elysées down to the Rond Point was empty: fading into a grizzly mist, the traffic lights all the way down springing up; red, amber and green with no one to warn save a lone parked taxi. The whole world was suddenly a void.

I had a business luncheon at Lippe: no point in cancelling it and sitting staring at the wallpaper in the Lancaster. Heat, cooking smells, laughter; plates of cabbage and sausage, carafes of wine; my host assuring me earnestly that if I joined his firm I would never cease working, there was already something he had in mind with Audrey Hepburn.

In the privacy of the lavatory of the suite in the hotel I suddenly beat the white tiled wall with my fist and yelled, "But why *him*?"

An absurdity.

Why not him? Everyone dies.

On Friday night there was a rail strike. There would be no ferry, but the train would go to Calais. We'd have to depend on British Rail after that. Calais at three-fifteen in the morning. A light drizzle, but hopeful news. A car ferry had been diverted from Dunkirk. We trailed aboard cold and tired.

At Dover at five-forty-five a.m. an officious little fellow in Customs called me over, examined every item in my handgrip; I had no other baggage and was travelling in a black suit which I had worn in the film. He was as tired, no doubt, as we, cap on the back of his head, cigarette stuck to his lower lip, shirt open at the neck, crumpled tie undone.

"I take it you're a resident of the UK?"

"No."

"Staying with us long?" he was poking and prodding.

"No."

"Come for a holiday?"

"No."

He grew impatient. "What have you come for, if I may ask?"

"To bury my father, if you will allow me to get there."

"Well then . . ." He closed the hand-grip, zipped it up. "Got an autograph book here somewhere." He fished about under the counter on which he had placed his foot, one knee bent in shiny blue serge. "Sign it, will you? It's not for me actually; my sister. Big fan of yours. Or *was*. Don't see much of you these days, do we? For Lorraine. With an 'e'."

The train was freezing and dirty.

"Didn't expect you lot," said a steward. "Supposed to be a strike. Take time to get the steam going."

We sat huddled in our coats for an hour watching, through frost-ferns on the filthy windows, the residents of Dover starting a new day. A woman in a pink quilted dressing-gown, and curlers. A man in his vest, yawning, tugging open curtains, standing in thought picking his nose unawares: someone shaking a packet of Corn Flakes, taking up a milk bottle; a woman opening a back door and pushing a reluctant cat into the frost and the scrap-yard of a garden.

The train lurched suddenly, clanked, stuttered, a long hiss of steam. We started moving slowly past the ugly grey houses towards London.

★   ★   ★

An ancient English country church: centuries of candle wax, varnish, dust. Stone pillars, pine pews, flagged stone floor. A muted organ, rustling of clothing.

Gareth, Elizabeth and I in a line: left in solicitous solitude by the others who had come to mourn him with us. Friends from the village; from his favourite pub; from London. The Chesterfields of childhood were there too, and, most movingly, some of his companions from *The Times*.

My mother had stayed behind at the cottage with Cilla and Forwood. "He's dead," she had said. "I don't want to see what happens. Please?"

152

They say that death diminishes, and it is so; at least it was that day. The coffin, of plain oak, carried by six bearers, shuffling past us along the flagstones, could not, I thought to my astonishment, contain my father's body.

So small, so humble; nothing to do with the man we had known and loved so well. But we were all there to bury him: so it must be.

For the first time, Elizabeth suddenly bowed her head and wept into a crumpled paper handkerchief. Not noisily, just hopelessly.

Gareth and I stood together stiffly upright, looking intently at the glass in the windows, the shine on the brass candlesticks; anything but the coffin.

And afterwards, in the gravediggers' pit, dug from the Sussex earth and flints, he was lowered carefully down on ropes, and as the first spade of frozen soil hit the coffin lid I heard no door slam, but the sound of bolts rammed home: a key turned.

And that was it. There was no more. We trailed in little groups up the path to the gate and the waiting cars: a woman said, "Must rush, but I just had to come; he was very much loved here, you know, in the village. We were all very fond of your father. A gentleman; not many left now. I've got to dash: just wanted you to know." She hurried away, unchained her bike leaning by the gates and rode off into the November light.

There was champagne at the house, smoked salmon sandwiches: the room was jammed with people. My mother sat upright in a large armchair, smiling, hands outstretched in pleasure and gratitude, greeting people who had come so far for this occasion. She was groomed, elegant in black, easy, calm, extraordinarily composed. She was particularly moved to see, once again, his colleagues from *The Times*, and particularly his devoted secretary, Mr Greenwood, but at no time was there the slightest sign of grief or sadness; sorrow perhaps. That. But masked. She was behaving with incredible dignity and grace.

I realised that in some strange way she was "on stage"; an audience had come to see her and she would not, under any circumstances, let them down. Or herself, her children or her husband. She had a "Full House".

This was no invalid who would not walk; no helpless

creature enveloped in her chosen aura of Tragedy Queen. Quite the reverse of these things, her eyes were bright, her hands eager, caressing, her laughter soft. She was straight-backed, confident, putting each and every one of her guests at ease.

"Oh! My dear! How wonderful of you to have come . . . Ulric would have been *so* proud."

What would happen later, when the curtain, so to speak, had fallen and this "full house" had gone, I did not dare to imagine. But for the moment the performance was spellbinding and the room, instead of being muted by grief, was, to my joy, gradually, cautiously, filling with laughter. People were mourning my father as they should, with the pleasure in the remembering of him; not with sadness.

The atmosphere was almost that of a party, which he would have enjoyed greatly, not that of a wake, which he would have scorned.

Elizabeth looked as if she had scrubbed her face with a wire-brush. I hugged her tightly.

"Do I look really awful? I know I do. I tried not to, you know, I mean, cry. So silly, and he would have hated it. But it was that coffin. So titchy . . ."

"I know. Thank God Ma didn't come. Much better here."

"Oh much! I think it might have killed her really: that little box; fifty-two years of a marriage, carried to that awful hole."

"But she's in good form now. She does put up a bloody good show when she has to; it's what's called setting a good example."

"Yes. She jolly well knows how to behave."

"Sad about Lally."

"Well, too far for her to come all that way, and it was a bit short notice, she's not getting younger either."

"It's later on I worry about for Ma. After . . ."

"Not now," said Elizabeth. "Not today. Talk about that later. But not now."

For some extraordinary reason Gareth and Elizabeth and I had never really thought that our father would be the first to die. We were almost convinced that Ma, who was growing ever frailer, losing her grip on life generally, caring less, having her "little falls" rather too often, catching colds and so on, would be the first to go. And then, in an abstract way, we agreed that Pa would come to stay with one or the other of us.

We even looked forward to the fact that he might, if the terrible day arrived.

I think that he had seemed to us permanent. A fixture in our lives, I can't imagine why, for it is patently idiotic to think in that way. Life is life, and short. But the human spirit is determined that it is immortal, and in some strange way I think we thought that he was.

The deep-rooted bitterness and despair in my mother had grown as she grew older; the years of disappointment, of long-quenched ambition, of smouldering fury at the frustration of her acting-life had started to emanate from her very body almost in the form of a corrosion. It was tangible now. You could, and did, touch it. And it was incurable.

On the other hand, Pa was like the cliché oak: flourishing, steady, no signs of malaise, of inner distresses, no signs even of aging. He had never been ill. Although he was the most secretive of men, he made no secret, whatsoever, of the fact that he loved life and all that it had to offer so, naturally, we were quite convinced that he must be the survivor.

But he had not been: he was not the stronger member of the partnership. He had gone. And that shock-wave was still to hit the three of us fair and square between the eyes.

"What about Christmas?" said Gareth quietly. "We'll have to do something about that, it's not far off."

"I'll speak to George and Elizabeth about it. Perhaps they'll bring her out to France, with the children. We'll have a non-Christmas."

"Best idea. I'd have her with us but we're a big family now, I think she'd be far happier with a trip to make. Take her mind off things, keep her occupied, it's the first hump we have to face. When's your flight tonight?"

"Sevenish. I'd better start making my farewells."

The next morning at eight-thirty, in the gilt and mirrored saloon of the Travellers' Club in Paris, I played my "marvellous scene" with Mr Fonda. It was all very simple, easy, and Mr Fonda expert, although still oddly mute; however, it was finished by five o'clock. The next day, I had one more small piece to do and that was that. I caught the Blue Train back to Nice, fairly sure that my first screen work, after two years' absence, had not been disastrous, and that I had not lost my "edge". Some months later, when the film opened in London, Miss Dilys Powell in the *Sunday Times* wrote: "Mr Bogarde, given too little to do, does far too much." I never saw the thing; but I am absolutely certain that she was right. She always is.

★ ★ ★

A week later I was back in Sussex trying to help Elizabeth to sort out the papers and belongings in my father's studio, a small room up a flight of narrow and very steep stairs.

"I really can't imagine how he got up and down here every day; *I'm* puffed already." She was leading the way. "You know he had a terrible truss-thing. A hernia?"

"No. No, I didn't."

"Said he did it heaving himself out of the sea on some rocks at Denia, when you were all there on some film. I can't remember what. Ruptured himself."

"But he never said anything to me! Never a mention."

"No. Well, he was secretive. Didn't give away things like that. I only found out years ago by accident."

She pushed open the door. A strong, familiar smell of oil paint, linseed oil and turpentine.

"I've been burning a lot of stuff this week; bits and pieces. Of course, trusses don't bloody well burn."

"Of course not. They're metal."

"Awful things. And his teeth . . ." She stopped herself quickly, hand to her eyes.

"Teeth? He didn't have false teeth?"

"A dear little plate. With two or three on one side. I wanted to get rid of all those things; shaving brushes, razor, well you know. Reminders. For Mummy."

On the easel I remembered so well, a big unfinished canvas of Windover Hill, the hill sketched in, the sky a great expanse of blue and clouds. I'd forgotten how good he was at painting clouds.

Bottles; his paint-box open; the tubes neatly stacked. A dirty paint-cloth on a nail. His brushes standing stiffly in an old Tate and Lyle syrup tin, cleaned, erect, ready. Canvases stacked against the walls, a hard wooden chair, a cushion with the imprint of his body. On a low yellow-oak bookcase a long row of old box files marked "Private".

"We'd better get to work," I said.

It was bad enough being in his empty studio, still so alive

with him, but it was utterly wretched for the two of us rummaging through his private papers, the personal hoarding of eighty years of a life.

Papers and papers. Letters, hundreds, it seemed; from *The Times*, from J. M. Barrie, from Pavlova, from Munnings with a drawing of a little horse, letters of thanks for photographs which he had used in the paper from a hundred names which he had chosen to keep. Then his diaries, dating back to 1910, all in an unbreakable code and the smallest, neatest, writing. They meant nothing to us. Cyphers, figures. There were old newspapers printed in Flemish, a few school reports, some sketches which he had made in Italy during his war, and then we found his Will signed and dated in 1954: leaving everything he owned to his wife.

Everything was the house and contents. And he was over-drawn at the bank.

"Why? Why in God's name didn't he tell me?" I said in anguish.

"He wouldn't. You know that. But did you know about this?" Elizabeth held up a fat pile of bills and receipts from a firm of undertakers in a suburban town for the upkeep of his mother's grave. Paid up to date. We looked at each other in bewilderment.

Granny Grace!

We had hardly heard her name mentioned by him in our entire lives. And yet right up until the present moment he had been paying for the upkeep of her grave.

All we knew of Granny Grace was that she had died in 1917 while he was fighting in Passchendaele. There was a three-quarter portrait of her hanging on the stairs. A pale, smiling woman; head to one side, wearing a black velvet coat with sable collar, holding a closed fan in gloved hands, folded before her. She was one of three sisters, the eldest of whom, married to an eminent lawyer called Nutt, became our surro-gate grandmother, the younger of whom, Rose, lived in a pleasant cottage in Sidcup, which was then, as far as I recall in the early twenties, still almost the country, waiting for the return of her husband who had been posted "Missing" in 1915.

The house, I well remember, was kept ready for him, just as he had left it. His slippers were in the hearth, his pipe and tobacco jar on the table by his chair, his raincoat still hung on the back of the kitchen door. Each night Rose, or Great Aunt

Rose as we called her, would unlock the front door, leave one small lamp burning, and fill a thermos with tea. "Because, you see," she said, "it is very possible that he will come home quite late. One can't tell."

But we knew very little at all about Granny Grace. She was not real as her sisters were; one had seen them and spoken to them and liked them well. She was unimaginable, a shadow. Never spoken of, a private part of my father's life. Except that once, when I was about eight or nine, hunting about at the top of my mother's wardrobe where I knew she used often to hide early Christmas presents from us, I found, to my astonishment, a steel-mesh purse full of coppers and shillings which I knew instinctively must have belonged to her. I stole from it from time to time.

I had a feeling of guilt, but it never lasted very long. She was dead and I had never seen her. It didn't feel like stealing at all. My logic satisfied me perfectly.

"Well, one thing is absolutely certain," I said. "Ma is broke."

For two days we sorted, sifted, packed and filed whatever seemed worth the keeping, and burned all the rest at the far end of the garden. I am certain that we made errors; it is impossible to sort through the hoardings of a man's lifetime in two single days, but we had to move quickly and cut away the undergrowth, so to speak, before we started the family discussion on what to do with Mamma, because something had to be done, and soon.

There was not the slightest possibility, now, of her being able to manage on her own again. For the last five years Pa had been her help, cook, cleaner, nurse and comforter. She was now bereft of all five: not just her husband. Her initiative had gone, she was lost and bewildered. I had feared that she might perhaps crumble the moment that the "full house" had left, and this is exactly what she did.

In the week since the funeral, the bitter numbness of her grief bit deeply. She sat for most of the day, in her deep armchair, in black, chain-smoking, offering us no help whatsoever simply because she no longer knew how to.

"Darlings, you do as you like. Please! I don't care. I really don't care. I don't even know what Daddy did with all those papers and things; I've never seen them, he never told me, just burn them all, burn everything."

We didn't, of course, and did our best to try and rekindle a spark of interest in her for some of the things which we considered must be salvaged.

"Gareth ought perhaps to have the diaries, don't you think? He's got all those sons, they may like to have them later."

"As you like. I don't care."

"And there are boxes and boxes of glass negatives. Some could be valuable. Records of things he did for *The Times* perhaps; of us even, family things; we can't just chuck them away."

"I don't know about any glass negatives. I don't know what they can be, probably all old-fashioned stuff. Do what you want."

And that is as far as we ever got.

Finally, Forwood called us all to attention and the family conference. Down to brass tacks. Very brass ones. No money. Alone. Helpless.

We talked about and around for far too long, deciding nothing, reaching no definite point of view, and finally Forwood, who listens a great deal before making any remark of importance, suggested that perhaps George and Elizabeth should move into the house, which they would buy from my mother at a reasonable price and then invest the money for her future. She would also, he reminded us, be certain to receive a decent pension from *The Times*, and my father's studio could be easily turned into a separate wing of the house, where she could be perfectly independent, still in her own surroundings, and among her family.

She agreed uninterestedly, and lit another cigarette. The possibility of her coming out to France to live with me had been firmly scotched. Too long a journey. Foreign people she couldn't understand; too many stone stairs in the house and, she added, shrewdly, too damn lonely. What was she expected to do when I "went off making films all over the place?" She'd go *mad* there. So that was that.

Gareth had already a large and growing family and she wasn't keen on a lot of children, and anyway she would pose a dreadful burden for him. She didn't, under any circumstances, want to be a burden. That much she made clear. She insisted that she could stay on in the house. Alone. She'd manage somehow.

We all looked at poor George and Elizabeth who were

obviously going to be the ones to face a sacrifice. Elizabeth loved her house by the sea, she loved her life there, but she bravely, if perhaps a little bleakly, agreed that it seemed to be the only possible solution.

"I don't know what else we can do, truthfully. She can't stay here on her own, that's certain." She shrugged. Her arms wrapped round her knees, squatting on a low stool by the fire, shoulders hunched. "We'll just have to try and see how it works out: it may. Nothing else for it really, is there?"

The next day I left for France feeling wretched and acutely aware that she and George had made an enormous personal sacrifice and knowing, even if she did not quite at this moment, that Elizabeth was now hopelessly trapped.

Before leaving the house I noticed, high up in a dark angle of the staircase, a small portrait of my mother, in chalk and wash. It had been drawn two years after I was born, and I had forgotten about it until that instant. I asked her if I might have it to take back to France with me.

She was suddenly alert, interested, eyes sparkling. "Oh do! Darling, do. If you want it, take it. Ulric always hated it, that's why it was always hidden away in dark places. He didn't ever want to see it: but it's really terribly good, he was a wonderful artist, and it is so *like* me. Amazing."

"Why did Pa hate it so much?"

"Because he was convinced that poor Hookway [the artist] was desperately in love with me, and Ulric was a very, very jealous man, I can tell you. It was all so silly. But *I* loved it, so it stayed: and you like it, so you have it. I want you to." She took the slim oak-framed portrait in her hands. "Yes. You take it. You won't stick it away in some corner. I wasn't bad-looking, was I? Really not so bad. I made the best of myself, your old Ma."

When Liliana Cavani saw it hanging here in the long room, she went to it instantly. "Who is?"

"My Mama. 1923."

"Ah . . . sì bella. Sì bella," she said, and then laughed softly shaking her head in amusement. "Oh ho, oh ho!"

"Oh ho, oh ho! What?"

"La Malcontenta, no?" she said.

★　　★　　★

The sweet-sour stench of naked bodies huddled in a frightened mass in the huge tiled room with a filthy concrete floor. Overhead, glaring white lamps in metal shades. Bitterly cold: no heating except for one big gas burner which roared away uselessly, blowing little gasps of warm air into the freezing room.

Old men, young men, old women, children, young women. Hands folded across their bodies trying to conceal, in one hopeless gesture, their sex.

A woman, heavy-breasted, pregnant, a child of about two slung round her hips looking more naked even than the others because she wore a hat on her untidy hair; gay with two bows.

In the centre of the crowd, which was filing barefoot towards the trestles at which sat a number of black uniformed SS men and women who were taking down their particulars, Charlotte was as naked as the rest; and she was clearly distressed. Her distress was sudden, and nothing whatsoever to do with acting. Suddenly she broke away from the crowd and ran blindly to Maria, the Wardrobe Mistress who had dressed me on both Visconti films and who now smothered her in a coat, clucking and whispering consolations.

Tears, which did not fall; her voice unsteady, fighting for control. "That *hat*. Why did she keep her hat on? Everything else has been taken from her, why the hat: those bloody bows. Why?"

"Because that is what she did. Last relic of dignity, of self, of identity perhaps."

"But it's true? It's not Lilly's idea?"

I found the large black folder of photographs from the archives which Liliana had collected together for just such a moment as this.

"No. It happened."

The blurred photograph taken in Poland in 1943 was an exact replica of the scene before us. And the naked woman with the child round her hips, heavy-breasted, pregnant, wore a silly hat.

In Vught Camp, or perhaps in Belsen, I can't remember exactly which now (both were as terrible) I had wandered through huts piled high with the relics of human life: hair in mounds, higher than myself, from shaven heads. Whole rooms filled with artificial legs and arms; metal things with joints and a single shoe, or one gloved hand, worse somehow, a gloveless hand in polished wood with articulated fingers. Rooms full of false teeth, hearing-aids, spectacles rimmed in tortoiseshell or dull gold, glimmering in the light; an avalanche of dusty metal, glass and porcelain.

In one shed, apart from the others, a rack of women's evening-dresses on hangers, swinging gently in the April wind. Another rack of tail-coats, the white ties knotted round the hanger-hooks like dead worms; top hats; gold and silver dancing-shoes, patent leather ones in a neat row as if in an hotel corridor waiting for a valet.

Appliqued flowers, crushed cotton roses on a thin shoulder strap, sequins hanging by a single thread.

"Dutch Jews," said my guide, an Estonian "Kapo"* who had over-eagerly offered to show me the camp. He touched the shabby dresses with indifference. "Is pretty, yah? They caught them at a big celebration. All." He pronounced the letter "c" like the word "sea", in a hissing sibilant. Turning back the collar of one of the tail-coats, he twisted his head about, squinted, read the tailor's label. "Is so. Yah. Dutch Jews. I remember. From Amsterdam."

"And they kept these things like this? On hangers . . ."

"Oh! Excuse me, please. Oh yah. Always very tidy. For the concerts we had: many concerts for the guards at Christmas and other times. Also we have orchestra. Very fine, this orchestra. Jews are good musicians, but this you will know; so. But not all the peoples here were Jews, we had many kinds, Communists, Socialists, religious ones, homosexuals, many kinds, and we had good orchestra. Ah yah, all this we had."

I am not absolutely certain of the camp, but I do remember the conversation with the "Kapo". I remember his shaved head, the striped suit of his prison garb, his over-eager smile, terrified, fawning, wanting to please. I gave him the "unexpired portion" of my daily rations, a bully-beef sandwich and an apple. I could not eat. He touched the newspaper packet with his lips.

"So thank you. So thank you. I taught English, you know, to the young ladies of my city by the sea. Thank you, chentleman." He was crying.

At twenty-four, the age I was then, deep shock stays registered for ever. An internal tattooing which is removable

---

*"Kapo", the local word then for a "Trusty" in the camps.

only by surgery; it cannot be conveniently sponged away by time.

Bombs, shrapnel, tracer-bullets in the night, even flame throwers, all the vile and ugly mechanics of war I had managed, over time, to accept, even the constant dead who *never* "lay serene, peaceful, as in sleep" but were sprawled and chunked by metal shards in the hedges and cornfields. These too I had managed to deal with. After all, I was in a war, and these things are part of war, and young men have to get accustomed to them. Or go under. I had become accustomed to them: they came to me gradually.

But I could not, and I never have, become accustomed to the rack of evening-dresses, floating, twisting silently in the soft spring wind. Nor to the mounds of stinking hair, tumbled; or the angled legs and arms. They were something so horrifying that my mind could not even accept them at the time, and even when my "Kapo" friend took me proudly to the long hut where the concerts were held, I still could not accept, though I saw the stage, the sagging red curtains, the rippled backcloth of a pretty Austrian lake with a white steamer crossing. It was only when I tripped over a scattered pile of tangled music stands in a drift of sheet music that I believed. And came to terms. The evidence before my eyes.

But coming to terms is not the same as becoming accustomed. That morning, in the bitter cold of the tiled room, among the naked people, the women with white hair and breasts as empty as old pockets, the hat with the bows, the smell of stripped bodies crowded together, Charlotte too had come to terms: suddenly.

Born long after the war, she had no conception of what had taken place in those camps. Reading about them is not the same; the written word does not, always, fully evoke the horror and the terror. But standing there, naked as the others, before a table lined with black uniforms, with the smell, with the shame, she understood.

★　　★　　★

When I first started in the cinema, in 1947, Mrs C. A. Lejeune was one of the most distinguished, and important, critics of the time. She and Dilys Powell were affectionately, and respectfully, known in the industry as "The Girls". They kept away from the junketing and the dreadfulness of the press parties, and their reviews were all their own work, unhindered by wheedling press agents or anxious film producers who always tried to buy good reviews by serving ghastly lunches and a constant flow of gin and tonics.

Mrs Lejeune and Miss Powell did not attend these orgies. But once I did meet the former, and her words stayed with me throughout my career. "It is not my business," she said, "to know what troubles you had, what problems you had to overcome, what discomforts you endured making your film. My business is simply to judge the finished result: nothing more."

She was absolutely right.

But movies aren't made the way we made them then, in the comparative comfort of a studio. Things have changed radically.

We had started the shooting of "The Night Porter" on a freezing day in January in a condemned TB sanatorium out on the via Tuscolona, Rome. It was, like all Liliana's locations, brilliantly chosen; for it had all the atmosphere of a Death Camp, and the years and years of sadness, illness and despair which had filled it originally were distilled into the air like a vapour.

Walking, or perhaps I should say strutting, through the empty huts and wards, the long dim corridors and the decaying scraps of abandoned garden surrounding the place, in my fine black-and-silver uniform and high-peaked cap with its Death's Head insignia, cracking my boots with a thin silver-topped whip, I had no illusions at all that I was *not* the man I was supposed to be playing. I felt exactly right. I felt frightening; powerful; commanding. The uniform did that; at least externally. The internal struggle of the man himself was my own affair: but I found it much easier to become him than poor Von Aschenbach, although the role was to prove equally demanding and draining.

The uniform itself had a curious effect on the inmates of the camp. Perfectly ordinary paid-up members of their actors' union, they had been carefully chosen for their thinness, drabness, age and general feeling of decay. They scurried away as I walked past them or hid, crouching, in corners, huddled nervously; and the more that they huddled and scurried, the taller I stood, the wider I strode. It was an interesting experience. The SS uniform had been extremely well designed for the purpose it was to serve: fear.

I remember how small, weedy and insignificant Himmler had looked lying dead on the scratched parquet floor of a bourgeois villa in Lüneburg in 1945: his feet thrust into a pair of old army boots, a blanket roughly thrown over his naked chest and belly, his hairy shins sticking out at angles, like broom-sticks on a scarecrow. They hadn't even given him a pair of socks: and his tongue hung limply from thin lips like that of a dead dog.

And dead dog he was that day, without his splendid uniform which had once inspired so much fear and dread in so many people. It seemed, that morning, inconceivable that this runty little man could ever have inspired terror, or had the power, the authority, and the absolute control over people's lives that he did, for he looked, lying there in the thin spring sunlight, as if he could never have had the force to push a barrow or hold a begging-tin.

A British Corporal beside me kicked him lightly in the ribs. The boots shuddered, eyes glazed, half closed, the head rolled.

"Nasty little bastard, wasn't he? Did 'isself in with cyanide or something. They had a right old scrum trying to get it from him, but he just bit it, I reckon, got it down. No guts, this one hadn't."

But he had had incalculable power over life and death not so many weeks before.

The uniform did a great deal to assist him in his lethal tasks: there was no goodness in a man who wore it; and this the huddled Italian "extras" knew only too well. They had known the Occupation; and the sight of that uniform on their streets. It was not easily forgotten.

If I had the wardrobe to help me with the performance, I still hadn't, quite, got the dialogue together; which was a little worrying.

Liliana and most of the crew had their scripts in Italian, Charlotte and I and the other actors had the English translation. This was literal; and being literal, far too long. Understatement is not an Italian virtue. Every day Charlotte and I would go through the script, cutting away and chipping at yards of over-explanation under the ever-darting, suspicious, eyes of our director.

To help us all get through this effort, she had brought a

splendid woman named Paola Tallerigo to join us as translator. Paola spoke every known language, as far as I could gather, and English fluently; her job, as go-between, was not an enviable one, but at least she got things wonderfully clear, and translated what I had to say to Liliana, and what she had to say to me. Constantly.

Charlotte spoke a little Italian, so her life was a bit easier, but it was Paola who held us all together and with the greatest tact. Each time I cut another chunk of dialogue Liliana, or Lilly as we now called her with affection, screamed as if stabbed, and shouted for Paola.

"What is he doing to page 56? He is cutting everything I have sweated writing!"

"He says he doesn't need so many words."

"*I* say what he needs! I *wrote*; he butchers! I have things I want *said*!"

"There are simpler ways of saying things in English. It is a simpler language than ours. He will say what you want, don't worry."

"Butcher! Will he say what I *intend*? Dio, Dio, I wrote what he kills!"

One day I managed to reduce almost half a page of dialogue to just the one word, "No".

Lilly stared at the offered page in stunned amazement. "What does he do?" she said. "He says one word. I say," she thumped her own original script with a clenched fist, "I say fifty, sixty words!"

"He says that 'No' is enough. You will see: in the playing."

"It is my *polemic*!" Lilly cried furiously. "He is ruining my argument!"

All this, I hasten to add, was done with the greatest good humour, although any stranger wandering on to our set could well have been excused for thinking that they had walked into a bitter battle in the life of the Borgias; but we knew what we were doing, we all trusted each other implicitly, and on the occasions when Lilly had thought, seriously, that I was wrong and she right, or that even Charlotte was wrong, she had watched the scene played and had come to understand that thoughts on film convey far more than words. And had given in gracefully. If sometimes grumpily.

In this odd manner of working, the only one we had, we came to terms with the script although it was often wearying and always exhausting. But it was, at the same time, exhilarating. I was back in full harness as a creating actor, and I honestly rather liked it.

It was far easier than mowing terraces: and much more stimulating.

After two weeks in the sanatorium, we moved into Cinecittà for a time and then out into the cruel world again. The cruel world was an empty villa built at the beginning of the century, which awaited the demolition teams. As soon as we had finished work it would be wrecked.

After a day or two of trying to exist in it, I didn't think this a bad idea at all. There was one working lavatory, with a cold tap for us all. It was arctic cold and damp. We ate, when we got the time to do so, in a small trattoria on a neighbouring corner.

For a dressing-room I had a vast empty room, in which the wallpaper had peeled in ugly strips, and somewhere above a pipe had burst, leaving a great fan of damp fungus on the wall. It was not over-generously furnished, with a chair, a table and a one-bar electric fire.

Charlotte was next door with her months-old child in a Moses basket on the floor, a double-barred fire, and an electric blower heater (which regularly blew up) to heat her freezing infant, and a small divan on which to lie.

All superstar stuff.

But we were happy together; all of us.

There is a strange moment, usually a couple of weeks into a production, when the crew, and everyone else, gets the feeling that what we are all doing is good: better than good, important. From that moment on, any sacrifice is made for the film, willingly.

However depressing the subject-matter of "The Night Porter" might be, the atmosphere was one of radiant hope and secret excitement. Something quite marvellous and strange was happening on the screen, and we were all responsible. It is a greatly rewarding feeling: and it doesn't occur often enough for one to become over-sure, over-confident. It is too rare.

But, alas, if all looked well on the surface, and even more than well, things below were not so good. We were running out of money daily.

The film story of my life, it seems.

We finished all the work which we had to do in the "Hotel"

(which the hideous house had been transformed into by brilliant designers) at the end of March, and on the last evening of work an exhausted Bob Edwards came up to my freezing room and announced sadly that we had no more money: he had tried, begged, implored for the extra needed to take us to Vienna for the last important segments, to no avail. I could go back to France leaving the film unfinished.

I was so used to this situation (it had happened to every film I had made which had been worth the making from "Darling" to "Death in Venice") that I accepted it as normal. There really wasn't much else to do. Back to the terraces.

In quiet despair we packed up, with three-quarters of the film finished, the last vital quarter to be shot in Vienna, abandoned. Anyway, for the time being. Charlotte was sitting in her room, humped in a chair, her hands wrapped round a big mug of coffee for warmth. Maria, with a face like granite, was packing up costumes in a corner.

"I mean, what's *happened*?" said Charlotte. "Why have we run out of money suddenly?"

"Spent the budget, there isn't any more."

"*How* have we spent the budget, for God's sake! It's been Economy Week every single week since we started. It's a small picture; we aren't making 'Ben Hur'."

"Well, they won't give us any more. I don't think they like the subject anyway, and so we won't be able to finish it. Basta."

Charlotte prodded her laughing infant with a loving finger.

"If we don't get the stuff in Vienna there isn't a picture anyway."

"Perhaps that's what the money gentlemen know. Abandon the thing."

"They'd do it on purpose? Scrap it all?"

"They've done it before in movies. Edwards says he's off to try elsewhere; he might succeed. He's determined."

"Money!" said Charlotte. "God. What they're paying me wouldn't keep a hamster for a week. I just don't see how we *could* have got into this state."

Maria bundled up a pile of clothing, stamped across the room, opened the door with her foot, slammed it with a kick behind her.

"Everyone is so miserable. We were all so wonderfully happy, so sure, it was a feeling so terrific. Oh well!"

Lilly seemed a great deal less depressed than the rest of us (she possibly knew a little more than the crew or the players did) and smiled away agreeably through cascades of Italian.

"She says," said Paola, translating carefully, "that we must not lose faith, we must hold firm, we will fight them to the death and, ultimately, we shall win."

"She's not on the bloody barricades now!" I said. "How *can* we finish without any money?"

"Lilly says that when she has cut this film together, and we have a lot already, they will be so excited that someone will give us money, not much, but some. And some, you know, is quite a lot. It is a beautiful picture."

And so I went off back to France, and Charlotte carried her Moses basket back to London. There wasn't any alternative.

A month later, in April, we were, amazingly, reassembled together in Vienna. Not one member of the crew had left to do another job, all had stayed, loyal and unpaid, so strong was their belief in the film, and waited: just as we had done.

And in pouring rain (not bitter cold this time) we finished the film as intended. Somehow, someone had got some extra money, as Paola had said; not much, very little in fact, but just enough to finish; with nothing left over or extra. So tight, indeed, was the budget for the final week in Austria, that we had a handful of extras only to fill the whole of the Volksoper. No mean task.

But Lilly, with careful camera angles, and by impressing members of the crew who were not immediately engaged, even Forwood, the publicist or the hairdresser, and any odd person who had wandered into the theatre, achieved an atmosphere of an "All Sold Out" performance from Gallery to Stalls and Boxes.

Working in Vienna, the crucible, once, of Nazism in Austria, in my black SS uniform, was not going to be quite the same as it had been in Rome. Wearing it at all was a provocative thing to do in that particular city, so I spent all my time draped in coats and hid the cap in a box. We were shooting in the streets and it seemed tactful, and wiser, to keep a very low profile.

The night I most dreaded was left until the very last day of shooting. A small shot, but it was to be in the eastern sector, the Workers' Quarter, which was well known for its toughness and also for the monolithic blocks of flats, the Karl Marx

Hof, to which people came from all over the world to admire the brilliance and advance of the design.

This was mainly a strong Communist area, one of the crew warned me thoughtfully, full of extremely rough people who would probably lynch me if they saw a swastika, let alone the hated SS uniform. His remark compounded my unease, so I sat wrapped up in a raincoat in a corner bar until the very last moment that I would be needed.

It had been arranged beforehand that I would be smuggled through the crowds, which were already gathering to watch, to a flat on the fourth floor from which Charlotte and I would make an exit, descend the concrete stairway, and so arrive on the street. I would be given a signal to start the action when the cameras were actually rolling so that no time would be lost. In lynching me, I supposed. Charlotte was perfectly all right because she was wearing a simple pink dress and long white socks; nothing provocative in those, except perhaps Charlotte herself.

These elaborate precautions had been taken so that I should have only a very few moments of vulnerability on the pavement below before getting into a car and driving off. Which was all the scene was about. I was terrified.

As the evening wore on, the crowds grew larger, attracted by the blazing arc lamps which lit the front of the monstrous block: children ran about screaming and laughing, clambering about the equipment, dancing in the light. There was a feeling of a circus in the air; and me skulking in the corner bar feeling exactly like a naked clown.

A polite, slightly uneasy, Austrian assistant came to collect me and hurry me through the seething mass outside the flats. We were nearly ready to "go". I had the cap well hidden under the raincoat; no one noticed the whip or boots because we were almost unobserved hurrying up the concrete stairs to the flat on the fourth floor, where an old lady, white hair in a knot, braids about her ears, shuffled down her hall to let us in, her face suffused with pleasure because she had been paid handsomely for the use of her apartment for just a few moments, and, as she said to the assistant, she lived all alone and it was much nicer than watching the television.

She smiled at me and "Grüss Gotted" quite a lot, bobbing her head like a swallowing duck: I was shown her two canaries, a bad colour print of two exceedingly plain women and a very fat man on a mountain who were, she explained, her "Kinder", and was offered coffee from a metal pot simmering on her spotless stove.

The Austrian assistant was leaning out over the balcony waiting for the signal from below for us to start moving down. Charlotte would be picked up half-way down the stairs. I stood clutching my raincoat about me, and the old lady kept saying that it was "kalt" this winter, when the signal came to move.

I threw off the raincoat, adjusted my cap and belt, took up my whip, and the old lady gave a loud cry, the coffee pot held in one hand, her other hand to her cheek. Her eyes were wide, watery, pale blue.

She was not shocked. The eyes were surprised: pleased.

She replaced the coffee pot briskly, wiped her hands on her apron and came towards me quickly, speaking as she did so to the assistant. Then, standing before me, she put out her hand and stroked my arm smiling.

The assistant was acutely embarrassed. "We have to go now, they are ready, but this woman says please to be so kind and shake her hand. She says that this thing . . ." he indicated the uniform with a slight move of his finger ". . . remembers her of the good old days. This is how you say in English, I think?"

I agreed and shook her hand. What else do you do?

The signal came up, "Rolling!". I left the little flat, the old woman nodding and smiling, hands clasped tightly.

"Camera!"

When Charlotte and I reached the blinding lights in the doorway below, there was a sudden, extraordinary, silence as I stood there in my glittering regalia and high-peaked cap: and then a great gasp of astonishment rose into the still air from a thousand throats.

My heart shamefully thudding, I supported Charlotte and started "acting" the finding of the car keys. I knew that there were a number of hefty crew members strategically placed around to hustle us away if any trouble broke out—the only member of the police I had seen had been having a beer in the corner bar.

The gasp faded to an intense, excited, silence. I walked Charlotte across the width of the street, got her into the car. Someone started to applaud. A lone sound. Then it grew, others picked it up, it mounted in intensity, there was cheering and somewhere I heard a voice shout "Sieg Heil!". Another whipped across the crowd. "Sieg Heil!" to an enormous roar of laughter and applause. "Sieg Heil! Sieg Heil! Sieg Heil!"

I got into the car and drove off into the darkness beyond the arc lamps. The crowds were cheering and laughing, applauding. They "killed" the lights. The laughter and cheers continued. The Sieg Heils rang in my ears.

"Probably a few drunks," said Charlotte.

"I don't think so."

"You take things so seriously! But do you *believe* it! It's amazing! They loved it. Just loved it!"

Not the "acting" alas: the uniform.

★   ★   ★

Ten months after my father's death, on her own in the house for the first time while Elizabeth and George were lunching locally with friends, my mother drank the contents of every bottle on the drink-table, plus a crate of Light Ale, replaced all the stoppers neatly, and plunged headlong down the staircase which led to her bedroom, breaking almost every bone in her body: except her neck.

At the hospital they regretted that it would take forty-eight hours to "dry" her out before they could operate.

The shock, which we had all expected, had finally struck her: and her purgatory began.

## 10

A trim, smug, Georgian house surrounded by green lawns still spiked with frost in the shadow it cast, on this brilliant January morning.

In the hall, polished wooden floors; rugs scattered; a brass bowl of dried grasses. Sunlight, the smell of furniture polish and Air-Wick. In a small room to the left, a little bar in a corner. Dubonnet, Cinzano, Booths gin, two bar-stools: a fire crackling.

"Oh yes!" said the matronly woman. "She's waiting for you: very thrilled. Up the stairs, first landing, then up four more little ones and hers is the first door on the left. Just knock and go in, she'll be so pleased."

As I started up, she said: "You'll be four altogether for lunch, right?"

"Right. If it's no trouble?"

"None at all. Your sister, Mrs Goodings, did warn us."

White paint shining, good quality fitted carpet, cleanliness. Almost, perhaps, a little spartan. I knocked at the door and she said, "Come in."

She was sitting on the edge of her bed, dressed, made up, hands folded in her lap. On her feet, heavy black lace-up shoes.

"Well then! Here I am." I stooped to kiss her, and put the big bunch of daffodils I had brought on a small table.

"Darling, you shouldn't have spent all your money like that."

"I could have got you some in pots, in bud. But I thought that these would be a bit easier."

"Much. Lovely. I'll get Mrs . . . I can't remember her name, my mind's gone; anyway I'll ask for a vase. Or vause or vaze."

I sat in a small chair opposite her.

"How do I look?" she said. A false smile; fingers pulling at the stuff of her skirt.

"You look marvellous! You've had a good rest."

"You're telling me. Five weeks. And then all that ghastly physiotherapy."

She had shrunk, she was old. Very sad. The fire had died, leaving nothing but a banked pile of greyish ash.

"It's not bad here, Ma. Really *very* pretty, the house . . . and it seems clean and all the rest."

"Oh yes." She brushed her skirt. "It's clean. Hellish."

"Oh come on! I mean this is very nice, this room. You've got all your little bits and pieces with you, I see."

"Bits and pieces. Yes. Elizabeth did that."

A photograph of my father, a heavy silver presentation cigar-box, a Staffordshire figure in a kilt; odds and ends from the house.

"You've got your Scotsman too."

"Who?"

"The Staffordshire thing; behind you there."

She turned without interest. "Oh that. Bonnie Prince Charlie. Yes, he's here. Poor bugger."

It was a figure of Macbeth, but we had never told her because she had invented him to be Bonnie Prince Charlie, and so that's how he stayed.

"Well," she looked at me straight in the eyes, unsmiling. "How do I look?"

"I really think you look marvellous. And you've done a terrific make-up job. Does it take ages now, I mean to do?" I was floundering.

"Oh yes, I still do my face. God knows why. No one ever comes, so why bother?"

"I've come."

"That's your answer. Why I did my face."

"Your hands are all right? I mean, after the fall?"

She looked at them lying in her lap as if someone had retrieved them for her. With vague surprise that she had lost them.

"That terrible fall. God. Yes. Oh yes. The hands are all right. They took my rings away. You see? No rings."

"Why did they do that?"

She shrugged, looked across the pleasant room to the window. "Don't know. Knuckles swollen up: something."

"Well, we'll get them back."

"Oh no! They won't go on now. My knuckles . . ."

"Ma, you said people didn't come."

"I said what?"

"People didn't come to see you. But they do. Elizabeth

comes every day . . . and Mrs Brown and Miss Smith, I mean people *do* come to see you, darling."

"Who told you that?"

"Elizabeth. I mean a lot of people have come to see you here."

"Some do. Some don't. It's too far out of the way. It doesn't matter."

"Of course it matters! But it's not too far out of the way, Elizabeth is literally ten minutes distance, I mean you're not buried on the moors or something."

She laughed dryly. "I'm buried. Your father buried me for years in that cottage. All the way up that bloody hill to the village to catch a bus: then all the way down again when I got back. You don't know what it was like. Where's darling Tony?"

"Gone on to collect Elizabeth, for lunch."

"Oh lovely! We're going to have lunch together, are we?" Without interest.

"Well, darling, I haven't come all this way just for a quick chat. And I need a drink. I saw a little bar-thing downstairs."

"It doesn't open until twelve o'clock."

"Not long to wait."

"Where have you come from then?"

"Home. In France."

"Oh yes. Dear France. I'm only allowed one small glass of wine with lunch now."

"Well, perhaps today we could go one more, celebration?"

"Some celebration. I really look all right, do I?"

"Terrific. A bit of nail varnish perhaps, that super red you always wore."

"They took it off in the hospital place. I had that terrible fall."

"I know."

"And I *have* got varnish on. You can't see it, it's natural."

We had lost contact. She was shy, nervous, possibly ashamed. Dreading that I should ask her questions which she would be unable to answer, that might perhaps expose her to criticism, to being cautioned. Blamed.

I walked across to the tall Georgian windows and looked down into the gardens. Frost under the shrubbery, a donkey standing dozing in the sun, his breath puffing from his nostrils like a small, fat dragon.

"There's a donkey, did you know?"

"Donkey? Horses too, I see them from the window."

"Don't you ever go out? You can, can't you?"

"In this weather?"

"No. But you can take a little walk?"

"Oh yes. I can take a little walk. Have to use that thing there. Impossible." There was a walking-frame in a corner.

"Well, we'll go out for a bit after lunch if you like. You could lean on my arm, couldn't you?"

"That terrible fall. No, you go if you want to see the horses. Mrs . . ." She stopped, smoothed her hands together. "I suppose that I've got to stay here for ever?"

"No, not for ever." I was lying, and she knew it. "But it's not a bad place, is it?"

"Too many stairs. I'm terrified of the stairs."

"Well, perhaps there's another room on the ground floor? I'll ask."

"No, no. Don't interfere on my account. For God's sake. I'm all right."

"Look, Ma. The main thing is that you are as happy as we can possibly make you."

She cut through my sentence harshly. "Really you make me laugh! Happy! Who is *we*, may I ask?"

"Elizabeth, Gareth and me."

"Well, I'll be happy only when I get back to my own house. Not in this bloody place."

The conversation, such as it was, had edged again towards the topic I dreaded most. Her return home.

There was no possibility that she could now. Without a nurse in constant attendance; and there was no room in the cottage for a nurse. The blunt fact was simply that she could no longer be left without supervision. She could not be trusted, for one second, on her own, and she knew this deep down in her canny Scottish way. She knew what had happened and why; and she knew damned well that we, her children, knew.

I had written to the surgeon who had performed some kind of miracle on her poor shattered body, asking him, in all our names, to explain to her, for we could not, why she had had to suffer such terrible pain at the very beginning, and what he had had to do before operating. But he had ignored my request, in a cold, if polite, manner, and I had obviously made an ethical blunder in requesting his help.

So it was up to me now, as the eldest, to try and get it over to her that for the rest of her life she would have to be under constant watch and care. And that Elizabeth, with a growing family and no help, could no longer cope.

But just at that moment I funked saying it outright: perhaps after lunch; after a glass of beer or a stiff Scotch. Perhaps.

I pulled a small packet out of my pocket and threw it lightly into her lap.

"What's this?"

"It's so odd about your rings, I know how much you loved them."

"I loved them." She took the packet in her hands. "Ulric lost them."

"Daddy did?" The childhood word came out easily.

"In France. Somewhere. I had a terrible fall. You remember?"

"I remember, yes, you were staying with me. I've brought you some new ones."

She gave a little cry of pleasure for the very first time, her eyes, wide and sparkling.

"For me? Oh darling, spending all your money on me."

"Not very expensive; no diamonds." I started to unwrap the jeweller's packing and tumbled three modest enamelled rings into her cupped hands. "I just hope they'll fit."

"My knuckles, you see?" She held them towards me. "Swollen."

"We'll try, give me your hand. Which for which finger? The green one on this hand, the red and gold?"

"Not near my wedding ring. Ulric lost that too, you know. It's a new one, this. He bought it for me. I was so sad, so sad."

We got the rings on easily; she spread her fingers before her face, admiring them.

"I'm so happy! They are heaven! Heaven. You *are* a good boy, where did you get them?"

"In France. Cannes."

"To tell people, you see. They ask and I like to know."

"And this. Look! Scent! 'L'Air du Temps' . . ."

She clapped her hands with delight. "I'm being so spoiled. Flowers, rings and scent."

"Remember your favourite one? 'N'aimez que moi'? You can't get it any longer, but this is good for you, I think."

"No, you can't get it. That was before you were born. In Paris. Ulric bought it."

She was tearing off the bottle wrapping; from somewhere in the house a couple of dull sounds. A muffled gong hammer.

"The bar's open," she said. "It's nothing but rules and regulations in this place. I could die."

I took the scent bottle from her, opened it, poured a little into the palm of her hand, she rubbed it carefully on to her wrists, took the bottle back, put some scent behind each ear, smiled at me, openly, easily, without constraint.

"How do I look? Do I smell all right? I can't smell a thing. Someone, I don't remember who it was, said that scent didn't stay with me, but tell me: all right?"

"You look ravishing and you smell marvellous. It suits you."

"Time for my glass of wine. It's Spanish, but I like it." She put out an arm. "Help your old Ma. God! These good-woman shoes. But I feel safer in them, and anyway no one ever sees me. No one comes."

We went out on to the landing; suddenly she stopped. "My flowers! Put them in the washbasin in my room."

"I'll take them down and ask for a vase."

"No, no! It'll cause a fuss. The woman gets fussy just before serving lunch. Do as I say, fill the washbasin and stick them in there. I'll do them afterwards." She followed me back into her room.

"When you've gone away," she said.

\* \* \*

A high-ceilinged room, sunlit. Tables round the walls, one or two in the centre, mostly single people. Perfectly silent except for a muted symphony of cutlery and the chink of china, a soft murmur now and again of conversation.

On each table a tin biscuit-box, little clusters of pill-bottles; when someone had finished eating they would play nervously with their napkin rings, turning them endlessly in a shrivelled hand, chewing thoughtfully, awaiting the next course served by a girl in a floral pinafore.

Our table was set well away from the main body of the room, in a window, "so that you can be a bit private", the matronly woman had said. The sun lanced across the polished oak table, the dainty place mats, Views of Olde London, a small pot of daffodil heads in the centre. It was all very dainty.

"I wish they wouldn't do that," said my mother.

"Do what?" said Elizabeth.

"These daffodils. Just their flowers stuck in a pot."

"Heads, you mean?"

"I mean flowers. Heads. I don't know. But they should be long, lovely. Dirk brought me a huge bunch."

"Well: they'd be too tall on a lunch-table, wouldn't they?"

"You think so?" She looked away across the room, humming under her breath, a habit she had when she no longer wished to pursue the conversation.

"I love your rings, terribly pretty." Elizabeth crumbled a piece of bread.

"From France," said my mother. "He's a good boy to me." The inference being that no one else was.

Forwood collected his glass with mine. "I think I'd like another; Maggie dear?"

My mother turned suddenly, questioningly, as if she had been mentally miles away, another trick she had of pretending, or choosing, not to have heard the question.

"Another little glass of wine? I think we can swing two today, don't you? A sort of celebration," he said.

She agreed, holding out her glass. "The girl will come if you can get her: you aren't allowed in the bar during meals. Strictly forbidden. I don't know why."

While Forwood was catching the eye of the girl in the floral pinafore and ordering the drinks, Elizabeth dragged her fork across the ugly plastic place-mat before her.

"When do you go back? To France, I mean?"

"Saturday."

"Just a quick In and Out then?"

"To see Ma, and I had a blood test. It's clear; but I haven't been feeling absolutely terrific."

"You look a bit thin: gaunt. You all right?" There was concern in her eyes; she still prodded the beastly table-mat.

"Fine. I have to go steady on the drink. No, I'm fine. And I wanted to buy a hand-fork and a trowel. Can't get them in France for some reason. Good wooden-handled ones."

"What sort of a trowel?" My mother returned from wherever she had decided to go mentally.

"Just an ordinary garden trowel; with a wooden handle."

"Extraordinary thing to come all this way for," she said.

Two women in floral pinafores arrived, one with the drinks, the other with a tin tray and four plates.

"Roast lamb?" she said, waving the plate unsteadily.

My mother offered her wrist to Forwood. "Can you smell me?"

He bent his head to her wrist. "Yes, I can. It suits you."

"Dirk brought it for me. From France." She put her wrist across the table to Elizabeth. "Can you smell it? I can't smell a thing."

"Lovely, it's flowery; hyacinths, jasmin . . ."

My mother sniffed her own wrist. "Floral scents aren't really me. I'm better with something heavier. I can't smell a thing." She started to eat her roast lamb. "Can't chew anything either. I'm a dead loss. That awful fall I had . . ."

"Well, anyway," said Elizabeth, "you look marvellous today." And appealing to me she said, "Doesn't she? Marvellous. Your lamb all right, Ma?"

"Yes. All right. I don't know why I bother: no one ever sees me. Who cares?"

★    ★    ★

We drove Elizabeth home through once-familiar lanes very little altered. A new house here, a copse grown thicker there; the land smiling, sharp, clear in the cold sunlight, the cottage (which I had always privately hated ever since my father had bought it as a row of three semi-derelict cottages set in the middle of the common, beetle-browed, sagging-roofed, viewless) shining with fresh white paint.

"Did you get a shock? Seeing her? She's had a terrible time." Elizabeth was opening up the house.

"A bit. She's different. Of course. God knows how you've coped."

"I'm glad *someone* does. Tea? Or too early?"

"Love a cup," said Forwood.

"The thing is, she's convalescing, and getting grumpy. Quite normal, but a bit hard to deal with every day. And people have been wonderfully good about, you know, going over to see her. She was popular with people. Her friends and Daddy's here. Mind you," she switched on the electric kettle, "I know that they think that George and I have just moved in and packed her off to a home. She tells them so. It's jolly hard."

"I know that. I, even, have had letters saying the same thing. In France, from the Old Brigade. I know," I said.

"It's been damned difficult. And it's just not true. I suppose that you didn't say anything to her? About not coming back, about needing supervision and so on."

"No. I couldn't. I mean, how could I? I'd just arrived there: but I think that she knows, deep down inside, I am sure she does. She's not a fool, whatever else she is. She knows."

Elizabeth was setting cups on a tray. "Can't find the sugar bowl. Can't find anything today."

I looked round the pretty sitting-room. She had made a lot of changes: the heavy oak and plum velvet which my father strangely liked had gone, the walls were white and no longer dull cream, the thick curtains removed, light streamed in.

"It's much better, darling; what you and George have done, it's all opened up, looks much bigger, lighter, cheerful."

Elizabeth came in with the teapot. "She hates it. Naturally, I suppose. Every time I bring her over, once a week for lunch, she puts things back where she liked them. She keeps on calling it her house and it's not! George paid a proper price. If it wasn't for that she wouldn't be where she is, and warm and comfortable, even if it is a bit awful and prissy, but she couldn't afford it otherwise. And the hospital! I mean, really, it is no joke to be ill today, National Health or not. She doesn't really understand all that, you see: Daddy took care of the money; what there was of it. You can't tell her about the decimal point, or how much a pack of cigarettes costs. She just says she doesn't understand."

"I'm afraid that Pa did her no good by taking over as he did."

"Had to," said Elizabeth, offering a tin of biscuits. "No alternative. It started with that first 'little fall' when she broke her wrist, remember? And just went on from there. I know she *hates* where she is, but what else can we do?"

"Nothing. You've done enough. You've been a saint: both of you have, and I think she'll be better off in her new room. It's on the ground floor, no stairs, which she dreads."

"You know it wasn't the first fall she had down these bloody stairs. It was the fifth, my dear. We just daren't risk it; I couldn't leave her here even to nip up to the village for a bottle of milk. You can't turn your back."

"Well, Mrs Whatevershe'scalled was very pleasant, and the room downstairs is vacant so she can move in, or you can move her in, whenever you like."

"It'll cost a bit." Elizabeth poured herself another cup of tea. "There's nothing to spare."

"Well, we'll manage that somehow."

"It might be a good idea," said Forwood, "if you got some of her personal stuff over there, her dressing-table, so on."

"That's just what I thought," said Elizabeth. "George can take things over in the van, anything she wants. Pictures, china, things to make her feel that she's in a little flat and not in a hotel. I mean it is an hotel, you know? It's not a home, as she keeps telling everyone: she really is awful about that, but I suppose I do see what she means."

"I just funked telling her the truth, which she knows anyway," I said. "Maybe when she starts to pick out the bits and pieces she wants for her 'flat' she'll realise it's for good. It's a dreadfully shabby way of saying it, not saying it, I mean; but I think it's the best way. She'll take it in gradually. To tell her right out would break her."

"She's pretty tough," said Elizabeth.

"Not as tough as that," I said. "I honestly think that she has given up for good. She's started to die."

★　★　★

With "The Night Porter" finally finished and ready to show, Bob Edwards flew off to California, as Visconti had done before, rather like a commercial traveller with a product to sell. The product, he felt, was pretty good: the few people who had seen it at private screenings had been enormously enthusiastic, and he felt we had a reasonable chance of making an acceptable deal.

He was wrong.

The reaction from the major company executives was one of stunned incomprehension; followed by charges of "offensiveness", an "insult to the Jewish faith" (although there was absolutely no Jewish connection anywhere in the context of the film), and "obscenity". Warner Bros, refreshingly, found it "dull and uninteresting".

I thought that "obscenity" might perhaps have interested

them, because obscenity always makes money, but this time they stuck to "incomprehensible"; and that was that.

Of course what they had entirely failed to understand was all Lilly's bitter anti-Fascist "polemic" and argument, and so they had just concentrated on the Love Story, and found it appalling, and the idea that a woman could fall in love with her gaoler completely unacceptable.

A brief cable from Bob said that the audiences at the screenings had been "very enthusiastic" but that the executives remained . . . "uncomprehending". He wished me a Merry Christmas.

The New Year brought a ray of hope: if the Californians had loathed it the French had liked it; and what was more important, understood the political background as much as the romantic attachment. There was a very good chance that we would open the film in France before anywhere else.

The French, and the Italians, had been through the hideous and humiliating process of Occupation, and they knew very well the strange relationship which can, and did, exist between captive and conqueror. They were much closer to the facts. America was a long way off and no one had invaded them since Columbus, Cabot and Amerigo Vespucci. Who didn't linger there anyway. The millions who followed in their paths were of no consequence; except perhaps to the unfortunate Indians whose land it once had been.

However, there it was. We might have gained a foothold in the European Market with France, but it was obvious that we had lost America. A serious blow.

One night there was a call from Los Angeles: Deena, an old and trusted writer friend who got herself about the town, and missed out on nothing.

"Happy New Year! I've seen your movie, at a private screening. And wow!"

"What do you mean, wow?"

"Well, it's strong stuff. I didn't know you were into soft porn, honey!"

"Soft porn? Deena!"

"Well, it sure as hell isn't Goldilocks."

"Not supposed to be: and I gather we've bombed with the majors?"

"You'll sure as hell never do a deal with them; anti-Jewish, and *black, black, black*."

"It isn't anti-Jewish. There isn't one frame in which a Jew appears or a Jew is mentioned. It's anti-Fascist, I give you that, but not anti-anything else."

"That's what it looks like from here. You know in L.A. it is considered the Jew's prerogative to die in a concentration camp. It's stuck fast. You can't make them listen to anti-Fascist speeches with all that sex and stuff going on, and the lovey-dovey stuff, in a *camp*! Be reasonable!"

"There is hardly any stuff *in* the camp. It's afterwards that counts, the present."

"Listen, the audience loved it, don't ask me why. I loved it, no, not loved it, I was shattered; but I've been around a bit, and you know some of it is a little melodramatic."

"Where?"

There was a crackle of silence for a moment.

"Well, I can't really remember now; the speech on the cathedral roof in Vienna? I mean, that's going too far . . ."

"You mean the 'I'm proud I did what I did, and I'd do it all again, Heil Hitler' piece?"

"Exactly. Now come *on*."

"We took it from the Austrian newspapers that very morning. It's from Eichmann's speech for the defence at his trial in Israel. Verbatim."

Another crackle.

"Perhaps you should have put in sub-titles. I didn't know."

"Well, we've made a deal with the French anyway: that's something."

"Oh the French! All that sex, naturally. *Amour*."

"Nothing to do with sex. With the Occupation, they know all about that."

"Listen, I just called to say Happy New Year! I was shattered by the movie, and I am sorry you won't make a deal this side. No way. Not even with the soft-porn stuff."

"There *is* no soft-porn stuff! It's all in the mind of the beholder, Deena."

"Sure is, and you give them an eyeful. This call is costing me the earth."

I wandered about the long room in despair. Soft porn? Sex and melodrama? Had I perhaps, and it was entirely possible, lost my head? Been away from the cinema for too long, not caught up on the current trends, made a mess of clipping the literal translation under Lilly's beady eye? Had we all really been having a happy time of self-indulgence? Been offensive? I couldn't answer the questions.

Perhaps the bucolic life I was enjoying had blunted my senses. I'd been out of touch for too long, lost my way as an actor; not just my sense of order. It was frighteningly possible that I had become like some of our kind in the profession who get stuck in the rut of self-satisfaction. Certain that they are right and that things are as they have always been, allowing no possible time for change, unaware that they are quietly, but deliberately, being moved from centre stage towards the Exit sign by younger, more dynamic and inventive players. I had seen it happen often enough. Had it now happened to me, all unawares?

Well: if it had, it would be better to pull out right away, draw a veil over the whole sorry mess, before I started shuffling off into playing cameo roles, or worse, featured bits, in a nightdress on some dusty location in Spain in "inspirational" epics about the Holy Family.

Scripts of this sort had started to arrive in the tin mail-box at the end of the track, overtaking the Spy Thrillers and the Schoolmasters.

I'd better get out, and try and find something else to do. Laying my metaphorical eggs had been a disaster. They had got scrambled.

But, before I made such a definitive move, such a crippling move, indeed, I knew that I must have advice. I had no intention of trusting the verdict of the major company executives; they never knew anyway. Forwood was probably too close; I had lost my confidence and could no longer judge.

Someone absolutely independent, unbiased, must have a look at the film and tell me that I was wrong and should pack it in, or that I was right after all and should fight for it. A tough assignment, but I had an idea how to go about it.

Bob arrived back from California tired, dispirited, very downcast. I called him in Rome and suggested an unethical and dangerous plan. We should have a private screening in London for four or five selected critics whose only job would be to pass a verdict on the film. It would be secretly arranged, no one would know beyond those invited, and all they had to do was to write to me, as the instigator of the scheme if it came off, and say exactly what they thought. Under no circumstances would they be asked to review the film because, technically, the film was *not* a film (as no one had bought it) and it was not mine to show anyway. It belonged, as it stood, to the company in Italy who had made it; to write about it could have serious consequences for me.

Although their verdict would not be law, it would however be an invaluable indication of where we or, more to the point, *I* had gone wrong. After all, it was I who tuned into that television and re-started the wretched project.

Bob agreed. He was so weary, so disillusioned, and it seemed a reasonable idea, if unethical. However, he said, he was on his way to London immediately with the film anyway because Columbia wanted to have another look at it; just to make sure.

I chose four critics, three of whom had known me since my earliest days at Rank, and all of whom had consistently influenced and encouraged my career. These seemed to me the best people to give me a clear-eyed verdict. They were Dilys Powell of *The Sunday Times*, Margaret Hinxman, then of *The Sunday Telegraph*, Felix Barker of *The Evening News* and Alexander Walker of *The Evening Standard*.

Knowing them as I did, I was certain that they would be unbiased, honest, and certainly pull no punches, however devastating their verdicts might be. They were, above all things, devoted to their craft and to the cinema. As well as being highly professional people.

I would not be present, for that would be inhibiting, so I arranged with Theo Cowan, who had looked after all my publicity through the Rank years, and since, and who was a highly respected figure in the industry, to take charge for me. He started to work immediately. We had four days in which to set the whole thing up, for Bob could not keep the film out of Italy for very much longer.

To my relief, all my guests accepted, even at such short notice. Theo suggested, quite rightly, that four people sitting by themselves in an otherwise empty projection theatre would be pretty soulless. Projection theatres are at the best of times, and this was the worst of times. So he arranged to invite a handful of my friends to furnish the place, people who could be counted on not to talk, and to keep the whole affair quiet; he also added a small bar for a glass of wine at the end of the showing.

I felt extremely nervous. I had never done anything as underhand as this in my life, and I was very well aware that there is always a risk in doing something unorthodox in secret: somewhere along the line there could be a disaster.

My heart lifted when Theo telephoned to say that the evening had been a minor triumph. People had been held in complete silence throughout the film, and had lingered a long time over their wine, discussing and talking about it: a very important sign. No one had actually sprinted from the building, no one had hissed or booed, although, he warned me, it was clear that Mr Walker had not liked the film at all. But that, I felt, was perfectly reasonable. Not everyone would. And after the general reaction from Los Angeles, the atmosphere at this special, private, showing was enormously encouraging. Perhaps the film would have a fighting chance after all? Maybe the three years which I had spent away from the screen had not, after all, impaired my work or my judgement?

All I could do now was wait, as patiently as possible, for the verdicts. They were bound to write in a day or so, and as the mail took so long, it would be at least a week before I would know anything. But six days later Theo telephoned to say that two of my guests, to my consternation, had gone into print and reviewed the film. While Mr Walker had slammed us with a scathing attack spread across two pages, Mr Barker, on the other hand, had been extraordinarily generous.

It was, of course, perfectly possible that the exceptionally private and sensitive nature of the screening had not been fully explained that evening. There very well might have been some 'human omission', so to speak, in the hustle of getting everything organised at such short notice. I do not know. In which case Mr Walker and Mr Barker were perfectly justified in going into print, and it was abundantly clear that the latter had done everything he could to draw attention to the fact that the film, in his opinion 'of extraordinary quality, terrifying but compulsive', was without a buyer. He had championed us in every way possible. But the fat was in the fire: the secret was out.

Meanwhile Columbia had rejected the enthusiastic recommendations of its London office, and turned the film down flat, and, in some dismay, Miss Powell and Miss Hinxman had no alternative but to follow their companions' lead and go into print themselves on the following Sunday, with the result that

"The Night Porter" was, to all intents and purposes, reviewed without having been sold to anyone, anywhere.

In contrast to Mr Walker's two-page spread of distaste and ridicule, the other reports (for, rightly, they stopped short of giving the film full reviews) were greatly comforting. Miss Powell praised both the film and the playing; Miss Hinxman compared Charlotte to Garbo; and Mr Barker proclaimed it, in a large headline, as "The Classic You May Never See".

Well, so much for that. Vindication. Four highly experienced critics had passed verdict on us publicly, and the verdict, of three of them, was favourable. Not a bad ratio.

Naturally there were distressing repercussions to my clumsy effort to save the film, or at least obtain a balanced judgement on it. As I had suspected, there was anger and disappointment from some of the critics who had not been privy to the event; but my almost abject letters of apology and explanation to them of the entire affair were handsomely accepted. A very unhappy experience, however. Very unorderly, and entirely my own fault.

This unexpected flurry of interest had other repercussions. The Americans immediately re-summonsed the film for another look; the London reviews could hardly be ignored. France made a definite deal, and the film, after all the months of trial and tribulation, opened in Paris in March to vast box-office business, even though the President, Georges Pompidou, died on the day we opened.

However, we had "arrived", and in thirteen days in Paris 98,000 people went to see our scorned effort, and the readers of *Elle*, one of the most influential women's magazines in Europe, voted it the Film of the Month. As their ages ranged from sixteen to seventy, I felt that this must be a good sign: if you have the women behind you it is difficult to fail. The rest of the press was, generally, highly favourable, and the only bashing we really got was, predictably, from the *Herald Tribune* which was a certain indication of how we should be received in America if we ever got there.

So there we were.

For a while only: a few days after our triumphant success in Paris, the Italian censor banned the film in Italy. Lilly hit the roof and immediately went into battle. This was her affair, in her own country; there was nothing I could, or would, do, to meddle further. She fought hard and won, in the meantime causing a tremendous scandal in the press, which was extremely useful publicity anyway, and with all the Women's Liberation groups behind her she stormed to glory, and the film finally opened in Italy in the major cities to unanimous press support and packed houses everywhere.

It closed the following day when all the prints were sequestered by the police.

Back to square one: even a 48-hour strike by the entire Italian film industry who had come out in sympathy with her, failed to budge the Police Chief from his verdict. Obscene.

And that, I thought to myself, is bloody well that. No more cinema, no more struggle and strife: I'd have to find something else to do to earn a living; this was just too much, and I was weary with the stresses and strains. Acting posed little, or no, problem, and could be greatly enjoyable. But all this clatter and banging was nothing to do with acting. It was politics, and I have always abhorred them.

"I'm not fighting anymore," I said. "You'll have to get your eggs elsewhere. I've got to try and do something else."

"What'll you do?" asked Forwood reasonably. "You can't do anything else."

"I don't know. I really don't know. The only other thing I have been trained to do is be a soldier. Or paint, and I'm no good at that."

"You wouldn't contemplate joining up again, would you? You're over-age now, and I honestly don't think you'd like it."

"I have to find another way to earn a living. Have to."

"Tough at your age."

"Practically impossible, but this business is strictly for lunatics."

That evening, Charlotte telephoned from Milan to say that she, Lilly and I were to be prosecuted by the Milan courts. For obscenity.

And that, I thought, really *is* that. I'm leaving. Order remained: but it was slightly pear-shaped. The frame had buckled.

I realised, perfectly well, that I had brought the whole thing on myself from the instant that I had fiddled with the neglected Television: that was my fault altogether, but what I could not come to terms with was the fact that after years and years of playing those wholesome, jolly, rollicking doctors, stiff-lipped soldiers, soul-eyed lovers who never, it seemed, got to bed with anyone and actually made it, I'd be summoned to a Court on charges of obscenity.

"But what in the name of heaven did we do that is obscene!" I said to Charlotte. "I mean, we never undid a button, untied a bootlace . . ."

"Apparently it's what we did *without* undoing shoelaces and buttons that has made them all so up-tight. God knows why. Don't ask me."

"But it's absolutely potty! We didn't do anything obscene! If Lilly had made us roll about naked on double beds, or if she'd used some of the archive pictures like the one of the people being hanged with a full orchestra playing the overture to the 'Magic Flute' behind them, I *could* understand. But she didn't; we didn't do anything remotely like that. I suppose it's a question of defining obscenity and a work of art? I mean, like Joyce, Lawrence, Epstein, hundreds of others. I mean, look at the lists throughout history."

"*You* look at them, love," said Charlotte. "I'm leaving Milan tonight; just thought you'd like to know the latest news. Lilly is on her way to Cannes for the Festival, and Bob is in America again. Stay where you are; keep a low profile, my darling."

Her advice seemed sound to me; but Lilly raged back into battle. Again, to tremendous publicity and championed everywhere, fought bravely, fiercely, and in the end victoriously. For the final outcome was that the Judge in Milan's High Court, the most powerful in Italy, pronounced "The Night Porter" to be "a work of art", and that meant that no one could lay a finger on it under any circumstances. We were saved at last.

But the relief was still soured by the bitterness of the whole silly business. Underlying all the banning and sequestering lay a distressing knowledge that, once again, politics had played a major, if not total, part in the scheme of things. The film was vehemently anti-Fascist and that, *not* obscenity, was what had caused the trouble.

Interested parties, and there were and are still a great number in Italy, had done all that they could to suppress the film, using the tritest excuse, as far removed from the real facts as possible. You cannot alter an entire nation's political belief overnight just by hanging its Dictator from a petrol pump. People slip into the shadows and wait. Lilly's attack on their beliefs had encouraged some of them back into action; but they had, fortunately, been foiled. For the time being at least.

She arrived here one evening, bright-eyed, victorious, bursting with ideas for her next effort, bringing with her an ecstatic review of the film by Edward Behr in *Newsweek*, which almost, but not quite, went to our heads, and the day before Visconti had telephoned me to say that he agreed with the Milan Judge that the film *was* "a masterpiece" and that we must go on fighting to get it shown in America and England.

But my heart had left the battlefield long since. I had had enough.

Down in the *potager*, wrenching about at the roots of a rosemary bush which had outgrown both its plot and itself, I realised that I had done the very same thing: outgrown the cinema and my place in it. However, if it *was* really the only way that I could earn a living then I'd have to try and adapt my feelings and plod on; but I was absolutely determined, after this experience, to wait until Disney made me an offer to play opposite a baby elephant, a pack of cuddly puppy dogs, or even a herd of bloody Bambi's. I'd even accept Mr Darling in "Peter Pan".

I was quite unaware that at that exact moment Forwood was starting negotiations for me to make a film in Austria. Playing, once again, Mr Philby. Or, anyway, "a kind of Mr Philby".

Some people never give up.

*       *       *

The happy furore which we had made in Europe, obscenity cases, vast publicity, law cases, police sequestration, and all the rest of it, finally crossed the Atlantic. The major company executives were still terrified of it, afraid of insulting a large part of the population and alienating their Jewish audiences, equally aware that there was the smell of profit around, but too frightened, in the final event, of losing their own heads. Heads roll faster, and more frequently, in Hollywood than they ever did in the French Revolution. So while they dithered and fretted, the film was sold under their noses to a gentleman called Joe Levine who was an old hand at picking up "difficult" subjects.

I knew Mr Levine fairly well. He had originally made a

fortune from a minor Italian film starring an American body-builder, and never looked back; came in at the eleventh hour and salvaged a sinking "Darling", which netted him a lot more loot, and had since become a very rich and powerful operator.

We met from time to time at various functions in New York and London and, when he remembered who I was, he always promised to make me a World Star. But never quite got around to it. My face, apparently, didn't "stick" with him. But he was always affable and did greatly entertaining tricks with dollar bills and dimes, for in his earlier days he had been a successful conjuror. It seemed to me that he was the ideal man to sell "The Night Porter" in the States. He was known for his lavish publicity campaigns and could have sold sand to a bedouin.

Lilly and Charlotte were flown out in great style to New York to assist him. I was not invited because once again, I think, he had forgotten my face. But I was perfectly happy to remain where I was, well out of things. I'd done all I could at my end to support the film; now it was over to them.

They settled down to enormous publicity and a disastrous press led by a more than usually loathing Pauline Kael and a review in the *New York Times* which for savagery could have felled the Empire State Building with its blows.

But the public flocked to the cinema. Which made Bob, who had also gone out, so happy that he sent constant cables to tell me how many records we were breaking. Apparently daily.

Charlotte and Lilly were bruised but brave, and Charlotte only gave up when she discovered that the press receptions to which she was invited were jammed with Girlie magazines and coaxing photographers, whereupon she silently fled, after two days of humiliation, and was not heard of again.

Lilly, bemused, battered, a stranger in a strange city, found herself not very much in demand for interviews, for once the press have failed you in New York no one is anxious to meet you. Failure is contagious. So one doesn't touch for fear of contamination. No matter that the film was a raging success at the Box Office and that Mr Levine was smiling broadly, the Nero's of the press had given the thumbs down sign, and so Lilly too fled away.

Mr Levine, faced with the loss of his two main attractions,

instantly remembered my face and insisted that I should fly out at once to fill the gaps.

"What happened to Charlotte and Lilly?" I asked.

"They just took off! I don't know why and we don't know where, and I've got a great campaign going! We're the hit of New York, and you gotta *get* here."

Prudently, I called a journalist friend in New York. She was to the point.

"Don't budge. Stay just where you are. The press have belted the movie, it's a press disaster, and a terrific box-office success. If you got here now no journalist would give you a quarter inch. It's a damned shame because it's been sold as a porno-movie, and there's as much porn in it as there are snowflakes in Hades, and what's more it's good. It's really a *great* movie. But the damage has been done."

Apparently the Press Show Luncheon was fairly odd. Tables draped in black vinyl, chains across every chair, black candles and book matches covered in fake leather embossed with boots and whips. A veritable sado-masochistic feast.

Oh well . . .

However, despite the trials and tribulations which we had all endured in order to get "The Night Porter" on to the screen, the struggles had been well worth it in the end. It made Charlotte a major star, confirmed Lilly as a director of great force and originality, and is now no longer considered as just a titillating piece of pornography but, as we had all hoped, a major film which is still being shown to this day.*

If I hadn't tuned in, by sheer chance, to "Galileo", gone down to the cellar to look among the slithery pile of slug-trailed scripts, if Lilly had lacked courage, if Charlotte had said "No" . . . all ifs. Life is full of ifs: I suppose it's part of the fun.

I traced Lilly eventually to Rome and explained that I would not be going to New York. She pleaded that I must go and "fight for the film, for its honour", but I read her two of the reviews which had come in the morning mail and reduced her to helpless weeping. With reviews like these there was nothing to fight for; except one's sanity.

London, a couple of weeks later, was not really very much better although we managed to do without the vinyl table-cloths and whips or chains, and the press were treated to a

*At the present time, March '82, the film is running in New York.

193

spectacularly lavish luncheon and a speech by Mr Levine in which he assured them all that very soon they would see, running about the "streets of London Town", a fleet of motorbuses, one of which would bear his name, another that of his wife, one his children's, and one the name of his "brand new grandchild". These buses were going to take "the poor little blind kiddies of London Town" to the seaside for a happy day.

None of us present was absolutely certain just what this gesture of quite astonishing generosity had to do with "The Night Porter", and it didn't exactly bring forth a burst of thunderous applause from the weary press. Neither did the film the next day. Notices were mixed. Some excellent, some disaster.

However, at the luncheon, Lilly, lost in a babble of American and English spoken too rapidly for her to comprehend, buried behind, and under, vast floral arrangements, and choked by the smoke from eight-inch cigars, assumed cheerfully that all was well. Realising her error the next morning when she had the newspapers read to her, she packed her bags and quietly returned to Rome, leaving me to do my final chore for the film before I, too, went into retreat.

\* \* \*

I suppose that of all the things which I have been required to do as an actor, the television chat show has always been the worst. And I've had to do a number in the course of my career.

Banal, facetious, ill-lit and as mentally stimulating as the information on the back of a cigarette card, they are, however, apparently essential as a method of plugging whatever it is you have to sell. Or so I am always assured.

I was once flown out to New York especially to take part in a Johnny Carson show to plug a long-forgotten (and never-to-be-remembered) film. It was considered a tremendous "scoop", and I dutifully went. Mr Carson, with an apricot face, a shiny blue suit of synthetic fabric, and small, darting eyes, received an hysterical reception from an audience composed entirely of U.S. Marines on leave, and introduced his guests.

Miss Zsa Zsa Gabor adrift in chiffon and diamonds, myself,

and a pleasant gentleman who knew all there was to know about chimpanzees.

Mr Carson got my name wrong, shook hands vaguely, pointed to a chair in which I might sit, and had a brief conversation with the chimpanzee expert who had, unfortunately, brought a live specimen of the breed along with him; which Mr Carson instantly gave me to hold for the entire programme, while he concentrated his confident charm lavishly on Miss Gabor. They had a ball together. So did the U.S. Marines.

But if you had stooped to pick up a hairpin you'd have missed me; I can't believe that it helped the film, I don't remember that anyone mentioned its name, and I couldn't believe that a chat show could sell anything; apart from the interviewer's ego.

Russell Harty, I was assured, was not at all like that. He was different from all the others, had been to university, was intelligent, sharp, and no fool. I'd like him. I did.

We had a congenial luncheon at the Connaught, during which I did all the talking, leaving him little chance to open his mouth, apart from forking a mouthful of Sole Véronique into it, or sipping his Chablis. This was less rudeness on my part than incipient hysteria.

I had been giving interviews for five days solid. Eight to ten a day sometimes, and although I was much moved by the warmth and kindness which I received from all those who came to talk to me, I grew progressively more exhausted, haggard, and hoarse, and feared that I must soon be reaching the edge of lunacy.

Conscious that this luncheon, and the show which had to follow it later in the evening, would be the last effort I would have to make for "The Night Porter", that the next day I would be on my way home to France, and that my host was sympathetic and interested, I relaxed: found a second wind, and chattered away like a demented parrot. Mr Harty gave no signs of minding. He listened courteously, even attentively, while I rattled away like an electric typewriter about everything from Hollywood to Belsen; with digressions in between. At the end of the meal he said that he would scrap his arranged programme for that evening and allow me to have the entire fifty minutes to myself on condition that I repeated the same dazzling virtuoso performance which he had just been forced to endure. To the letter. I accepted from sheer exhaustion.

It was, as it happened, a great deal more fun than sitting slumped behind Miss Gabor with an incontinent chimpanzee in my lap.

Mrs Norah Smallwood, a weekend guest of friends in the country, happened to switch on Mr Harty's programme. And stayed to watch.

My second "needlewoman" had arrived.

THE mail strike which France had endured for seven long weeks finally ended; without having done anyone very much good, or harm; and every morning an exhausted postman trailed up the track to the house bearing bundles of accumulated letters bound in lengths of rope more suited to a hangman.

Personal mail was easily set aside by the particular "code" I use, and then there were scurries of fan letters from Japan (where, it seemed, the young were taking "A Tale of Two Cities" for their English exams, but had ducked reading the book and caught the movie version, which I had made in 1958, instead), appeals from earnest Reverends for the roofs of their churches or gifts for their tombola stalls, early Christmas cards and, naturally, bills.

Among the litter of Robins-in-the-Snow, stage-coaches and "Snoopy" Santa Clauses, the ever-arriving bills and the fan mail ("I have seen every film you have ever made, and I love you. Please send me your photograph. Sandra. Age 10"), I one morning came across a letter addressed to me at the Connaught Hotel in London, and sent on by them. As it bore the "code" and was therefore Personal, dated November 1st which made it just over a month old, for the date was now December 6th, I thought that I should open it before settling down to the Tombola Stalls and the anguished letters from Kyoto and Yokohama.

It was from a publisher. Chatto and Windus. Brief, ten lines in all. But ten interesting lines. It read, in part, as follows:

"*Dear Mr Bogarde,*

*Several of us here saw your television appearance last week and were most impressed. Have you ever considered writing about your life? If so, on the strength of having heard you speak the other night, we have no hesitation in saying that we would be delighted to publish it. . . . If the idea appeals to you at all . . . we should welcome an opportunity of discussing it in greater detail.*"

It was signed in a generous, but firmly upright, hand: John Charlton.

"*No hesitation in saying that we would be delighted to publish it.*"

That was fairly amazing! No one had said, or written, anything like that to me ever before: it was not something to take lightly. Pretty impressive. And Chatto and Windus themselves, I knew, were pretty impressive also.

But had they, perhaps, taken leave of their senses? Together with The Hogarth Press, their list of writers was formidable: Aldous Huxley, Henry Green, Virginia Woolf, Isaiah Berlin, Iris Murdoch, and even, I remembered, Freud, among others. Not to mention M. Proust himself.

There must be something wrong here. What on earth was a firm of such exalted reputation and grandeur doing making overtures, for that is surely what it was, to a film star? Perhaps they were going bust? It was always possible. And who was this upright fellow Charlton?

I took a look at the list of directors on the letter-heading, and yes indeed, there was a J. F. Charlton. I had been written to, not by a literary tout, but by one of the directors no less.

There were five of them; all with initials save one who declared proudly, with her full name, that she was female. The rest I assumed to be male. One of them had a slightly Alpine flavour, but the rest were unmistakably English in every way: Parsons, Smallwood, Trevelyan and Charlton.

Safe-sounding names. To be trusted absolutely. Like a list of bishops. Could anything be more sober and reliable?

But did bishops ever watch television? Did they know anything remotely about film stars? It seemed to me unlikely: but here was the letter of proof in my hand, that one had written, and that "several of us here" had indeed seen television. Now Chatto and Windus were not merely Tom, Dick and Harry in publishing. They were far above the rubies.

I had lunched with many a Tom and a Dick, and not a few Harrys in my time: bland, charming, manicured, perfectly tailored, they would chat away happily over oysters and chicken pie, or roast beef and bread-and-butter pudding at the Connaught, and not come down to business until we had reached the coffee and liqueurs.

What would I say to writing my memoirs? Eh? After all, Brigitte Bardot, Ava Gardner, Judy Garland; what? It was unfailing. And unfailingly tedious. "A book about your film life . . . so *much* to tell, such a tremendous innings . . . so many *glamorous* people."

There were one or two alternative suggestions, on occasions, that I should only write a little book about my craft. As if I were a weaver or potter, or beat pewter into bracelets. Educational stuff.

The problem was that I didn't know much about my "craft", as they insisted on calling it, because being mainly an instinctive actor I didn't go by any absolute set of rules, preferring to make them up for myself as I went along. I could no more have set these down on paper, like the instructions on the back of a seed packet, than swim the Channel, because I couldn't explain them even to myself. And if I couldn't do that, then how on earth could I write them down for a clamouring horde of hungry-to-be actors who wanted to know all?

Impossible.

"Nonsense!" cried the educational Toms and Dicks and Harrys, and immediately tried to prove how easy it was by sending me slim books written by distinguished players who had already done it before. It was always perfectly clear to me, after about two pages in, that they had been spoken to a tape recorder and had as much life as a smoked haddock and as much inspiration going for them as the Albert Memorial. What they did, they did supremely well: they crushed for ever any remote curiosity I might have had about acting as a craft. Or writing about it.

However, I tried to be absolutely fair at all times: and after listening to them all mutter away about the extraordinary career that I had had, the incredible amount of people I must have met, the enormous interest there would be for future actors in what I had to say, I would start my hesitant suggestions that I *would* like to write. One day. But that when I did it would not be about the cinema or the theatre as much as about my childhood, my family, and the countryside which I loved. The eager light died in the eyes behind the cigar smoke, and I usually ended up paying for the luncheon while they fussed about with credit cards and cheque books. It seemed only fair that I should pay, for after all they had gained nothing from their efforts to cajole me, so I might as well feed them. Lunch was over.

Of course it was always made perfectly clear, at the start,

that there was nothing more than an interest being shown, nothing else was suggested; nothing outlined, it was simply a preliminary discussion and no offer, of course, was made. Which was hardly surprising, for I hadn't, as far as they knew, written so much as a baggage label in my life. And what they wanted really, when all was said and done, was a tell-all, rough-and-tumble, film-star book, including, one supposed, immodest chunks from my most flattering reviews, blow-by-blow accounts of my best acting-scenes and, most important of all of course, succulent pieces about Veronica Tishtush or Monica Mishmash: those would be *certain* to secure serial rights in the cheaper papers, and that could mean a great deal of money. They smiled enticingly; I shook my head.

So the lunches always ended amicably, if disappointedly, and I nodded to a waiter. Which saved all their fiddle-faddle with wallets and leaking fountain pens. Having rejected so many ideas, I thought it wiser to part as soon as possible. There was no use in prolonging the subject. It was tidier my way, and much more orderly. And no one ever complained. After all: the Connaught has the best restaurant in London.

Now, it seemed to me that the upright Mr Charlton might well be one more of these smooth, plump, manicured gentlemen; how could I possibly tell? And as I was just about to embark on my "Mr Philby" role in the film which Forwood had started to negotiate some time before, I felt it wiser to reply to his letter out of simple good manners, and at that same time do my best to "put him off": I felt almost sure that even so imposing a firm could only want from me exactly what all the others had wanted, either a slim book on my "craft" or else, which seemed rather unlikely but which was always possible allowing for the problems which were besetting publishers, a rollicking film-star book full of hilarious anecdotes and tales of indiscretions written, of course, in the nicest possible way.

I wrote, immediately, to Mr Charlton, apologising for the delay, thanking him for his kind comments on the Russell Harty show, and adding that I *was* writing, in a desultory fashion, a series of essays on some of the highlights of my life, but that I really didn't want to write a film-star book and that what I had to say had already been said; and much better. I added, as a further dampener, the news that I was almost immediately off to Vienna where I was to make a film and would be there until mid-March, and that what I had written so far was probably libellous.

I felt perfectly safe with this gentle refusal. Essays and so on would surely put him off, just as it had the Toms and Dicks and Harrys chumping cheerfully through cold chicken pie at the Connaught.

Quite unaware, of course, that behind Mr Charlton lurked the deceptively gentle-sounding female on the directors' list on the letter-heading: Norah Smallwood.

Satisfied that both honour and good manners had been saved, and that I would never hear from them again, particularly after my carefully planted suggestion of libel, I bundled up all my old cardigans and knitted ties and headed off to Vienna to start work on the film in which I would be required to play Mr Philby. Or rather, "A kind of Mr Philby". No one ever seemed quite certain. Least of all myself.

I was egg-laying again. So far the earlier results, I had to confess, had been moderately successful: "Le Serpent" had allowed me to rip out the dreadful black pit and replace it with a splendid, gleaming kitchen. The struggles on "The Night Porter" had produced a modest terrace at the back of the house at which meals could be taken during the summer heat; and this present effort, I hoped, would help to re-tile the roof of the house, since the original ones, which had lain there since 1641, had a heart-chilling tendency to zip away across the valley during every mistral, exposing both rats' nests and the bed-rooms below, to the rains. It was time to secure them.

I had known the Chinese Suite in the Bristol Hotel, Vienna, for many years. I had lived in it, and almost died in it, trying to come to terms with playing a piano (thoughtfully supplied by Columbia Pictures) and the genius of Liszt for months. I had since made other films in and around the city, and the Chinese Suite, or the Red Room as I called it, was always my base, my home, my womb. A shelter from all the idiocies of filming and the people who make them.

Red flock paper, heavy, black, carved furniture. Chinese bowls and plates on every inch of wall; what-nots of alarming intricacy stuffed with smiling buddhas and bent, aged fisher-men. Lace table-cloths and hard, over-stuffed, upright chairs under an enormous chandelier. The windows looked down on to the Ring and the Opera House on one side, on the other up the glittering length of Kärntnerstrasse. In the spring, with the windows wide open, a blackbird always nested on the top of the Opera House and sang until dusk swallowed the great bulk of the building and the lights sprang up along the Ring. Over all the years I had stayed in the Red Room, nothing had ever changed; not even the blackbird. Joseph Losey had once filled it with bowls of white cyclamen while he forced me to sit and read three scripts, one after the other, to advise him which one he should make. I suggested he made none of them; which he accepted with extreme good nature. Elizabeth and George and the children had come out for a Family Christmas, and all caught 'flu which put a damper on the festivities. I had played night and day on my beastly piano, with my despairing music coach shrieking out the beat. Capucine had had a mild form of hysterics in it from the sheer terror of starting her first film, and was only brought to her senses by a glass of vodka so strong that it would have dissolved a spoon; and Charlotte Rampling had gone from it one evening in furs and a snowfall to her very first Opera. The room, therefore, was full of memories. A secure place, a loved place, nothing unpleasant could intrude whatever the problems were, which I always tried to leave outside and never bring home.

I took no account, of course, of mail. That intruded, and could not be avoided. I had been there three days only when a letter arrived. From Mr Charlton.

He was certainly wasting no time. He was, he said, delighted to know that I was writing about some of the highlights of my life. He said that he felt very encouraged, brushed aside the problem of libel, which I had hoped would dissuade him, and said that "we" (Who were they? All the directors, one wondered?) would be extremely happy to see what I had written so far because they would have a "better notion of the terms that we would offer you if you would like us to draw up a contract".

Mr Charlton was not giving up easily. Was not giving up at all, it appeared. He was, politely, using force. As I can only ever do one thing at a time, lacking as I do any form of co-ordination between left and right hand, I decided that I would have to write to him immediately and stop all this nonsense, for nonsense is what it seemed at the time.

I had to go off and "be" my Mr Philby. This would take three months of work: I couldn't possibly deal with a publishing house which had either lost its head or gone into the red and needed a rib-tickling anecdotal film-star biography to save it. Ever since the amazing success of David Niven's book, every publisher, it was known, was trying to tap another gusher.

I wrote, that afternoon, a polite postcard saying that I was extremely busy on a film and would write again one day; "when the dust has settled". And hoped he'd take the hint.

It is strange, but I remember graphically, sitting down at the black carved desk in the corner of the Red Room, facing a painting of two Chinese ladies messing about in a boat, and scribbling this card urgently.

For some reason his letter, which was a long one, had filled me with a sense of unease and fear: I felt that I was possibly being forced into making a promise to do something which was far beyond my powers. I couldn't get caught up in something as complicated as writing, whatever it was, or on whatever scale. Although it had been the determined wish of Mrs X, and although I had felt it might be something I could have a shot at one day, she was no longer there to advise me or, more important, to correct me when I went wrong. The essays which I had mentioned were only that: exercises in writing to amuse myself. They wouldn't stand the cruel scrutiny of all those directors.

I was not about to attempt something in which I would fail, for if that happened at such an early stage, when I was only just playing about with an idea at the very back of my head that I might one day develop, I should be cast down and would lose all confidence and never try again.

I knew the length of my corridor: I was aware of the doors on either side, of the inevitable final one at the far end. But what I did not realise that afternoon in the Red Room was that a corridor is not necessarily one long walk in a perfectly straight line; there are corners there too.

And a corner is not for standing on only; you can turn left or right and alter your direction absolutely. With courage, support, and encouragement.

I know today what I did not know that afternoon, that Mr Charlton's letter had indicated a change of direction.

I mailed the postcard and put Chatto and Windus out of my mind while I concentrated on assuming the mantle of my cardiganed imaginary Mr Philby.

★    ★    ★

The film was certainly no Disney frolic with a pack of Bambi's in a bluebell wood, and I was not playing Mr Darling. However, although it was a pretty ho-hum kind of story, the script was at least literate and at worst a re-tread of countless secret agent stories. But the Company was pleasant and I was working with Ava Gardner once again, and in Vienna. Those were two particular pleasures.

Ava and I had not worked together for fifteen years, when we had made a perfectly frightful film about a priest and a tart in Spain during the Civil War which, when it opened, apparently to ten Eskimos in North Alaska, closed the next day and sank without trace.

It was a sad blow to us both and also to our gentle, civilised writer-director, Nunnally Johnson who, after trying to battle with the Hollywood company who wanted the whole thing made pretty and glamorous ("A Man and a Girl in Blazing Madrid" kind of thing) threw his cap in the air and gave in; as both Ava and I had been forced to do. It is impossible now, and it was even more impossible then, to try and buck the studio system. We ploughed on in misery, and Nunnally was once heard to say that although he had ruined my career I was a really very nice guy, because I still talked to him.

Nothing to do with Nunnally or careers being ruined; but that was the tenor of the times; we were a dispirited, battered group, and parted, when the time came, with relief that it was all over.

But here we were again, Ava and I, reunited and full of that idiot optimism which all actors have to carry with them as part of their survival kit.

At least the film was peaceful: there was no polemic, this time; no arguments about Jew or Aryan, not a whiff of obscenity, and nothing that could possibly cause crowds to march in the streets as they had done in Germany when "The Night Porter" finally opened there and Jews marched to demonstrate against the film for being anti-semitic while on the next night a large Arab contingent stormed the cinema protesting that the film was pro-Israeli.

This was going to be a good old-fashioned spy thriller, without any complications, and as such was surely going to be a relief. All I'd be required to do this time was act: I hoped. After a couple of halcyon weeks in Vienna we all set off for the location work.

For countless days, it seemed, we sailed up and down a frozen lake in Upper Austria in blizzards, chased about for endless nights in the very bowels of Schwechat Airport, or stood freezing to death in melting snow among mournful black fir-trees, desperate for the arrival of tea-urns and something hot to eat. When the tea arrived it was usually stone-cold. The sight of a pile of cold, boiled spaghetti on a sagging paper plate, a plastic cup of cooling milkless coffee on the upper deck of a listing lake-steamer in a biting wind is engraved on my mind for eternity.

Finally, one bitter day, I lost both my head and my temper and raced back to the Unit Hotel in the motor-boat which came out daily to supply us with this congealing muck.

Snug in the hotel dining-room, just finishing what seemed to have been a splendid luncheon, puffing contentedly at their cheroots, the money looked up at me in some surprise, and went white to their collars when I demanded their presence in a less public place. I rather think they thought Ava had drowned and I had come to break the tragic news.

Crushed between the service door of the kitchen, the telephone booth, and the gentlemen's lavatory, I exploded.

I don't often lose my temper; about once every twenty years perhaps. But when I do, I am informed, it is a pretty spectacular business, not because I shout and rail or wave my arms about, but because I am deadly cool, brutally accurate, and the hundred minor, or major, faults which I have noticed about my victims over the years are suddenly, vividly, and with appalled dismay on their part, laid before their eyes. Naked, as a skinned rabbit.

I, the good-natured, understanding, co-operative, reasonable, orderly man, suddenly erupt like Mount Saint Helen's, and my flow of molten fury and dislike engulfs them. I strike so far below the belt that they are often severed from their feet.

It would be wrong to think that I leave these encounters with a manly stride, proud of my success in the worm-turning act: far from it. I am so unnerved and shattered that I manage, usually, to blast my targets, and stagger off in desperate need of a bed in a sanatorium; so much does my fury and anger exhaust me.

So, naturally, I am careful not to do it very often, and spend months, even years as I have said, holding firm. Storing up my bits of shrapnel. Not a very attractive part of my make-up, I agree.

This particular encounter, as it happened, didn't do much good. All that happened was that the coffee urn arrived at blood heat, and the food still stuck to the paper plates in hardening fat. Naturally, the weather, and the freezing conditions, were to blame, and all that could be done had been done.

Eventually, Ava finished her part, leaving a loving note for me filled with relief, and saying that she was not "saying goodbye", but that London called to her "quite desperately" and she was off.

I worked on in my knitted ties for a little longer until I too, thankfully, reached the end of my assignment and was free to leave the gloomy little town on the lake, the mournful fir-trees and melting snow, and fly home to clear skies and the swelling buds, heralding a warm spring. God knows why people always think that filming is a glamorous business.

Sadly, I was not to see the Red Room again: it passed, as so many other pleasant things have done, into the mists of time and memory.

Home, then, to capering dogs, a welcoming Henri and Marie, a neglected garden, and an ungathered olive crop, fallen into the wild anemones and bee orchis. At the pond a last pair of toads lurched about obscenely, the willow trailed greening ribbons, and the first leaves of the water lilies lay on the still surface like pink plates. There was a great deal to do before the sudden burst of summer, which in this climate seems to happen almost overnight.

And it promised to be a busy one, for now the house boasted a Guest Room, and people had already started booking.

The year before, Henri and Marie, getting on a little, and no longer wishing to continue working after years of labouring for other people, decided to retire, but promised that they would always come to care-take if I had to be away for any length of time. This suited me perfectly, and so the staff room was stripped out, re-carpeted, re-curtained, and Antonia's selection of pictures, tom tits in apple blossom, and autumnal views of Burnham Beeches, was replaced.

And I, once known as the Idol of the Odeons (sic), could be found daily in the bright new kitchen, up to the elbows in detergent, washing up burnt saucepans, scrubbing out the dog bowls, and doing all the jobs which had been done for me for over thirty years by other people. The pleasure of having the house to oneself far outweighed the mundanity of the daily chores: it also saved a good deal of money.

★   ★   ★

The trim, smug, Georgian house in which my mother was living had suddenly raised its prices to an alarming degree, and it was necessary to find an alternative place for her; and one in which she would be happier. This Elizabeth managed to do eventually, and Ma was installed in a big comfortable Edwardian house, set in attractive gardens, and had her own self-contained flat full of her own furniture and pictures, into which she seemed to settle very well.

Elizabeth, on the other hand, was exhausted. I telephoned every Sunday to keep a check on things, and every Sunday her voice was more and more dispirited and weary. She needed a break from obligation desperately, and now that Ma was settled, and in good hands, she found it possible to come out to stay, with the intention of just sleeping for days, or mucking about in the garden.

It was a brilliant spring, and the garden work went apace. She found that, after a day's complete rest in bed with a couple of books, the extreme tiredness, most of which was mental strain, had almost worn off, and together we planted and mowed and dug, trimmed the bay trees, and brought out all the terrace chairs.

"It's a funny business, isn't it? Growing up, I mean," she said one morning while we were filling buckets from a great truck-load of earth which had been dumped at the back of the house and with which we were replenishing all the ornamental pots on the terrace, since my own mix of limestone, shale, peat and local earth dug, at great effort, from the *potager*, had produced nothing but spurge and chickweed. Naturally.

"Growing up? What do you mean, it's funny?"

"Well. I mean, take Ma. She looked after us and now it all goes in a full circle and the children start having to look after her."

"She's all right where she is now, isn't she?"

"Says she is. Difficult to tell really. But it's a terribly pretty place, very much like a private house, you know? Not imper-

sonal. Big bowls of flowers everywhere, the rooms are aw-
fully nice, and the man who runs it is charming. Ma took to
him right away and he's told her she can do as much gardening
as she wants to. Well, it isn't much, she pulls up a weed here
and there, feeds the birds. But she's happy, yes, thank God,
this time I think it'll work. She's even using a walking-stick
now."

"And the penny has dropped? About staying there?"

Elizabeth stuck her spade into the earth pile. "I think so.
Yes. But it's going to be a long haul. She still comes over to the
house every week, for lunch. I take her out in the car twice a
week, to all the old places we used to know as children: Lewes,
Alfriston. She likes that: and we usually have lunch at 'The
Five Bells'. They make a terrific fuss of her there, she and Pa
went so often. She likes that best of all."

"Doesn't leave you much time, for yourself I mean, does
it?"

"No," she laughed shortly. "None. You know what she
says every single time I arrive at the house? 'Well,' she says,
'and where have *you* been? Haven't seen you for weeks!' I
could kill her sometimes, quite cheerfully. Oh well . . ."

"Well, as long as she's happy."

"She thinks the people at the hotel are a better class. She
hated the ones at the other place. Not her type, she said.
'Nothing to say for themselves.' Fact is, they got bored stiff
with her stories, poor old love, and when *this* lot get bored
she'll say *they* aren't her 'type'. My dear," she said half
laughing, "you and Gareth simply don't know what it's like to
be the daughter in a family, don't know at all."

She was right. Growing up was a bit funny. Here we were
together, messing about with buckets and earth, filling urns
and pots, talking to each other as we had in the days of
childhood. Comfortable in each other's company, knowing it
so well, trusting it so deeply, relaxed, continuing. Aware that
we knew each other better than perhaps anyone else would
ever do. Conscious of each other's doubts, apprehensions, and
private joys, which were not private between us, because one
flick of an eye, caught suddenly in a crowded place, amid
laughter or conversation, struck instant, private responses
which no one else on earth could ever share, and comforted us.

Here I was at fifty-five. No longer the skinny boy in
plimsolls and baggy shorts, and she no longer the thin child in

a cotton dress and sandals skipping high over the tussocks of grass in Great Meadow lest she be bitten by an adder: the exteriors had altered, but the minds, and above all, the affection, had stayed constant.

We remained the original children, on our own together; while all about us had quite altered. Pa was dead; Ma in a private hotel with some of her personal possessions and whatever memories she had chosen to retain; Forwood was now a grandfather; my young brother had five children of varying ages; and Lally was a widow with two children of her own to care for, although she was always to refer to us as "her children". But at this moment, shovelling earth together under the olive trees, it felt almost as if we had stopped the speed of time and had gone back: an illusion. Time is not stoppable.

"Are you managing? I mean, without Henri and Marie? Running the house?" she said suddenly.

"Yes. Very well really. I can't iron, though. Well: only tea-cloths and napkins, square things, you know."

"They're easy. Wait until you get to collars. And you can't separate the yolk from the white of an egg: I saw you yesterday when you were doing the dogs' dinners. You just bunged the whole lot in. Awful."

"Oh! Come on! Now be fair. Not the shells."

"No, not the shells. I'll show you how, it's easy. And they hate the white and it's not good for them."

"Well, I don't make too many mistakes, really. I mean, I know about mitring sheets, and Harpic down the lav, and I'm really pretty good at washing up. I learned it in the army, in the Tin Wash. I can gut and skin a rabbit, scale and clean fish, and pull a chicken. What more do you want?"

"Can't boil a tin of soup, can you? I mean *in* the tin. And I just hope you know how to cut out that little green bag in the chicken's inside: the gall-thing."

"I do now."

"Jolly well better. Perhaps you should have got married really: a nice wife who would iron your collars and sew on buttons."

"No thanks. Set in my ways now. I don't believe that marriages are made in Heaven: they're made in a double bed, and when that wears off there's not much left except habit, or duty."

"What a dreadful thing to say!"

"I know. And I know more married people who are un-happy than unmarried ones. It's all right for some, of course. If I'd become a schoolmaster after the war, remember?, at Windlesham, things might have been different. But marriage and acting don't work: I know, I just didn't want anyone to get in my way. Wanted it all for myself. No school fees and fret, no four-door saloon and a mortgage on a house in Barnes or somewhere."

"Dreadfully selfish, honestly. And when you're old and grey, what then?"

"You'll come and look after me."

"Silly fathead. Some hopes. I've got my own problems, thank you."

"It's not easy, marriage, mate."

She stuck her spade in the earth pile, brushed her hands on her jeans. "No. It's not. I'm going up to get the salad and stuff out of the fridge," she said.

And Forwood called down from the kitchen balcony to say that Alain Resnais wanted to speak to me on the telephone.

★  ★  ★

After seeing "Last Year in Marienbad" and "Hiroshima Mon Amour" I knew that, as an actor, life had nothing more magical to offer than to work with Alain Resnais. But I suppressed the idiocy of the idea almost as soon as I had thought of it; and never spoke of it to anyone lest they think that I had taken leave of my wits, for a sea separated us, literally, and I was certain that he would never have heard of me anyway and, in any case, being a Frenchman working in France, would be sure to use only the local product.

One evening in 1966, his wife, Florence Malraux, tele-phoned me from Paris and asked me, in perfect English but with a slight frill of uncertainty in her voice, if I had ever, perhaps, heard of her husband? When I said yes indeed that I had, she asked if one day I would have lunch with him? If I said "Yes" he would come over from Paris right away; he hadn't telephoned himself, she added, because he was afraid that I would not know who he was, and was shy of being rebuffed. I said that I would be greatly happy to meet him anytime, anywhere, in London and when? She said, "How about

Thursday?" (which was two days later). And I said that I would be at the Connaught at twelve-thirty sharp.

He arrived, this tall, pale, grey-haired man, bundled up in a shabby raincoat, a red wool scarf round his neck, for comfort not politics, and slung over his shoulder an old airline bag with the letters BOAC peeling from the canvas.

Once he was unburdened, of all except the BOAC bag, to which he appeared permanently attached, we went into lunch. He spoke English impeccably, he knew every film I had ever made and wanted to know if I would perhaps be prepared to work with him? When I agreed without hesitation, he nodded contentedly, and sipped his Perrier. I asked him when this amazing event, at least for me, would take place. He said he was not absolutely certain; but perhaps in two years or three.

My heart slid.

He then asked, looking anxiously at his watch, what play in London I should recommend him to see; he only had the afternoon, for he was leaving for Paris that evening, and therefore the play must be a matinee.

"It's a quarter to two now," I said. "The matinees start, usually, at half-past two. Will you have time?"

"I will have time," he said. "I eat little."

He had eaten a small omelette and salad, refused all wine, wiped his lips with his napkin and I dropped him off at Wyndham's Theatre, with ten minutes to spare, so that he could see Vanessa Redgrave in "The Prime of Miss Jean Brodie". And that was that.

But he did not forget me. In time to come two quite remarkable scripts, "The Adventures of Henry Dickson" and one on the imprisonment of the Marquis de Sade, came my way. But although we battled hard together, no one would touch them as commercial subjects, and they lapsed into the dead-letter box finally. And tragically.

Both were too expensive to make, neither of us was safely "bankable", and the conditions under which he was expected to make them, even at the preliminary stages, were so unacceptable that neither of us wanted to be a part of them. So they died. We had last met together in Venice at my house on the Giudecca during work on "Death in Venice" to discuss the de Sade subject, but long before the shooting on "Death" was finished, de Sade had folded, and the rest was silence.

Until this moment. Filling pots and urns, starting the

terrace off for the summer. We went through the obligatory signals of greeting. How are you? How is Florence? I am well. It's so good to hear from you. Where are you now? And then he told me that a Swiss company had offered to finance him to make a film on two conditions: one that David Mercer, the English writer, should script it, and two, that I should star in it. Would I?

Naturally, unthinkingly, happily, I agreed. When?

In a year, maybe longer, about a year. There was no script, not even a subject. He just wanted to know my reaction before going any further; now that he knew it, he could put things in motion and would go to London for the first discussions with Mercer. He would, he assured me, keep me informed at all times on the development of the script.

Having battered through "The Night Porter" and the film on the lake in Upper Austria, cutting lines, adding lines, re-writing, and all the rest of it, I knew I wanted no more of that. All I wanted to do was my job, to act. Nothing else. "Just," I said to M. Resnais, "wind me up and point me in the right direction." I am not certain that he understood exactly what I meant, but he got the point.

"I'll see the script only when it is completely finished and when you are certain that it is the film *you* want to make; and then I'll do it," I said.

He seemed satisfied with the remark, but added that, just the same, when he and Mercer had worked out a story-line he'd send me a synopsis, to which I agreed. No harm in that.

"One thing, Alain, I beg you."

"Which is what?"

"Well, if you are writing this for me, will you please give me some rage?"

"Rage?" He sounded startled. Rage in French also means Rabies.

"Anger. Fury. Let me rage somewhere, I'm sick to death of all the enigmatic, silent creatures I have been playing. I want *anger.*"

He agreed, I would have some "rage" and a synopsis quite soon.

I went out on to the terrace into the early sun. At last, I thought, well into my fifties, it's going to happen. After a decade of waiting.

"Tea?" said Elizabeth, coming out with a tray and cups. "I

can't remember where you keep the biscuits; can't be bothered anyway."

Forwood came walking slowly up the steps with a watering-can. "What did Alain want? They down here or something? By the way, I've fed the dogs."

"Wants me to do a film with him. This time it seems it might be definite."

"How lovely!" said Elizabeth, pouring tea carefully into the Italian spode.

"When?" said Forwood.

"Next year. Anyway, a year's time."

"A year!" Elizabeth cried. "My God! Who knows where we'll all *be* in a year. Milk?"

★   ★   ★

In July the sky was white with heat: roses opened, bleached, and scattered crumpled petals across the cracked earth of the *potager* within the day. Lizards lay still on the hot stones of the terrace, golden eyes shut, only the gentle throb of their green-scaled bellies betraying that they lived.

Under the vine the shade was green, dark, cool; no breath of air. Occasionally a fat blue Provençal bee would drone past, swing about among the swelling grapes, soar up and away into the white afternoon; and down the hill, in the speckled shade of the olives, the summer guests lay in angular groups, knees bent upwards, arms thrown wide, heads to one side, inert; bodies by Stanley Spencer.

I had been foolish to believe that no one would ever come to this house, as I had on the very first day that I had taken the key from behind the orange tree and let myself into the long white room. Everyone had come, in time; and only one had considered me mad.

"Bumble" Dawson arrived on a summer's night, driven up the bumpy track by two over-tanned gentlemen in sailors' caps and striped shirts, in a white Rolls-Royce which looked as out of place, as it inched up the hill, as a double-decker bus. "Bumble", a-flutter and a-swirling in printed voile, unsteady on high heels, bade them goodbye (for they were off to Monte Carlo for dinner) and reminded them to come back to collect her before midnight. They had crept down the track, wincing, one thought, with every bump, each caress against the pristine white coachwork from every unpruned bramble, thankful to get away.

"Bumble" had been a weekly guest at the Bendrose-Beel-Nore gatherings, and her arrival, a little disapproving, for she disliked the French and France, was a moment of charming emotion generally; and then she saw the house for the first time and was deeply shocked.

"This is *it*?" she had said. Her voice had a dying fall. "I thought the servants perhaps . . ."

"No, this is it. All of it. Come and look."

She was not impressed. Hated the "things which fly about at night and bite" and shook her head sadly. "The furniture looks so sad here. So out of place. It's simply not *you*. It's not your background. You'll never stay here . . . too lonely, too far away! Who'll ever come all this way, up that ghastly road and then that track. It's not *possible*, darling. You don't *fit*."

But I did fit. And I did stay. And everyone else came up that ghastly road and the track, but "Bumble", alas, never did again, and although we met at suppers in her elegant London flat, stuffed with china cats and tight satin settees, from which I constantly slid, she never mentioned the house, and died one New Year's morning in her bathroom at Castle Howard, where she was staying, in far more suitable surroundings.

In August the weather sometimes makes an abrupt and surprising change. At first the clouds appear, high above the crest of the hill, which grow as one watches into enormous hammer-heads, colouring from ice-white to deep copper; the birds are silent; the air still.

"There's going to be a storm," someone will say with blinding obviousness, and we hurry about closing the shutters, dragging the cushions from the terrace chairs, gathering up the books and papers and all the symbols of a lazy summer day.

With the first, tremendous, zig-zag of lightning comes a gust of hot wind, as if hell has opened its doors for a brief moment, scattering the lizards, the first yellowing leaves on the vine, bending the last of the hollyhocks, ripping the flowers from the fuchsias in their pots, and sending wild scurries of dust and leaves spiralling high into the air; and then the rain roars in, beating down like steel beads, as everyone hurries to shelter in the house and the dogs flee, tails between legs, to the darkest corners of the long room. A cruel, and

15. The first script-conference for "Despair". March 1977
L/R. Peter Martesheimer, R. W. Fassbinder, self and Tom Stoppard.

16. Cannes Film Festival. The reception after the showing of
"Despair". With Andrea Ferreol. May 1978.

17. "I can't go on trying to understand what you want through a translator. Please help me," I said to Rainer. "Despair". R. W. Fassbinder, Munich, June 1977.

abrupt change of season, after which the weather will never quite be as hot again, for the first fingers of autumn have laid themselves upon the parched earth.

It can (and often does) rain for days; sometimes it clears away, racing in great black clouds down towards the coast, tumbling and rumbling to spend itself far out in the ocean. But in general it marks the end of summer on the hill and the arrival of cooler, moister, days.

September came treading with suggestive steps across the land, the evenings became cooler, the vine started to turn from vibrant green to pale yellow, the wasps arrived and every morning the grass was wet with the early dew, and the sun began to sink each evening a little earlier behind the big oak by the front gate as my summer-guests prepared to pack and head slowly home. The last of the holiday postcards had been sent: summer was over.

But for me September meant that Alain Resnais would soon be arriving. Bringing with him both Mercer's synopsis and a thousand photographs which, he had warned me, he had taken during his hunt for locations. In Providence, Rhode Island. Which meant, naturally enough, America.

This last piece of information about Rhode Island had, when I heard it, sent me into a mild state of depression. I knew that the film was to be a twelve to fourteen week business, and even though that was far too long by my standards to be away from the house, I had willingly, deliberately, insisted that I should have nothing whatsoever to do with the script, and only read it when it was quite finished. Of course, having an obvious mind, I had reasoned that as Resnais was French, and his film French, he would, of course, shoot it in France. That seemed perfectly logical to me. But then I have such a depressingly literal mind; and it often kicks back at me. To my constant surprise.

I had forgotten that Resnais had once confessed that, among the main passions in his life, one was America, like most intellectual Frenchmen for some reason, and the other was ordering breakfast in bed at Claridge's in London. Pressing the bell in that hotel, he said, gave him profound pleasure. The breakfast "arrives almost before you have removed your finger from the bell!"

However, of the two passions it was clear that Rhode Island had won over Claridge's. Which was a pity. The thought of spending all those weeks in America, so far away, was very depressing. I'd never be able to get home for a week-end.

★ ★ ★

If September had begun the dispersal of holidaymakers, it hadn't finished the job; some would linger on as the crowds departed, enjoying quieter, if cooler, beaches, less congested restaurants and roads, and on the first Sunday one telephoned.

"This is John Charlton speaking," said a brisk voice.

Who the hell was John Charlton?

"I'm down here with the family, only a little way from you, I think. The other side of Grasse. I wondered if, perhaps, I could pop over one day; just for a few minutes? You *did* mention in your last letter that you had written some essays, if you remember?"

I remembered all right. Chatto and Windus. With its apparent list of Bishops, and a Nun.

My last letter had been written years, it seemed, ago. And the postcard scribbled from the Red Room in Vienna was supposed to have put them off, but had obviously been filed in "pending" rather than thrown into a wastepaper basket; as I had hoped. But one couldn't be impolite: the man was only fifteen minutes away, and nothing could possibly be lost by seeing him for a glass of beer or a cup of tea, because my time, from April anyway, would be fully occupied, and I'd be far away in Rhode Island, America. I was perfectly safe now. We arranged a rendezvous at the house for a couple of days later, after five o'clock, he stipulated, because that's when everyone got back from the beach.

So after five it was.

What on earth, apart from a drink, could I offer the man? Certainly there were some essays; small bundles of ill-typed stuff, nothing which would interest him or the row of names on his letter-paper. For the most part they were enlarged versions of some of the things which once I had written to Mrs X in her hospital bed so long ago. A story about, for example, Visconti: of a morning's shopping in the Marché Forville in Cannes, of the wild flowers high in the back-country in April, of my days with Rank, of my first sight of a grass-snake devouring, alive, a slightly anxious toad. There was nothing here for those distinguished directors to look at with anything but a shrug.

The row of files which contained these pitiful pieces nudged those which contained all the returned letters to Mrs X. She had always encouraged me to try and edit them, had even offered to do so herself, for she was certain that they would make a book, apart, as she had said, from the fact that, "*books of letters are really very difficult to publish. No one seems to buy them except University people.*" So that didn't appear to me a very good idea. I *could* offer them perhaps, and that would be the end of that. Mr Charlton would finish his drink, thank me, and go on his way back to his family holiday.

And then, just as I was stuffing some of the letters back into a file dated 1972, three pieces of writing, stapled together and obviously not letters, slid to the floor. Chapters 1 to 3 of the tentatively titled book of childhood stories which I had started to write for her called *The Canary Cage*.

These will do, I thought; they are cleanly typed, stapled, self-contained. Essays in fact. He'd certainly not find them of any interest, like all the other Toms and Dicks and Harrys in the past. But I'd have at least kept my word, he'd have his wretched essays and a drink and that would be that, and the hundreds of letters which, after all, were extremely private, would remain where they were, in their files, unread by strangers' eyes. They were far too personal to be picked about by the directors of Chatto and Windus with all their initials.

John Charlton didn't look remotely like a director of an extremely august publishing house. A tall, lean, angular man with a strong nose and an absurdly boyish cockscomb of hair which sprang in a high curve from the back of his neat head, he seemed, in his flannels and plain tweed jacket, far more suited to a sports field blowing a whistle, perhaps, on the sideline, or shouting L.B.W.! triumphantly to some unfortunate youth in cricket pads and gloves.

An illusion which he quickly dispelled.

I have an uncomfortable feeling now that I greeted him with some reserve and even vague hostility: I was fully aware that I had no need to fear anything, the essays would see to that, and also I had the safety-net of the Resnais film to sustain me. I can't remember what we talked about, but I do remember that I paddled about for quite a while avoiding the subjects of writing or books as if they were sea urchins, until he decided that we had had enough of pleasantries and reminded me why he had come.

"Well, yes: I have got a few bits of stuff, as I said. Really nothing much and I haven't written anything for ages: nothing which would interest you anyway."

"Well, those of us who saw you on that television show were deeply impressed."

"I was pretty exhausted. I'd been doing publicity all week and that was the final chore. I think I must have been hysterical. I do apologise."

"Oh no! Not at all, don't apologise. It was first-rate, and we wondered if you felt that you could, perhaps, write about some of the things of which you spoke. If you felt that you could put it down, I can truthfully say that we would be more than happy to publish such a book."

The man is going potty, I thought. How do I get out of this one? Perfectly simply, by using the same suggestions which I had used at all those Connaught luncheons with the bland, well-tailored, plump gentlemen, Tom and Dick and Harry.

"Well, the point is that I do want to write one day, and I *have* set down a few bits and pieces, but I honestly don't think they'd interest you."

"How do you know until I have read them?" he said perfectly reasonably.

"But it wouldn't be a film star's autobiography, you know. All my films, full of randy jokes and who I slept with, that kind of thing."

Mr Charlton looked calm. "I don't think that we would want that kind of book," he said.

Which caught me off guard.

"What I'm actually thinking of is a book about my early childhood with my sister and our nanny in Sussex."

If that doesn't squash it, I thought, nothing will.

It didn't. Mr Charlton leant forward. "That sounds a bit more like it," he said. "As a matter of fact I'm a Sussex man myself. Have you got something written in that vein?"

"Yes," I said, fairly ungraciously, and handed him the three thin chapters of *The Canary Cage*.

He took them politely, flipped roughly through the pages. In his hand they looked suddenly not thin, but famished.

"The title is only a working title," I said; as if I knew what I was talking about.

"Might I take these back with me to the house? I'll send them back to you as soon as I have read them."

"That won't take you very long," I said with a laugh which I hoped was deprecating. But I agreed; said I had a carbon copy anyway, and after a few more moments of not very much, he left amid handshakes, and I watched him drive down the track with extreme care. And that, I thought, is that.

Two evenings later he telephoned to say that he had read the chapters and that he had enjoyed them thoroughly. Couldn't I be persuaded to carry on, and meanwhile he'd like to take what he had back to London for his colleagues to have a look at?

"Are you sure?"

"Perfectly sure. It could be a very charming book; I really think you ought to carry on. Really. Of course it's difficult to judge from just *three* chapters, but I am convinced you've got something very good there, you must write a little more, say another five or six, in the same style; exactly the same style."

Praise, when it comes, often embarrasses me, and I don't handle compliments as well as I should. Judy Garland once told me that all one had to do was say, "Thank you", or "Thank you *so* much", or, if things persisted, "You're *very* kind"; which helped me greatly. But encouragement is something absolutely different.

Encourage me and I will part the seas; if you want me to.

The morning after Mr Charlton's telephone call I bought two trestles, a thick piece of planking, took one of the chairs from the kitchen, and my typewriter, and locked myself in the old olive store above the woodshed and started to write.

I am still there today.

## 12

THE quinces were already yellowing on the bough when Resnais arrived, bringing with him his wife Florence, a thousand photographs of the locations which he had chosen in and around Providence, Rhode Island, the second synopsis, and the first draft of the first two acts of the film. Which I politely declined to read until it was final and he had approved it fully.

The first synopsis had arrived in April. It was extremely detailed. The film was to be set in some city in the West: that is to say, the West as opposed to the East, but it must have nothing identifiable about it; it was not America, England, France or Germany, just vaguely in the West. We would start shooting in February 1976 for twelve weeks, eight in New England, the rest in Paris; the title was "The Stadium"; and the provisional budget was set at a low 2,700,000 dollars.

We were a small company of seven. I was to be a barrister with a wife and a twenty-four-year-old daughter who was in love with a footballer whose brother was a soldier in a paramilitary unit. There was also a cancer research pathologist, male, and a female American journalist who was dying of leukaemia. We were about to be taken over by a military junta and, in bewilderment and disarray, herded into a football stadium from which, eventually, we were to be driven to an, obviously, unfortunate end just as a World Cup football match began under the new regime.

Not a lot of laughter there, I couldn't help thinking. And not a lot of the rage in my role, for which I had asked Resnais long before. Perhaps there would be in the complete script: this was after all nothing more than a synopsis and one couldn't be absolutely certain of anything. However, it was perfectly clear to me, even at such an early stage of events, that I was going to be exposed to a good deal of political-hype (little of which I should be able to understand) and that Mr Mercer had determined that his audience would be spared no kind of brutality, interrogation, torture or death.

But by September all that had changed radically.

Among the scattered photographs in the long room, I read the second synopsis, now called "Providence", to find that I was still a barrister (rageless) with a wife but no daughter. She had faded away, along with most, but not quite all, of her footballer-lover and almost all of the cancer pathologist: the paramilitary brother remained in a different guise, as did the ailing American journalist, and I discovered, with a deeply-rooted sense of unease, that I had suddenly acquired an aged novelist father with a vicious tongue and a love of the bottle. I had a pretty shrewd idea that this could be a most commanding role: I've been an actor long enough to know about those rascally father parts with bottles and vicious tongues. They invariably take the picture.

Nervously, or perhaps I should say cautiously unnerved, I turned my attention to the photographs which had spilled about the room. Some were exceptionally interesting, some extraordinary; all conjured up a strange and unidentifiable place. But I became overwhelmed by the plethora of roots, tree trunks, boulders, rocks, oddly shaped houses, hideous streets, and in particular one exceedingly ugly house standing on a bare knoll high above the Hudson River. This was to be our main location, and Resnais was obviously as delighted with it as he had been with room-service in Claridge's. It had been photographed from every conceivable angle and still, to my mind anyway, looked like a mill owner's house in Ramsbottom, Lancashire.

I held my tongue: but I couldn't help feeling that all these items, so carefully recorded on large glossy prints, could have been found a lot nearer home, without us having to trail all the way across the Atlantic. However, Resnais was adamant; as he was about everything, with a quiet, still, polite, firmness which could not be budged. Providence, and a singularly unpleasing little town nearby, were to be our bases; so be it.

The photographs were collected up, the script and the synopses filed away, and I turned my uneasy mind to more pressing things: for this was September only. The film was still a long way off, and Resnais had promised that by the end of the year I would have the final, approved, script from him. I'd waited a decade for it, so four more months wouldn't make much difference and would give me time to get on with the job which now awaited me, daily, up in the olive store.

Encouraged by John Charlton's reaction to the first three

chapters which he had read and taken off to London with him, and following his suggestion that I would have to write "five or six" more before anyone could possibly say that a book was underway or not, I wrote and wrote daily, sending him each chapter immediately it was finished.

By the time that I had written three, or perhaps it was four, his letters became more encouraging and his use of the words "we" and "colleagues" more frequent. Obviously his were not the only eyes to scan my tumbled sheets: he was distributing my chapters like tracts all about the lofty halls of his firm for the bishops on the letter-paper to read; and from his remarks, which were extremely guarded, they appeared to like what they had read also. Which was comforting.

Once the name "Norah Smallwood" appeared; in October. A throw-away reference in a P.S. reminding me that *our Managing Director* would welcome an opportunity of meeting me, should I be in London at any time, and reminding me that it was *she* who had first heard me talking about "The Night Porter" on the television, *"which was the start of our* [his and my] *correspondence."* This was the first *I* had heard of it.

I looked at the letter-heading and noted that the name of Mr Parsons was now no longer at the top, but that the nun among the bishops had slipped into his place. No nun this: rather the Reverend Mother. Or, to be accurate, Managing Director.

So, with an approving, I gathered, Managing Director behind me, I wrote on furiously, and by the time that I had completed six chapters, to universal approval, it became pleasingly apparent to me that, with luck, I might actually be writing a book, and that in that case I would be in need of literary advice, perhaps an agent, and most certainly a typist who could deal with my dire spelling and lack of punctuation, for I was still using dots when in doubt, and from the look of my pages I was in doubt most of the time.

Robin Fox's partner, Dennis van Thal, who still looked after whatever theatrical ventures came my way in England, had just such a person to hand in his own firm. His brother Herbert, or Bertie as he is called, was a literary agent, had been a publisher himself, written an impressive number of books, and was gentle, witty, unassuming and much respected in the publishing world. I liked him immediately. Fortunately, he liked me, and what he was given of my work to read: dots and all.

"Don't worry about the dots, dear boy," he said. "We'll get someone to clean them up in a trice. A couple of margins would be attractive, I think, easier to read. And then we'll sort out the paragraphing."

And one afternoon at the Connaught he produced a slight, fair-haired girl, in a pale blue trouser suit, who took my mangled pages in capable hands and read fluently every single hieroglyphic with which each page was liberally covered. For it was not my practice, and still is not I regret to say, to retype my corrections. I prefer to write them all in afterwards, scribbling them over and about the page like lengths of bent wire, spiked with directional arrows, erasures, and far too many capital letters.

I was much impressed at the speed with which she managed to decipher this stuff, but she was as sure and calm as if she had written it all down herself, and Sally Betts became (and still is) the only person living who can make head or tail of my typescripts. She accepted the marathon job cheerfully.

So now I had a literary agent, a typist, and could, with extreme caution and a good deal of finger-crossing, murmur the magic phrase "my publisher" to myself. Caution and finger-crossing were important: for there *was* no publisher as yet, just an interested one offering encouragement.

It is strange now to remember that, almost six months to the exact day that John Charlton had come to the house, in the middle of his family holiday, and faced my slightly hostile (or perhaps indifferent is better) reception and read my crumpled chapters from the file of letters which once had belonged to Mrs X, I completed an eighth chapter, and Bertie telephoned to say that Chatto and Windus had accepted the book. Half written.

He said that just to be published by Chatto was something which he himself had dreamed of for many years, and hoped that I was very proud.

More amazed than proud. Still half a book to finish and quite the hardest part. For it was obvious to me that after eight chapters of childhood and a continual summer sky, I had to make a change, otherwise the whole thing could slide down into a soggy mess. A different flavour, sharper, had to be injected, and Bertie agreed.

"Go on with what happened after that summer-childhood. The growing-up part. Never much fun, that. But you *can't* stay embalmed as twelve years old. Make a switch, dear boy. Won't be easy, but just knuckle down and try. Remember: you have half a damned good book already, a marvellous firm to publish it, so finish the job."

Which, on February 24th 1976, assisted by all the bits and pieces which my father had collected for me in a large cigar box and which I had found in his studio during the clearing-out process after his death, at the trestle table in a howling draught in the olive store, I did. For a few moments I sat staring at the final page. Battered out a row of asterisks below the last line to indicate that I had finished, and realised that I had actually written a book.

I never expected to write another.

*　　*　　*

It would be unwise to think that this astonishing creative effort on my part had taken place in monk-like calm and serenity in the room above the wood shed. Far from it.

There were still the daily chores to deal with: the dustbins to lug down to the end of the track, logs to split, dogs to be fed, and the telephone never stopped ringing with urgent calls about "Providence" which, like every film I had ever really wanted to make, was proving to be as difficult to get started as any. It was on and off with the amazing regularity of a conjuror's trick-hat. Resnais kept me always closely informed: sometimes filled with happy optimism, on other occasions as drab with despair as a potential suicide case.

Contracts, mine anyway, got altered. Billing was changed, dates were scrambled, even though the contract itself had already, months ago, been signed. And only the force and determination of my agent in Paris, Olga Horstig, and my own stubbornness, got things sorted out, although it meant that on two occasions I withdrew from the project altogether, causing a tremendous flurry and fuss but instant withdrawals of unacceptable alterations.

None of this had anything whatsoever to do with Resnais. He remained aloof from this as much as possible and pro-ceeded with his wooing of Ellen Burstyn (who had just won the Oscar) to play my wife, John Gielgud to play my rascally old father, David Warner and the splendid Elaine Stritch; and by the end of October he had them all. It was a most impressive company of players. Resnais was to call us his quintet. A violin, a piano, a cello, a harp etc. Although I was never absolutely sure which instrument I was; perhaps a tin drum.

Through all these trials and tribulations I worked on at my summer recollections and slow approach to adolescence, grateful for the diversion, and comforted enormously by the fact that I was working towards an end-product which someone actually wanted and believed in. But it wasn't very easy: every day brought a new cry of disaster or joy from the "Providence" company, culminating in Resnais' sudden decision, for reasons I no longer remember, to postpone the whole thing until April. So I had plenty of time to start on my "revisions", another new word I learned from Bertie, which meant that one had to do a bit of re-writing here and there, but that the book, although finished and delivered, was still very much a part of my life. Thankfully; for with all the fizz and fuss about the wretched film, I think that without it I might very likely have finally pulled out in disenchantment. Which would have been a grave error.

In December I received the final draft script. I was the last member of the company to read it, as I had insisted. I remember that it arrived on a mild, wet day. The vine was bare against the low cloud scudding towards Corsica and the coast of Africa: far across the valley and beyond the mountains there was a thin saffron light over the Var. I sat alone in the long room and started to read.

It was a marathon. Page after page of dialogue, little of which I can truthfully say I understood. My earlier feeling that I should be subjected to a heavy exposure of political-hype seemed only too obvious; and my deep-rooted feeling of unease about the rascally old father with the vicious tongue was fully realised. It was a brilliantly placed role, and I knew that with John Gielgud playing it none of us would stand a chance. He'd pinch the picture. Which he did.

When I finished reading, two hours later, I knew three things were certain: I had lost the film for myself; I had no rage whatsoever; and I had to do it without question. What I was not certain about was whether it was a work of genius or one of pretentious rubbish. I secretly suspected that it was the latter; but I also knew instinctively that it was brilliant rubbish and would play, with the given company, as magic.

Forwood came down into the long room.

"Finished? What's it like?"

"Extraordinary. I'd be out of my skull if I said that I understood what the hell it's all about, but it's marvellous: quite marvellous."

"And your part?"

"Enormous. All chat. Pages and pages. Big black chunks. I don't know what it means, it all sounds to me like a lot of intellectual twaddle: they all take themselves *so* seriously. I honestly don't think that much of it makes sense really, anyway to me. But then Shaw didn't always make sense when one analysed his stuff. Remember that big speech to the Doctors that Dubedat makes? *It's* all nonsense; always has been."

"But you want to do it?"

"Oh yes! God yes! I'd be dotty not to: all my instincts say I must, but I can't really think why. It's a long, dull, barrister-part. No rage, as I asked, and a mass of chatter. A dull man: with a lot of intellectual nonsense to spout. I'll never be able to learn it."

"You'll just have to work extra hard."

"I'm getting a bit long in the tooth for learning. Anyway: I'm probably wrong. Remember I was brought up for years on a very simple diet. Boy Meets Girl . . . and even though I have a shrewd suspicion that they won't be actually beating down doors to see it in Preston, Cricklewood or Putney, I reckon that if it ever does get made it'll still be showing somewhere in a hundred years. A typical Resnais classic."

"Which is what you wanted."

"Which is what I wanted. Funny. I don't understand much of what I've read but what is really extraordinary is that I have a terrific lump in my throat. So there must be something working: something's got to me. I'm *very* moved. I wonder why?"

Outside on the terrace the last of the day was fading into night. Across the valley and the mountains the saffron light which had hung over the Var had died to a sullen, smouldering, crimson thread. I stood leaning against the iron trellis in the thin December rain, watching until it had gone.

★　★　★

The battle of the budget for "Providence" was waged well into the New Year. I don't know what happened in Paris, Zurich or Geneva or wherever the action was, but just as I was starting on the last chapter of the book, Resnais called to say that he was going to postpone the entire project for a year, to give him time, I assumed, to get enough cash to enable him to cart us all off to the location work in Providence, Rhode Island.

That was the main stumbling-block. We didn't have enough money to go to America. Which didn't worry me in the very slightest, but obviously distressed him very much indeed, for the locations were an integral part of his film and its particular atmosphere. I remember begging him to reconsider this drastic action, and reminding him that he had a magnificent company ready and waiting, some of us for months in fact, and that if he disbanded us now it was almost certain that he would never be able to assemble us again in a year's time. I said that I was certain that the script was so strong, so magical, and the cast so perfectly balanced, that if needs be he ought to "make it in a tent" and forget the locations. We were all ready and anxious to start; we were ready to begin the next day even.

I think that I had had my second whisky when I spoke to him that evening, and he listened in his usual, cautious, silence, saying nothing. In truth I hadn't left him very much of a chance to get a word in anyway. After I left the telephone I felt a surge of anxiety that I might perhaps have been discourteous, the very last thing that I would have wished to be to the director I wanted so much to work for, and for the rest of the evening I felt an anxious nagging of doubt. I had probably been extremely rude; but at least I had spoken, and I had meant everything that I said.

Two days later I was informed that we would be shooting the picture in Europe: America was out, and Resnais was going off to Belgium to inspect alternative locations.

The day after I finished the book, Olga called to say that the film was now firmly "on", but that it would take time to find the new places in which to work and we wouldn't start shooting until the end of March or late April at the earliest. But we were "on". That was the main thing. I was delighted, now I had all the time I would need for the revisions which were to come.

And the drawings.

Mr Charlton had written one day suggesting that he "*felt more than ever that the book should have some illustrations. I had no idea when I raised the subject before that you yourself had had artistic training . . . and what distinguished tutors you had.*"

Graham Sutherland and Henry Moore, to be precise, but sadly the fact that they had tried to batter some "artistic training" into my eighteen-year-old soul didn't mean much more than that. It didn't mean, by a long chalk, that I could actually draw. I could scribble, yes. But not much more.

However, as Mr Charlton and I now seemed to be joined at the hip, so to speak, and as I listened to his every word like a pupil at Plato's knee, followed his suggestions as much as I possibly could (well aware that there was another voice echoing his wishes), I decided that I'd better settle down in the time I now had free to do some free-line scribbles with which to decorate the book.

I was aware of the other voice, softly echoing his own, simply because the names Mrs Smallwood or, on occasions, Norah Smallwood, began to thread themselves through his letters like a scarlet ribbon weaving a pleasing pattern of managerial approval.

I was, frankly, enjoying myself tremendously. I had written a book. I was about to be published. I would do everything within my powers to assist them, so I put my long-unused pen to work recalling a myriad things which I had let lie buried in the dust of childhood and uneasy growing up. I remembered the privy, the pump, the cabbages in the cottage front garden, all the simple symbols of happiness, and fixed them on to paper to pleasure Mr Charlton.

I was always very pleased when I read in his letters that Mrs Smallwood had been "delighted" with them also.

*     *     *

At the beginning of March, Resnais called to say that he had found his locations, and that we would start shooting in Brussels on April 20th; and a few evenings later Simone (Signoret) telephoned, just as I was sitting down to supper, to tell me that Luchino Visconti was dead.

I remember that all I could say was, "Oh shit." A hopeless, useless, despairing oath at such a moment, and a very few minutes later, Joseph Losey telephoned; in tears, to tell me the same wretched news.

I sat for a time in the long room alone and in silence. Firelight flickered; a log settled. The Emperor had gone, and with him much of the splendour of the cinema.

We had spoken together not long before: he had a cold, wheezed slightly. "Is influenza. Is not serious, only annoying. I am thinking of *The Magic Mountain*, you remember we spoke of this?"

"Very well indeed."

"You are interested to work with me again? Or are you still feeling distaste for my work?"

This was a direct, and sharp, reference to the fact that I had declined, a long time before, to play a character based on himself in a film which he had made as soon as he was given permission from his doctors. The set of the film was built on one level so that his chair could be wheeled easily from place to place, and was to be very lavish, but I had disliked the script and knew that I could not possibly play a role founded on himself. He was furious. And for a time I was banished; I didn't even get the usual card at Christmas, nor were messages sent by mutual friends, as had been the case before.

"Luchino! I have *never* felt distaste for your work. That is a terrible thing to say. I just didn't like the role in 'Conversation Piece'."

"And you were right. You would not have been any good. Burt Lancaster was *much, much* better. He has brio!"

"Well . . . there you are! But 'Mountain' is something else, when would it be?"

"We have problems with the Germans about the rights. Always they make difficulties. But we will work this out. I must think if you are right for Peeperkorn or for Settembrini: I am not sure; perhaps Settembrini, we see. Now I go. I talk too much. We speak later. Ciao, Bogarde."

But there was not to be a "later", and sitting in the long room that evening I knew that another door had closed: softly; with a terribly final "click!". He would always be a major figure in my life even though, strangely, we hardly knew each other off the studio floor. Socially we met very occasionally: a Christmas party in his house in Rome; two days when he had come to my villa in the suburbs of the city, once bringing the book of *Death in Venice*. The fact that I could not, and would not, learn Italian irritated him to fury, for he thought that as I was a guest in his country, the least I could do was to pay it the compliment of speaking its language. When we spoke, which was not often, he would frequently force me to speak in French because, although he spoke English very well, he said that it fatigued him. The fact that I have a tin-ear as far as languages are concerned was of no consequence; he dismissed my excuses with an impatient wave of his hand.

But I know that he respected me, and I know that he knew how much I respected him. During the whole five months of work on "Death" we were never far apart, and at all times extraordinarily close: without ever speaking, or very seldom.

Each day I was bidden to lunch with him at whatever location we were working, and each day it was I who sat on his right as he poured his olive oil on his garlicked *bruschetta* while I ate my usual small boiled sole and three potatoes: for any other kind of food repelled me. And this he understood completely; without words. He knew that I had brought Von Aschenbach to the table, not myself, and respected that fact above all other things. Forgiving even my lack of Italian, and my solitary, unsocial life which had surprised him, until he realised that I had to live in that manner in order to contain the intense concentration which I needed to give him the performance he wanted.

He had marvellously curious ways of expressing his pleasure in the work one did. I never heard him ever say "Good" or "Thank you" or "Perfect" or any of the other cliché words a director will use to his actors. His thanks, if they came at all, came in a surprising, touching manner.

Once on "Death" we were working at night in a tiny square in the centre of Venice. It was raining; it was cold. The little square had been scattered all about with the contents of stinking dustbins in order to give the impression of the squalor and muck that existed in the city in the middle of the cholera plague in 1910. In the centre of the square was a small, much-used, marble well-head, against which I had to lean, laugh, and slowly sink to the ground: laughing in hopeless misery and despair at the tragedy of life.

A simple enough shot, one might think. Except for the fact that I had only one white suit; and that meant that there could not possibly be a chance of doing a second shot if the first did not work. Lying in the rain, the filth, the mud, I'd be a ruin. The laughter, plus the bitterness, pain and disillusion which it must express, had to be absolutely correct. Otherwise the shot would be ruined as well as the suit, and we'd have to do it all over again the next night after the thing had been sent to the cleaners. It was a "one off" job. And I was petrified.

So petrified that I mucked it up. The laughter was, Visconti said quietly, "too aware, too knowing; too young, above all. You must laugh old. We go again."

I had pulled myself up from the filth in which I had lain, and was suddenly surrounded by the entire troupe; cameraman, wardrobe, props, electricians, carpenters, everyone whispering "Bravo! Bravo!" and smothering me in handfuls of white chalk-powder. The suit was clean again. We did a second shot which satisfied Visconti, and I heard him say, through the snot and tears which coursed down my face, mixing with the fine steady rain, "D'accordo," as he came across the filthy square to help me to my feet.

"Bogarde," he said. "I have something *incredible* to show you: look!"

With one arm around my shoulder he pointed to a tall, arched, pillared house across the little square, roped about with washing-lines, tilting against the night sky.

"You see! Only the Venetians know. It is not in the guide-books. *We* share the secret, eh? Is the house of Marco Polo!"

Visconti had said, "Thank you."

*   *   *

We finally started shooting on "Providence" on a bitterly cold day in an ugly, and extremely busy, street in Brussels. I was not "called" but, as I always do, went down to see the first shot put in the can, and to wish the troupe, and the actors who are breaking the ice, good luck.

Ellen Burstyn I found in the make-up truck, reading a thick paperback on some form of psychology or other, dressed immaculately in her Yves St Laurent costume and looking just a little tense.

"Is it normal," she asked, "that on European movies a star doesn't get to have a trailer dressing-room?"

I admitted that it was so; but that there was a small bar across the street which had an area reserved for the players to relax in.

"I don't relax in small bars," she said. "Is it going to be that kind of a film?"

"It's that kind of a film."

She returned to her book. "Just as long as I know," she said.

And it was that kind of a film. We shuttled about from Brussels to Antwerp and Louvain, taking in sundry squalid, and depressing, locations on the way, eventually ending up in a château, empty and deserted since the war, which was a kind of bastard French-Scottish baronial, turreted pile set in an immense and beautiful park some way out of Limoges, a peculiarly ugly industrial town.

By this time we had all started to settle down together: the troupe was marvellous, all hand-picked by Resnais himself. Ellen had very quickly come to terms with the sort of European movie she was in and threw in her not-inconsiderable lot happily with the rest of us; and Resnais himself, although seldom seen to smile much, was proving more and more to be the supreme example of an *auteur* director, and gave a very good impression of being happy: now that we had at last started and got under way.

Our close-knit group was joined at the château by John Gielgud, for his two-week stint on the film, bringing with him tremendous zest and pleasure and an inexhaustible fund of reminiscences. The Resnais quintet was, at last, complete.

If I had thought, at my first reading of it, that the script was difficult and at times obscure, the playing of it proved my point. It is one thing to read words, quite another to say them aloud. Mr Mercer's enormous blocks of dialogue were exceptionally difficult to learn but, more than that, they were extremely difficult to speak. The root of the trouble was that the verbosity lacked any form of rhythm, nor did it flow.

Although Resnais spoke impeccable English, and wrote it even better, his ear was still unsure and not quite in pitch with the poetry of our tongue. Which was hardly surprising, because there was none whatsoever in what we had to say: the players had to supply the poetry themselves, infusing the strange torrents of words with some kind of form, pace and, hardest of all, meaning. Because unless *we* believed incontrovertibly in what we were saying, no audience would.

Often, preparing at night for the work of the next day, I would discover that the removal, or even the substitution, of a word could make all the difference to a speech, but the script, as far as Resnais was concerned, was as sacred as the Turin Shroud, and although he would listen to my feverish explanations with the greatest politeness and attention, he would not budge, or permit an alteration unless I telephoned Mr Mercer himself and got his personal approval.

Since Mr Mercer lived at the time in Haifa, Israel, and we were stuck in a small village in central France with a distinctly uncertain telephone link even to the next village, to call him was, to say the least of it, difficult. It seemed to me a bit idiotic to telephone so far just for permission to alter a word like, say, "because" to "become". But if, by any chance, one thought that one was being clever and simply left the offending word out of the speech during playing, Resnais would instantly notice the omission, and one would see him huddled over the sound recorder, ear-phones on his head, playing back the error, detecting it as he read the script. So it was wiser to telephone.

"For God's sake!" cried Mr Mercer one evening when we had finally tracked him down after a long day on the beach with his family. "The script isn't sacrosanct! I'm not that kind of writer: change it about if you want to, if it's easier to play. I haven't written the Bible!"

"You have as far as this end is concerned."

"Well, for God's sake, if something bugs you, alter it. I won't sue!" He was at all times trusting and generous.

But having to stand in the office of the little house which Florence and Resnais had rented near the château, while he sat upright, silent, unsmiling, calm, attentive, made me feel like a delinquent schoolboy in a headmaster's study while I yelled down the telephone to a very distant Mercer in Haifa asking permission to alter a word here and there to simplify a complicated sentence, or speech. But it happened very few times: it caused too much trouble. So one gave in, but fought on with the words.

John's arrival caused a different form of reverence. One which was well justified, although it fussed him greatly.

"I do wish they wouldn't keep *on* calling me Sirjohn," he said one day. "It's so frightfully inhibiting. Couldn't you ask them, and Alain as well, just to call me 'John' as everyone else does on a film? It saves time, you see. Of course I have asked them not to but they still do. I know Alain thinks that it is disrespectful, but *do* please ask them."

I promised that I would try. "It'll be difficult. After all, you must realise that you are one of the greatest living actors in the English-speaking world, you are knighted, you have had a tremendous career . . . they *will* find it disrespectful. The French hold their great performers in high esteem."

"Well, it's very nice of them: but be a dear, and do what you can."

"It'll be almost impossible. But if you find it irritating . . ."

"Well, you see," he said, "I've always been lucky in having very unsycophantic friends around me, who just say, 'Oh! Stick a crown on his head and shove him on.' It's *so* much more relaxing."

In time he got his way: his very modesty, his generosity and warmth, made it possible; although I know that behind his back the troupe only ever referred to him as "Sirjohn". And that was that.

Shortly before he was to work, for the first time, Resnais suggested that I might have a little supper party and invite John to dine. I was staying in a small, isolated hotel some way out of town which had an excellent restaurant. Forwood arranged a perfect supper in a private room one evening for Resnais, Florence and John, whom we placed at the head of the table with Resnais at the other end; in this way he could observe his actor closely. Such was the entire nature of the exercise, and John caught on quickly, in spite of his asparagus, fresh river trout, and an excellent champagne.

He talked and talked, happily aware that he was holding the table and that no one would interrupt him. I don't know what Resnais knew before about Ellen Terry, Marie Tempest, Peggy Ashcroft, Edith Evans, or the third act of "Lear", but by the end of supper he should have known all that he ever needed to know. John's fund of stories, funny, and often gloriously irreverent, was limitless, and he was enjoying himself tremendously.

Once, while plates were being changed for another course, he leant across to me and murmured in a low voice: "You've fixed all this up! I know. I'm under observation, aren't I?"

I confessed that it was true.

"Most unnerving," he said, and started off again on a long, moving story about Eleanora Duse.

Resnais watched him with the rigid attention of a cat at a

mouse-hole: it was a happy and extremely useful evening. We had all relaxed in John's company, and the first morning's work he did was comfortable and easy, and although Resnais found it difficult at first, he managed to drop the Sirjohn and called him simply, John.

Towards the end of work at the château, on June 3rd to be exact, Resnais had a birthday. The troupe decided to club together and get him a tape-recorder because he didn't own one, so we all put our offerings in a hat and someone went off to Lovely Limoges (as it had now become to us all) and bought the best model available. Which wasn't much of a deal. Nevertheless it would be the main offering from a devoted and loving troupe and actors.

There was one small problem. They felt that it was essential that the first voice to be recorded on the virgin tape should be John's. And that he should say, "This is John Gielgud wishing you a happy birthday, Alain, on behalf of the troupe and actors of 'Providence'." Or words to that effect. We all knew that Resnais was passionate about John's voice, indeed he had told me long before that he was determined to immortalise the splendour of the voice and the actor on film; which is what he was doing at the present moment. It seemed ironical that such a signal honour should come from France, and not his own country . . . however: Resnais did so.

The troupe left it to me to ask him to speak these lines on to the tape and dispatched me across the grassy terrace to where he was sitting doing *The Times* crossword. He heard me out politely and refused absolutely.

"But John, why? It's such a little thing." I could see the troupe standing some way off watching anxiously.

"My dear boy," he said. "*I'm* not the star of the film. You are. It's *your* job."

"You *are* the star, for God's sake."

He looked up with a grin. "You have top billing. So *you* are."

I walked back to a saddened troupe. "He won't."

Their disappointment was so obvious, so dejected did they look, that I decided to go back and have another try. I knelt beside John's chair in my most supplicatory manner, and spoke to him in a low voice. For the troupe had inched nearer anxiously.

"Now John, listen. They want Alain to hear your voice on

the tape; for it to be the first sound recorded on the new machine. Their gift."

He didn't even look up: shook his head, printed a word, deliberately, in the white spaces of his crossword.

I was desperate. "John. Please. You probably have one of the most beautiful English-speaking voices in the world . . ."

He looked up over the top of his glasses. "THE!" he said sharply.

And spoke the message.

That evening, before the presentation and the Troupe Feast (a whole sheep roasted in the orchard behind the house), he did his last shot in the film and the one which would, eventually, be the final shot of the entire picture. As night drew great dark clouds from the west, as the wind started to blow and cut with cold, he sat alone at a long table among the debris of his film-birthday-party, an aging, bitter man in solitude below the huge turreted house in which he lived and would shortly, one knew, die.

The table-cloth on the deserted, plate-littered table fluttered and bellied, a napkin was caught by the wind and whipped across the darkening terrace, his body crumpled slowly, his eyes rimmed with unshed tears, and then he reached for a bottle and poured himself unsteadily a glass of wine.

"Just time for one more," he said, and night hurled black shadows across his face and the towered house and it was dark.

I knew, in that magical instant, why long ago I had said to Forwood after reading the script for the first time, "There must be something working: something has got through to me. I am *very* moved."

\* \* \*

We broke up shortly afterwards: John went back to London, and the rest of us went on to do the major bulk of the film in the studios in Paris in the hottest summer for seventy-five years; some said one hundred.

In the simplest possible terms, "Providence" was about one long night in the life of a dying novelist who, racked with pain, filled with drink and pills, is struggling to create a new work. Using the members of his family for his characters; muddled with the past, in terror of the future, filled with anger, spleen, and guilt, aware of swiftly approaching death.

This was the first two-thirds of the film; the final third (which we had all been busy working on) was the next morning, the day of his seventy-fifth birthday, and only then, in the sun and the brilliance of the day, when his sons and his daughter-in-law arrive to greet him and celebrate the occasion, did the film become "real".

The rest was all in his morbid, cruel imagination, and we, his family, were cruelly distorted puppets. It was this part which we now had to face in the Paris studios: the imagined section in which nothing was real, or true, at all. There was no sunlight in this part of the film, no light, except a cold one. Everything which we wore, touched, or through which we moved, was in sombre colours. Wedding rings were silver, not gold, our make-up was greenish-grey, the clothing dark, unmemorable; everything was, in fact, almost monochrome.

"Memory is colourless," Resnais said. "If you fill your car with petrol at a garage on the autoroute, what colours do you remember, *as colours*? Perhaps the overalls which the attendant wears? The petrol pump? Perhaps a door, a fallen leaf . . . nothing more; all the rest you will only remember without colour."

Memory was a rather depressing place in which to work.

The playing in this long section, two-thirds of the film, had to be larger than life: for everything that we did or said was only in the aging novelist's mind, an imagination heightened by pain and pills and drink. This called for a particular "style" in the acting, totally different from that which we had used in the summer garden and the sunlit reality. There it had been relatively easy; we were free, relaxed, laughing, real.

"How am I going to play this cold rage-less barrister my father has invented?" I asked Resnais. "Obviously he is detested for some reason so I suppose that he must show detestable signs? Have I got that right?" I was never absolutely certain.

Resnais smiled his cool Breton smile, shrugged, spread his hands; inferring, in those eloquent movements, that it was up to me to work out.

I was very perplexed; but suddenly I hit on an idea that I should play the role for him in three different ways, and whichever performance of the role he liked, and thought correct, we would stick with.

"You could play it three different ways?"

"I think so. Let's try. I'll play it absolutely straight—cold, attacking barrister; then in the style of, well . . . Congreve, the Restoration comedies; and then I'll give you my impersonation of Rex Harrison being bloody. Which shall we try first?"

I think that it was really the only time that I saw Resnais laugh with pleasure. But he also considered the suggestion with care. He was undecided how it should be played himself.

We did the scene three times, as suggested. He thought the Rex Harrison effort was possibly going a little too far, although it was funny, and finally settled for the high style of Restoration to begin with, mixed with the cold, attacking barrister, and here and there he suggested that I might add a pinch, just a pinch, of Rex Harrison. Which when I did always broke him up, to such an extent that he once fell off a chair.

I had started to shape my character, bearing in mind at all times that I must carry with it echoes and traces of Gielgud's *own* personality. Like father, then like son.

The supper which we had at the hotel, when John was under close scrutiny by his director, had proved immeasurably useful to me also: for I was able to recall, when I needed them, many small mannerisms and characteristics of the man, with which I could flesh out my playing of his "son". And so, for some days, until the performance finally "firmed", I did two, or even three different interpretations of every scene, and left Resnais to choose the one which he preferred.

The *auteur* director at work.

It is the parrot cry of many actors, especially those with a mainly theatrical background, that a screen performance is "manufactured in the cutting-room", which is as idiotic a remark as it is ignorant, and equivalent to saying that Van Gogh or Vuillard painted pictures by numbers.

To be sure, a bad, poor, even appalling performance can be saved by a brilliant editor, and often is. God knows, I have seen enough dreadful performances in my time lifted to a higher plane than the actor would ever have dreamed of, or been able to perform by himself, by the judicious use of a pair of scissors; but it happens very seldom (it's easier to recast, and cheaper), and if the player has learned his film technique, which is essential, and his director knows exactly what he wants and how to obtain the results, there isn't anything an editor can do, one way or another, to "manufacture a performance" of any importance, because that has already been done, and *fixed*, on the floor by the player himself through his thoughts and the force of his concentration.

A great many actors don't know that the camera actually photographs thought; which is a pity. For if there is "no one at home", so to speak, there won't be much on the screen in the final result, and no amount of work on the editor's part can magically paste together millions of scraps of film in the cutting-room and come forth with a *thinking* performance. It really doesn't work that way.

A very distinguished actor recently said in print that all the waiting about he had to do while filming dissolved his concentration to such an extent that in the end he was only able to play himself; rather than the intended character. A very sorry admission. Another, equally distinguished, complained that the nerve, energy and concentration needed to act were easily lost when "simply" performing *before* a camera. I don't know what he meant by the word "simply"; I imagine he has had more luck than I, for the last thing I have ever found it to be is simple. And *performing* before a camera is what you don't do. You work to it. And beyond it.

However, they both used the word concentration, and that is the main key to cinema playing; without it you are lost, and the retaining of it, through thick and through thin, is essential, exhausting and sometimes so hard to contain that one is brought to the edge of madness. It is a lesson that many actors never learn. But you have got to have it, and the strength to hold it. Resnais perhaps had it to the highest degree: and he fired us all with his firm, quiet, determined force, and drove us hard.

Now that we knew the form of the film, the texture as it were, the quartet, Burstyn, Stritch, Warner and I, found the going a little easier; although the heat nearly killed us, and the work left little or no time for any form of relaxation, and we ran with sweat constantly (Ellen's hair going, literally, straight before my eyes on one exhausting day) under blazing lamps in the hottest summer known, we were all extraordinarily happy because there was a feeling in the parched and burning air that what we were doing was not only pleasing Resnais, with his pitiless demands for perfection, but that we were actually playing together as he had first requested we should, as a full, perfectly balanced, quartet. Or quintet: even though our main instrument, John, had performed his solo, and left us.

I saw the film, eventually, at a press screening in Paris. It was exactly, for me, the film I had always hoped to be a part of; for it did all that I ever desired a film to do. It disturbed, educated and illuminated, and above all it made me laugh, much to the anger of some of the French press who hissed at me furiously like geese, thinking, I suppose, that I was being irreverent.

It opened in New York to savage reviews from the Three Butchers of Broadway as they were, and probably still are, called, who took axe, cleaver and saw to our effort. But this produced an immediate and exciting backlash of dismay and rage from their more discerning colleagues, and others, who had been overwhelmed with pleasure, all of whom wrote reviews and personal messages which they sent to Resnais with permission to use them for publicity.

So the *New York Times*, which had damned us cruelly, carried enormous advertising bearing lavish words of praise from Susan Sontag, Judith Crist, Rex Reed, Liz Smith, Sidney Lumet, William Wolf and a great many others. It was a brave, moving and generous gesture, but it failed to save the picture in that strange city of paradoxes.

I don't suppose that it would have troubled the Butchers had we worn wigs and breeches, carried tricorn hats and simpered under our patches. Restoration Comedy they might just have managed to cope with; especially in fancy dress. But not in a modern lounge suit. That became something quite else.

It has to be remembered that America is more a continent than a country: it takes over five weary hours to fly across it in a jet. It is an immigrant land, made up from every known race on the face of the earth.

The English language which was inherited from the earlier British settlers was, of necessity, rendered down to a simple mush, so that everyone from North to South, from East to West, could understand readily and simply. Instant recognition.

But in the simplification, the wit, the nuance, the irony and, perhaps above all, the *style* of the English language have been eliminated: they have no meaning for the vast majority of Americans. And the majority *is* vast. It is little wonder, therefore, that a film like "Providence", based on these very essentials of speech, should founder as it did.

Resnais, who had been present at the New York opening,

later said, with a wry smile, that perhaps he should have shown the film there in the French-dubbed version. With sub-titles. It would have made all the difference, and New York would then have understood the film better.

He proved his point some years later, with his next film, "Mon Oncle d'Amérique", which opened to rave reviews, not only in New York but across the entire country. In French. With sub-titles.

In Paris, we were an overwhelming success, and the smash-hit of the season, with reviews of a kind which I have never seen before and probably never will again, going on to win seven Oscars (French) with embarrassing ease, including, justifiably, one for Mr Mercer from Haifa.

And so it was over.

The wait of a decade had been worth every minute and I had, at last, achieved what was perhaps my greatest ambition as an actor: to work with Alain Resnais. It was, I couldn't help thinking, a hell of a long way from being The Idol of the Odeons.

# 13

IT was also, as it happened, the last major film I was to make. Three weeks after finishing work on "Providence" I was on my way to Holland to play a small role in Richard Attenborough's epic war-film about the disaster of Arnhem.

My sense of order, at this point, had completely broken down. I had sworn never to play featured-bits, or slide off towards cameo-roles, but reversed that decision, unwisely as it was to turn out, by allowing myself to be persuaded into joining the massive band of superstars and lesser mortals who had been gathered together to recreate one of the most appalling defeats the British had had to suffer in the Second World War. One at which I had personally been present: not in the city, but just across the river. I am still not clear, even today, why I broke my rule. My valued friendship with Attenborough certainly had a great deal to do with it: he and his wife, Sheila, had been the only people to show a modicum of kindness and thought towards me during my fledgling days with Rank, and I have never forgotten that kindness. Also I reasoned, I suppose, that it wouldn't take me long to do (it was a very small part) and would round off the summer's work admirably.

I took from the vast script the few pages in which my role appeared and, following Henry Fonda's trick on "Le Serpent", stuck them into a plastic cover; this was lighter, and so made packing easier.

The set-up in a small town in Holland was quite different from the one in Lovely Limoges. No small troupe of intimate friends here. Rather a crew of some hundreds, all, apparently, aged about nineteen, all running, all wearing walkie-talkie sets which screamed and bleeped endlessly. Every player had his own private trailer dressing-room complete with flush lavatory, his name in large letters on the door, and a private servant (usually an out-of-work Dutch actor or student of drama hoping for a "break", in the film about their own agony) to bring food, and run errands. I found it rather uncomfortable and uneasy.

There were trucks and trailers, generators and jeeps, an enormous "Honeywaggon" (the Unit lavatory; neat little stalls in a row), luxury cars to ferry the superstars from their hotels in Amsterdam, two hours away, and at all times the wail and scream of the walkie-talkies bringing a surreal air of hysteria to the whole vast safari (for that is really what it looked like) through which, with his stick and an affable, even jovial, demeanour, stamped Mr Joe Levine, whose extravagantly budgeted production this was. Some said twenty-seven million dollars, others thought perhaps a little less, at twenty million odd; in any case Alain Resnais, the poet-director, could have made his film ten times over, and still had enough left for breakfast and room service at Claridge's.

Mr Levine's presence was there mainly to encourage everyone to finish on time and, if possible, under budget. We finished on time I know, because I was in the final shot: I have no idea what happened to his budget.

Alas! My performance caused an uproar when the film was finally shown. There were cries of fury and distress from the widow and family of the man I was representing, and anger was expressed, so I was reliably informed, from Windsor Castle to Clarence House. Letters were even written to *The Times* (of *all* papers) complaining of my interpretation. I was crushed with dismay.

I didn't see the film, so I am not qualified to make any comment, nor can I judge where, or if, I went wrong. I had known the officer I played, in Normandy and in Holland: the very last thing I would have dreamed of doing was to defame his character or reputation, but both of which I was told I had; God knows how.

Such distress did this cause me that I considered making an apology in the press and sending my salary to an army charity. It wasn't much, as it happened, but I was determined not to retain one farthing.

After thirty years of working in the cinema and sixty odd films, this was the harshest blow I had had to take. And it taught me, for the last time, never to go against my sense of order again. At least, in the cinema.

However, my hysteria simmered down after two trusted people had seen the film, at my request, and instructed me to make no apology but just shut up. My work, I was informed, was "professional, straightforward, military and cold".

"Which," as one said, "I suppose, is what Generals were meant to be."

So that was a relief; but it took a long time to set aside. Forgetting, however, was different.

This unhappy business meant flying to and from Amsterdam for short spells of work from July until the final day of shooting, on October 6th, and it was extremely difficult to think of the book under these circumstances.

Finished even though it was, there was still a certain amount of work to do on it, not least corrections, which were sent by Mr Charlton, and extra scribbles for chapter headings or main page illustrations which he flattered me into providing. Not to mention the cover itself.

At first I had thought of using a fragment of Van Gogh's "The Cornfield", but then realised it was an impertinent thing to do to use a master's work in which to wrap up the writing of an amateur; so I decided to have a shot at doing my own. It would all then be of a piece.

Throughout "Providence" I had never lost contact with the book, even during the hardest and most trying times. I drew on hotel letter-paper whenever an idea came to me, and Mr Charlton kept me in touch with anything which he thought I should know; although he was very careful to leave me in tactful peace to get on with my proper work. But like all beginners, I constantly brooded on the things I had written and kept finding different, or better, ways to express myself, because I had been told that once the type was set up and the book in proof, corrections would be unwelcome—they take time and cost money. "Print is not made from india rubber" Mr Charlton reminded me.

Thus I abandoned a number of ideas which I had let float about in my mind for the re-writing of certain paragraphs and even, in one instant, an entire chapter, and concentrated on ideas for the cover design, finally roughing out the one I thought would fit the subject well enough on the back of a page of one of the sheets torn from the Arnhem script during a flight from Amsterdam to Nice. I then got down to work with long-disused brushes and a box of paints on the trestles in the room above the wood shed.

Ignorant as I was about anything whatever to do with publishing or printing, I did a happy, colourful, design and sent it off to Chatto and Windus, only to discover that it was the wrong dimension, and would have to be done all over again. However, Mr Charlton (who now had become "John" as I had become "Dirk" during our lengthy correspondence, and also due to the fact that he had come all the way out to the house for twenty-four hours to discuss minor alterations in the work and to sift through the many photographs which I had assembled for him to choose from as illustrations for the final book) indicated that the cover design, though far too small, was "excellent", and thus encouraged once again, I started from scratch with the correct dimensions; thoughtfully provided.

Sometime in late October, I can't be absolutely certain, he wrote an enthusiastic note about the new effort, and down at the bottom of his page I saw an odd block of red ink scratches which were obviously not from his clear, upright hand. These were spiked, angular, and quite unreadable.

I pondered over them for a very long time and finally came to the conclusion that whoever, or whatever, had penned these fascinating scraps was either "sad" or "mad" about the design.

A difference.

The only part of any kind of signature that I could make out was a probable letter "N".

On the telephone the next day, John assured me that the word *was* "mad" and that the writer was Norah Smallwood. Overcome by this nod from the Top, I suddenly decided that I would draw her a small remembrance of Virginia Woolf as she had appeared to me in those distant days when I was an "embalmed twelve" sitting by the River Ouse fishing, and she would sometimes walk along the river bank, singing to herself, carrying an enormous golf-umbrella. It was not for the book.

It was a personal gift of gratitude, modest though it was, to my, as yet, unseen needlewoman.

★　★　★

My sister-in-law, Cilla, on a wet camping holiday somewhere in northern France, with her two small children, once sent me a postcard on which she said that the holiday had had some benefits, in spite of rain and a series of minor accidents: she had been forced to learn a little more French than the phrase "Help! My postillion has been struck by lightning!"

I took the old phrase for the title of my book, and here at last it was before me in "proof". A pale green paper-covered volume, which I held as tenderly, as proudly, as filled with awe as a mother with her first-born child.

The fact that I had to correct the thing didn't worry me at all: I sat and read it through three times right off in a daze of pleasure, and self-congratulation. I was absolutely amazed. I had written a book.

Naturally I hadn't the least idea how to go about the corrections, but bearing in mind John's firm edict that print was not india-rubber, I started off with a light heart and a red pencil.

And work began again in earnest. Not only on proof corrections.

October is a hellish month on the land here. The last terraces have to be mown and raked before winter, the grapes picked, a venture spiced with danger from a million wasps, and far more tedious than it is romantic; the beds made ready for the spring with wall-flowers and ten-week stock, the pots and urns emptied and cleaned and, finally and with regret, the terrace furniture put into store. Summer is over.

Azis, the crazed Arab who helped with some of the heavy work, had long since wandered off. Probably back to his village in Tunisia.

He had finished some of the walls, and kicked the smaller lawn-mower to pieces in a fit of violent rage which overtook him one blistering day during Ramadan. As he appeared to be spending most of the day with his head stuck under one of the garden taps I offered him, unwisely, a cold beer, not knowing if he was a faithful Muslim or not: he was not. He accepted the beer with grateful signs (we still had no common tongue) and shortly afterwards I found him jumping up and down on the top of the mower, screaming hysterically and calling on Allah, waving his arms about like a demented semaphore, so that any move towards him must prove dangerous, while the mower shook to pieces under his fandango until, with a hefty kick, he sent a bit flying in the direction of Mecca and went to sleep curled up under a tree. Although it had been entirely my fault, I felt that the time had come for us to part: however, the following week he didn't turn up, or the next, and was never seen again. Which was a relief: except that we were now minus

18. " . . .Hermann in "Despair" was the nearest thing to a complete mental and physical take-over I had endured since Von Aschenbach. . . "

19. 'The Idol of the Odeons' (sic) awaiting the Jury's verdict on "Despair".
". . .so I was photographed, walking dutifully, among my olive trees. . ."

one pair of hands and a strong back to do the heavy work. But the mowing went on, we grubbed up the big stones for the walls, and hacked away at the summer's growth of brambles and broom.

The book still simmered among this activity; corrections were finally done, the photographs chosen, and John telephoned from time to time to say that the paperback people were "very interested", the Book Clubs "excited", and that there was heavy interest being shown in publishing it in America.

I drew a firm line at this. Or tried to. I had no desire that my modest child should be thrown to the wolves there: I told John, whose voice, after I had refused to consider this suggestion, showed definite signs of distress for the first time since I had once blithely decided to re-write an entire chapter long after they had started setting. Normally calm and unruffled, he now betrayed slight tremors of anxiety.

America was a big market, he assured me, and begged me to re-think my decision. I pointed out, I thought rather sensibly, that the Americans would expect a very different book from the one I had written, full of film stars, confessions, and film-hype. They would expect an index bursting with glamour.

All that I could put in the index were some vague names which would mean nothing to them: perhaps Henry Moore would pass; but I really couldn't see them going a bundle on The Sun Engraving Works, Watford, or Cissie Waghorn. Could he?

I suppose it was the first time that I had realised that, like the cinema, publishing was "business". A sale was a sale, a profit and a loss the same as they were in my profession, where no one was actually employing one for anything other than money. But, even if the thought saddened me momentarily, I wriggled clear of depression by consoling myself with the thought that in publishing everyone was gentlemanly, calmer, more elegant. Nothing could be as ugly or deceitful as the cinema.

Could it?

Not with Chatto and Windus, Bertie assured me cheerfully, but there were some very dark corners in publishing, into which I must not stray. "I know some who'd have your guts for garters, my dear," he said brightly. "You are with the best firm in town, with the best boss. I'd listen to her advice if I were you."

On the last day of October I was listening to another voice. A rather high, anxious one, which sounded on the telephone, as if it was coming from the middle of a bus-station. "Hello? Hello?" it shouted, and I shouted back.

"My name is Tom Stoppard," cried the voice. "We haven't met."

"No."

"I'm at London airport."

So I wasn't far out with the bus-station sounds.

"Oh, are you?"

"I've just got in from Munich."

"Splendid!"

"I gather that you aren't making any more films; am I right?"

"No. Wrong. I'm not making any more crap."

There was a short pause.

"I don't write crap," he said crossly.

"I'm sorry. I wasn't talking of *your* work."

"I've just written an adaptation of a Nabokov book, 'Despair', which Fassbinder is making in Germany and we both think that you would be marvellous for the leading character."

"When do you start?"

"Oh . . . *I* don't know. Early next year. Can I send it to you; the first draft?"

"Well, I am supposed to be doing 'Under the Volcano' for the Mexican Government . . . but I don't know exactly when; anyway there are a lot of problems there. So do send your script if you are certain I'd be all right?"

"I'm certain and so is Fassbinder. I thought of you on the flight out and when I got to Munich they told me that you were his preferred choice, coincidence?"

"I've got a book coming out," I said in a casual throwaway voice. "In March. I don't want to miss that."

"I think they'll probably start some time in April, anyway must go now, I'll send it tomorrow."

He rang off. Stoppard, Nabokov, Fassbinder.

Not a bad package: and he had said "leading character", not just "a part". The old surge of excitement welled up again: after all it *was* my job, and those three names were not easily dismissed.

248

The first draft of "Despair" arrived a few days later with a hastily scribbled note attached to it explaining that there was still a lot to be done to it, begging me to wait until a final draft was ready, in December. Which, when it arrived, had enough exciting material in it to persuade me, for almost the first time, to go against Forwood's advice and accept. He didn't feel it would be the commercial success which my career needed at that moment.

I reasoned, I think very sensibly (all order restored), that my book would be out in March and that after the hullabaloo, if there was one, it wouldn't last more than a week; after which I would be left with absolutely nothing to do.

Nothing to create either theatrically or in written words. There would be a silence. A blank.

Far better, therefore, to have a project in mind and a script in hand, and the fascination of working with Fassbinder was overwhelming. If, as I felt certain in the deepest recesses of my heart, my days as a working actor of the kind I had been for twelve years were beginning to fade out, I was determined that they would not fade out on a cameo role.

At least I would go out above the title; a position to which I had grown accustomed ever since my first film in 1947. The only slight twist of doubt I had was that, if indeed it was to be my final film (and who could possibly tell?), it had a most unfortunate title for the closing of a career: "Despair".

But I accepted—the temptation was too strong: a new director, a new country to work in, a new type of role altogether. And quite apart from anything else it had become increasingly clear that the Mexican Government was unsettled; to say the least. So, R. W. Fassbinder.

★   ★   ★

In January I finished lagging all the outside water-pipes in the garden, and then went off to London to start the promotion for *Postillion*, rather bemused by the interest it had so far engendered. Little, I thought, do they know what they are in for. No True Confessions here, just a rural ride through a time which had gone for ever: but before I started work I insisted on going down to Sussex for the family reunion luncheon with Elizabeth and George.

Ma was there. Brought over from her flat in the comfortable

Edwardian house a mile or two away. She was frailer than the last time I had seen her, but immaculate; sitting in what she insisted was "her" chair by a blazing log-fire, a wide scarf about her shoulders, pinned by Capucine's gift, of many years before, a Chanel clip of false pearls and emeralds; the heavy black shoes.

"Well. And how do I look?"

"Marvellous. You look terrific, Ma."

"I had my hair done especially. Elizabeth took me last week. Do you remember the brooch?"

"Of course I do. Cap gave it to you."

She looked vaguely about the light, pretty room. "Who?"

"Capucine. One Christmas. It's a Chanel original."

"Oh yes. I know. I love it. I'm never without it." She lit a cigarette, picked a piece of tobacco from her lip. "Your brother's gone to America. Chicago," she said, and put her lighter into the big black bag she always carried.

"I know. Very sensible. All those kids to educate: far more chances for them all in America."

"He took all my furniture."

"Darling! Not *all* your furniture: you know that. A few pieces only. And you told him that he could."

"Well. I hate them being in America. Ulric's dressing-chest went too . . . and all my babies."

"Ma dear. They *aren't* your babies, they're Gareth's."

She stared at me with defiant hostility. "*I'm* his mother!"

"And he has a wife. They are not *your* babies. Anyway it'll be super for them there, it's a young country."

She looked away, interest lost. "I don't know," she said. Then suddenly, as if remembering something, "And why are you here all of a sudden?"

"My book. I've written a book, remember? About us all, years ago, at the cottage. I'm here to do the publicity stuff."

"Will you be on television?"

"I think so . . . and the BBC."

"I must know when. To tell the maids at the home, they like to know."

"Ma darling, it is not a *home*, it's an *hotel*; that's quite different."

"It's a home to me. So that's your answer. When's it coming out, this book?"

"March. Just before my birthday."

"This room looks bare without the furniture."

"I think it looks lovely: lighter. The things Gareth had, the wine-cupboard, the secretaire, were a bit heavy, weren't they?"

She smiled. "Were they? *I* never thought so. Daddy and I liked them: I must be getting senile or something."

I poured her a glass of wine.

"What's that? Not my stuff?"

"No. It's a Chablis. I brought it: no good?"

She savoured it for a moment. "Personally I like a sweeter wine. That Spanish stuff suits me. I have a glass at night." She set the glass down carefully on a small table. "It helps me to sleep. So that I don't have to think. Where is this book then?"

"Oh. It won't be out until next month. You get the first copy, then Elizabeth, and one for Lally."

She suddenly looked up sharply, stubbing out her cigarette. "Why Lally?"

"Because she's in it. A lot of it."

"I see." She began to hum softly to herself, brushing imaginary dust from her arm.

Elizabeth came in from the kitchen, an oven-cloth in her hands. "Just about ready. Guess what? Boiled beef and dumplings!"

"Oh Lor' . . . your rotten old dumplings. All soggy: and hard in the middle."

"You are a beast. Quite vile. I bet you can't get them in your soppy old South of France."

"No, thank God."

"I'm simply not taking any notice of you. Ma? Ma, will you be warm enough in the dining-room?"

My mother started to ease herself out of her chair. "I always *was*. It's a cold room. Ulric blocked in the fireplace. Useless to argue. I told him not to. Anyway: I have my scarf." She raised an arm towards me for assistance. "Help your old Ma: getting so stiff. I do if I sit for too long: but I can't walk much now. My legs. You remember when I was in the Munitions in the first war, we all had to volunteer, and I dropped a shell on my foot? An enormous thing . . ."

"Yes. I know."

"Oh. Sorry you've been troubled. I've told you before. Well, I'm paying for it now, can't walk anywhere. Don't forget to tell me when you are going to be on the BBC or the television, I have to tell the maids at the . . ." She stopped, and waved a slender hand vaguely in the air as we walked slowly together to the dining-room. "The *hotel*. Is that right?"

"Absolutely right," I said.

★   ★   ★

William IV Street is short and unexceptional, linking St Martin's Lane with the Strand. On one side stands the ugly bulk of Trafalgar Square Post Office, on the other, and directly opposite, the unremarkable building which has housed Chatto and Windus since 1936.

No strip lighting here, no drooping rubber-tree in the reception area: no reception area in fact. A step up from the pavement and one is in a sort of hallway; on the right a glass case in which George the telephonist sits, an amiable spider in a web of wires and plugs before the aging switchboard. A little beyond, an elderly lift, and a sagging staircase, offer transport to the higher realms of literature. The lift is lethal; a shuddering coffin which holds four crushed over-intimately together, hauled aloft by greasy cables and rumbling wheels. It very often doesn't work at all and sulks in its well. In any case it is usually wiser, and safer, to climb the wooden staircase, an inelegant structure, mottled with years of chipped paint-scars, one's feet clattering on the worn linoleum. There is a "smell" of paper, of cardboard, of print, of dust: above all an atmosphere of work, and serious work at that.

It reminded me when I arrived there, that first morning, of *The Times* and Printing House Square, and I was strangely instantly secure in the familiar feeling of the place. The same sagging floors, scratched linoleum, narrow corridors, central-heating pipes strung about like macaroni, the coming and going, the rustle of papers, the grimed windows, the unlovely loveliness of it all. For an instant I had the impression that I had been here before: to ask my father for a loan, which I did often enough, receiving half-a-crown at the most, a florin at the least. And usually given to me by Mr Greenwood, his secretary, because, as my father would always say, "Greenwood: I've only got a ten bob note . . . what have you got?" Mr Greenwood had inexhaustible pockets.

A fragment of memory induced so easily by an atmosphere I knew so well.

John had hurried along a corridor to greet me. "Ah! There you are."

"Not late, I hope? I hate to be late."

"No. No. Absolutely on the dot."

Rosalind Bell, the PR girl, joined us, looking, deceptively, like a Dickensian waif dressed at a Women's Institute stall. "Everything all right yesterday? The interviews?"

"*The Spectator* was well-intentioned; there was a maddening woman from *The Observer* who had just sent her child off to its first Day School and kept telephoning the place to see if it was 'happy' . . ."

"Had she got the proof copy? I sent her one?"

"Hadn't read it."

Miss Bell almost shouted—for her. "Hadn't read it! I've *told* them all . . ."

"Well, by the look of it she'd had a bash at the first two chapters. The rest was unthumbed, and she'd lost her biro."

"I think," said John, "that Mrs Smallwood is waiting. Just round here a little."

A half-open door and a crisp voice came ringing through. "I thought I heard visitors!" The door flew open and there before me stood my second needlewoman, my "patcher". After all this time.

She was tall, very slender, elegant in a white silk blouse and a coral-red wool skirt. In her hands she held two books, one bound in blue, one in yellow; she thrust them towards me.

"Which colour d'you like?" She left the books in my hands and turned back into her room. "I'll get my jacket."

I stood there in the corridor holding two copies of *A Postillion Struck by Lightning* and knew that nothing as wonderful could ever happen to me again. Norah Smallwood came out directly, shrugging on a jacket, a wide-brimmed Herbert Johnson hat on her head.

She moved swiftly; sharp, brisk movements as if even going from point A to point B was using up time and had to be done as rapidly as possible.

"Have we got transport? It's the Garrick. We've booked for one o'clock."

We hurried down the stairs behind her, John, Forwood, an American publisher's representative and scout, and a pleasant young woman in paperbacks, much as if the Garrick Club was a ship casting off to sail.

Mahogany, oak; I don't know now. An impression of a fireplace, high, sombre rooms, portraits everywhere, a hat-rack, a porter and signing registers. A gathering of figures whose faces one remembers, actors or writers; the actors tightly clothed in lounge suits, sipping glasses of sherry in their double-breasted waistcoats; the writers, if that's what they were, less formal, more relaxed, the hand which did not hold a Guinness thrust into a pocket.

At lunch a long table. I beside my "patcher" who had taken her place, naturally and with ease, at the head and ordered oxtail stew. There was wine; waitresses in black with white aprons, muted conversation from other tables, the shine of silver on the canopy of the carving-trolley, and I haven't the least idea about what we spoke.

Before me, high up on the wall, a full-length portrait of Gladys Cooper: a sudden jump of pleasure, a tug of familiarity again. My marmalade Aunt. Marmalade because, years ago, in her garden in Hollywood she had shown me a giant orange tree heavy with fruit.

"What to do with it all? Such a wicked shame to throw them all away."

"Make some marmalade."

"I can't boil an egg! Marmalade . . . "

And later, one evening sitting in her cluttered, comfortable, very English sitting-room in Napoli Drive, she handed me the first pot. It had a label. "The Other Cooper's Marmalade". Written in her huge, looping, generous handwriting.

And now there she was before me, coolly watching as they picked through the oxtail stew and spoke of American sales, paperback rights, and press promotions.

"I've written a book," I wanted to say to her. "All by myself. How about that?"

Not quite by myself.

There was no portrait in this calm, high-ceilinged room of Mrs X from New England. No portraits of those who, so long ago in a dreary NAAFI, had welcomed me into their reading group and offered me unknown, unexpected, unbelievable treasure: Isherwood and Waugh, Surtees and the pale Brontës; Owen and the bewilderment of Wyndham Lewis and so many others.

No. I hadn't quite done it all by myself. There had been a little help from my friends; and from my second "needlewoman" sitting reassuringly beside me now, alive, touchable, tangible, spooning up her apple pie.

"Scrumptious, isn't it?" she said suddenly.

"I'm having cheese."

"You'll need a lot of strength in the next two days: there are masses of interviews laid on."

Of course, the thing was, she didn't know that she was my "needlewoman"; my "patcher". She didn't even know that I knew her voice had echoed quietly behind many of the letters which John, sitting opposite me, had written: didn't know, at this moment, that I was aware that she had watched a television chat show so many months ago and that I knew perfectly well that "*Several of us here . . .* " was, in reality, only herself.

I looked up at my marmalade Aunt. "I've got a hell of a lot of responsibility to this little group down here. Pray God I don't come a cropper and let them down: they seem confident; too confident. You once told me that you thrived on responsibility, absolutely loved it, you said. I wonder if I will too? It's a different kind of responsibility in the theatre or the cinema; this has become extraordinarily personal; I'll do my damnedest, even though half the time I don't understand a word they say. Wish me luck. Cross fingers?"

Suddenly, with courage gained, I leant across the table and told John, and the pleasant girl from paperbacks, almost the entire plot of a novel which I wanted to write. One day.

And did.

*  *  *

Elizabeth wrote immediately after she had received her advance copy of *Postillion*.

*Cherry Tree Cottage. February 4th '77*

". . . *I LOVE IT DESPERATELY! Not because I am in it, and, may I add, you have made me much nicer than I ever was, and brighter.* (sic)

*Was I as bossy as that!? . . . I long to talk to you about it all. What bliss to be taken back to one's happy, sunny, days even for twenty-four hours, and how lucky to be able to go there through a book.*"

And Lally.

*The Street, Steeple, Essex. March 10th '77*

*"Dirk darling,*

*The book sounds just right, don't change anything, I hope I shall always be 'Lally' to you whatever happens, dear . . . it is a great day for me to know you still remember all the lovely times we had together. Take care of yourself, darling."*

My mother didn't write. This was not surprising because she wrote very occasionally and when she did her letters were sad. *"I've no news to tell you, people don't come to see me now because of the petrol."*

I went to see her just before publication day. Her little flat in the Edwardian house was comfortable and warm, with a pleasant view across the lawns and gardens. It was furnished with "bits and pieces" of her own. On the walls were some of my father's paintings of places which she had known with him and loved, Alfriston, Berwick, Firle Beacon; a portrait in chalk and wash of herself which someone else had done and which she treasured. Everywhere there were pots or jars of flowers and plants and, here and there, small piles of paperbacks, mostly by Barbara Cartland and Georgette Heyer.

"All paperbacks!" I said.

"Easier to read in bed. I can't hold a real book. I get them from the maids."

"Where's mine?"

"Your what?"

"Book. *Postillion?*"

"Oh!" She began to twist her rings. A sign I recognised very well. "Oh darling: yes. Of course. Your book. I gave it to one of the maids."

"Ma!"

"Well . . . she's a dear soul and she has been so kind to me; wonderful. She saw it lying here and begged for it. They all know who you are, you see."

"But you read it first, didn't you?"

The rings again.

"Looked at the pictures. God knows where you found some of them. There's *one* good one of me, with Elizabeth when she was in the WRENs. Daddy took it. But that terrible one of you both sitting on the stairs like a pair of slum children. Elizabeth looks as if she was knock-kneed."

"Most people seem to like that one. But did you read nothing? Nothing?"

"It's heavy for me to hold in bed." She reached out and took a cigarette from a paper packet, lit it. "Anyway, it's all about children."

"I know, darling, yours. Elizabeth and me."

She put the lighter down, closed the cigarette packet carefully. "Elizabeth tells me that these cost a fortune now. I can't think why. Taste of straw. Aunt Belle won't be very happy: with what you've written about her and that man she married; Duff."

So she *had* read something. Aunt Belle was her elder sister and there had never been much love lost between the two.

"I've been a damned sight nicer about them than I needed. And changed all their names. You don't mind, do you? Not angry? About the Scottish part?"

"Good God, no! I had to come all the way up to get you away, if you remember; the most awful row."

"I know. It's in the book."

"She wanted to adopt you, did you know that? When you were born. She thought that I wouldn't be able to bring you up properly. Too flighty, she said. She didn't approve of me. The Scarlet Woman. An actress."

"I'm jolly glad that you didn't let me go."

"Narrow-minded, awful. *I* brought you up."

"Marvellously."

She tapped her cigarette deliberately on the edge of the ash-tray two or three times. "Lally didn't: that's all I'm saying."

"I know she didn't."

"She's all over your book. Lally this and Lally that . . . I don't understand it."

"It's all about the time when we were on holidays with her at the cottage. We had a wonderful time. You know what it's like. When the cat's away the mice will play, and when you and Daddy weren't there we ran riot . . . I mean that's all it is."

"You don't mention Daddy and me at all."

"I *do* darling! You just haven't read it so how can you tell? I wish you'd read it."

"Oh, I will. I will. I've plenty of time. I've always got plenty of time. I could go mad."

"Well . . . just as long as you aren't upset about your family in Scotland . . . the Aunts and Uncles. I've been very tactful, you'll see."

"My dear boy! I'm not upset. Your father couldn't stand

them. He wouldn't even go up there; he dreaded me suggesting it. I'm not upset."

But the Scots family were. From the moment that *Postillion* was published they never wrote to, or contacted, my mother again. Punishing her cruelly for a fault of mine. Once, some years later, a gentler sister-in-law sent her a small calendar for Christmas. It was about the size of a postcard. The price, in pencil, was thirty pence. It had "Views of Bonnie Scotland" on the cover and she pinned it on the wall at the foot of her bed: but we never spoke about them again. Although she had all their photographs in a frame beside her bed. It was the nearest they would ever be to her for the rest of her life.

I walked across the room to look at one of my father's paintings: trees, sun slanting through them; a road.

"That's down at the bottom of Great Meadow, isn't it?" I said.

"Somewhere. I don't know. I like it."

"Anyway: you're coming up to lunch at the Connaught on Friday. Celebration lunch for the book."

She stubbed out the cigarette. "Darling Connaught. How am I getting there?"

"George is bringing you up by car. Friday, remember."

"*I've* written a book," she said suddenly.

"You haven't! God knows, we've been trying to get you to for ages: when?"

"Oh . . . someone came to help me. Suggestions. She was fascinated; encouraged me."

"Remember Daphne Fielding?"

"No."

"Well, she gave you a note-book once, with 'Maggie's Story' printed on the cover. Is that what you used? That what you've done? Your own story?"

"That's what I've done. It's not much. Tragic. The woman was fascinated. It's too far for me to go all the way to London now."

"Don't be daft. You just have to get in the car and you'll be there in a flash."

"I'm not keen."

"I won't see you for ages if you don't. I'm off to Germany to make a film."

"Oh. Is my hair all right?"

"You look lovely."

Someone tapped gently at the door and said that lunch was ready.

★   ★   ★

I liked Rainer Werner Fassbinder the very moment that I saw him. Thick-set, wordless as far as I could tell, his inscrutability increased by tin-rimmed glasses and a thin straggly moustache.

He sat at supper that first night at the Colombe d'Or listening intently to every word spoken, but never made a sound himself, reaching for what he wanted and eating bread as if he was starving. I was assured, by his pleasant producer who had come with him (as well as Mr Stoppard), that he would not speak English, so he would translate any problems we had with the script.

And there were quite a number.

It didn't take me long to realise that Fassbinder probably spoke fluent English, or if not, that he understood it perfectly: for he laughed often at our remarks, and shook his head in angry disagreement from time to time at a suggestion made, or else nodded happily in agreement. I couldn't help thinking that he must be pretty well aware of everything said: his mother, after all, I had been told, was official translator to Truman Capote or Tennessee Williams, so it was very likely that he spoke English himself. It was going to be a hell of a problem working together in an English-language film with no common tongue.

The next day everyone came up to the house to have lunch and "iron out the bumps" in the script. We sat round the tin table, pencils poised, scripts before us, while Mr Stoppard feverishly re-wrote passages and then read them, eagerly, aloud, while Fassbinder shrugged from time to time, showing a marked indifference to what was going on, and frequently yawned.

It was perfectly clear to me, after half an hour of this, that he would make *his* version of "Despair", when the time came, and do exactly what he wanted. Which is precisely what he did.

At one moment during this somewhat lethargic conference I said to him, in English, that I had a feeling that he and I had nothing more to say to each other, that we both understood each other very well, and knew that we would work together easily. He grunted something, grinned, nodded, and finally said, "Ja". So I took him into the long room where he spent the rest of the morning lying prone among a pile of old motor magazines while we still battled away "ironing out the bumps", which were of no consequence to our director, who only appeared again when lunch was served.

His apparent refusal to speak English caused a good deal of confusion when we got to the studios in Munich; but I had been given a translator/interpreter through whom I had to make some form of contact with Fassbinder. His name was Ossie. German-English, born in Egypt, he had a fantastic ear for language and dialects. But he didn't find it easy on this assignment; nor did I.

I *knew* that I knew the man inside my director, but I was never going to be able to reach him, or give him a perform-ance, under these circumstances. After two days of mistakes and misunderstandings, I took him aside and said that I was certain that he spoke English, perhaps only a little, but that unless he tried to speak to me in that tongue we would be lost. I'd pack it in.

He trod on a cigarette butt in his heavy motor-cycle boots, rubbed his eyes with a nicotined finger under the tin-rimmed lenses, and said, in English, that he would try. But he was shy of speaking before his Unit.

"For heaven's sake, Rainer, I'm shy too! Just because I made a movie almost before you were born doesn't make *me* any the less shy: nervous, terrified! I'm a foreigner on a completely foreign set. I know that I'm old enough to be your father, but that doesn't alter the fact that you are my director, the boss. I need your help if we are to get this film off the ground. And I can't contact you if I can't speak to you."

He ground the squashed butt deeper into the floor.

"I can't go on trying to understand what you want through a translator; it just won't work, and we'll lose the picture. And it's much too good to lose. Please help me."

Rainer never spoke German to me on the set again, leaving Ossie, who had fast been approaching a breakdown, thank-fully relieved.

If Rainer had a fault it was that he found it completely impossible to concentrate, think, or create, in anything which remotely approximated to silence. He had to work in a vortex of sound: torrents of sound; it was something with which one quickly came to terms. Or perished.

From the moment that he roared up to the set (wherever it was) in his vastly expensive motor car, until the moment that he left, usually far later than the rest of us for he stayed on writing, planning, and setting up, in detailed drawings, his shots for the next day, he worked in a shuddering blast of music. Maria Callas at full pitch in both "Tosca" and "Norma"; sometimes, as a light relief, the entire score of "Evita", which made the very air vibrate, on other occasions "Der Rosenkavalier" over and over again.

A very different atmosphere to the saintly, cloistered, hush which had reigned at all times on "Providence".

But then this was a film about madness: perhaps it all helped.

One important problem, the first to arise after the discussion about what language to use between each other, was the fact that among a whole group of English-speaking Germans, plus my superb co-star from France, Andrea Ferreol, who had learned her English in a crash-course at Berlitz a couple of months before, my Home Counties accent simply wouldn't do. It sounded absurd in every possible way, I didn't fit in with anyone: I'd have to use an accent myself.

Ossie, now relieved of his main job as translator and interpreter, came to the rescue with a splendid Prussian one. Prussian, because I was playing a Russian émigré, and my German accent could not be that of Berlin, or Hamburg or Munich. The nearest accent that a Russian-trying-to-speak-German could have would be Prussian. Very complex. It was all extremely interesting: but when was I to learn it?

The fact was that I hadn't time to learn it: work had started, and I had to jump in with Ossie holding me, at a distance, like an anxious father with his infant in a swimming-pool.

We did it. God knows how, but we did. I made many errors at first, but these were gradually eliminated, and in time, in a remarkably little time in fact, I settled down as comfortably as a hen on her eggs, secure with the accent, secure in the role of poor, demented, Hermann.

In truth, the part of Hermann in "Despair" was the nearest thing to a complete mental and physical take-over that I had endured since Von Aschenbach had eased silently into my existence: it is an extraordinary experience in every way. The actor has to empty himself of *self*, completely, and then encourage the stranger he is to be into the vacuum created.

It is not easy. But once caught, and it takes a time to do the catching, one's whole personality alters, and it is not at all understandable to "civilians", as I call non-players, to comprehend. It is more of a mental alteration than a physical one, but sometimes in a bar, in a shop, at the reception desk of an hotel, even talking to Forwood at a meal, I would find that I was speaking, and more than that, behaving, exactly as my alter-ego would have done. This is not affectation: it is possession. But it is a curious experience for outsiders to observe.

Rainer's work was extraordinarily similar to that of Visconti's; despite their age difference, they both behaved, on set, in much the same manner. Both had an incredible knowledge of the camera: the first essential. Both knew how it could be made to function; they had the same feeling for movement on the screen, of the all-important (and often-neglected) "pacing" of a film, from start to finish, of composition, of texture, and probably most of all they shared that strange ability to explore and probe into the very depths of the character which one had offered them.

They took what one gave and built upon it, layer upon layer of physical and mental strata, so that eventually, together, we could produce a man, entire. Plus soul.

Exhausting, exhilarating, rewarding and draining, finally. But that was the way that I liked my cinema. It was the only way I could really work.

Which was just as well, for we had a pretty rugged time. We started work in Interlaken, moved up to Munich, to Brunswick, Hamburg, Berlin and then came to our final location, a small town near Lübeck in the north, only about a mile from the Wall. There were no luxuries: as on "Providence" so on "Despair", we were a tightly knit group and worked like a band of travelling players—which, I suppose, is exactly what we were, after all. Andrea and I, and the rest of the cast, changed our costumes in the back of cars, in the corners of sheds, once in the back kitchens of a filthy Berlin restaurant where today's food lay on the floor amidst the debris of yesterday's, and the air was full of droning bluebottles. But we were all tremendously happy. That strange feeling that things were going better than well took hold of us all, and Rainer, I was told, had never been seen to laugh so much or show such evident signs of pleasure.

I finished my role three days before the film wound up, and Rainer decided that there would be a big farewell party in the little hotel in which we were all staying. It was pleasant, quiet, set on the edge of a vast lake, with a terrace overlooking the town beyond.

I was sitting in the last of the sun having a beer when Rainer came and joined me. This was unusual indeed. He always went off to his room with his close group of friends after work, and one seldom saw him again until the next morning on the set.

He refused a beer, lit a new cigarette from the butt of the old one which he spun into the still evening water of the lake.

"I come to thank you," he said, "for the Hermann you made possible for me: I hope it will be our Hermann, like his madness is a little bit our madness."

He was smiling; extremely shy.

"I hope so too. I should be thanking you."

"No! I thank. I thank you for the things I could learn from you, things I never learned before. I thank you that you showed me authority, without fear. Normally, you see, authority goes with fear; but you did show me a way how to combine authority with freedom." He stopped and looked out across the lake. "I knew that only theoretically; so far. It is one of the most important things for work and life."

"I've been very happy working with you, you know that. I don't mind now if I never make another movie! You have spoiled me for any others."

He grinned, rubbed his eye with a stubby finger, dropped the cigarette into the puddle of beer on the table.

"In life . . ." he shrugged, crushed the cigarette ". . . it is more likely there is more despair than anything else. But, and this is what *I* think, life is timeless and end is endless. And this means it is not so sad; like it seems."

He rose suddenly. "Danke," he said, and walked quickly away.

People were calling from the bar, the evening had begun. Rainer didn't come to the party. I knew that he wouldn't. We had said farewell.

There is no question in my mind that "Despair" should have been a major film: as it was, it became a critical success and a box-office failure for reasons which I cannot fully determine. A sort of Jacob's coat of a film: a curate's egg somehow. Whatever went wrong, and something did somewhere along the line, it was, however, an incredible, detailed, study of madness by a brilliant director.

And that, of course, might have been one of the faults. Madness embarrasses people to watch; it makes them uneasy and uncomfortable.

However, for better or worse we were chosen, many months ahead, to represent Germany at the Festival in Cannes. Perhaps being chosen so far ahead was an error, for I have a feeling that Rainer grew weary of his production and started to clip away at it with his scissors, thereby carrying the abstract motive too far.

Anyhow here I was, once again, representing a foreign film at Cannes. This time with a splendid Prussian accent; and what is more, once again I was tipped to win.

Well: I'd been through all that nonsense before, and although the rumours which drifted up from the coast became more than usually insistent, I set them aside and got on with more pressing concerns with which I had to occupy myself. My second book.

*Postillion* had jumped into the best-seller lists, gone into a second printing, and had been sold to paperback: I had not let my "needlewoman" down after all, as I had feared, and with her encouragement had started off on *Snakes and Ladders*, which I finished in the year before "Despair" came to Cannes. All I really had to do, apart from the usual proof correcting, was the cover design, and the end-papers, which I decided to do myself.

But the rumours persisted as the Festival wore on, and I was haunted by television teams who wanted interviews "in depth", from Italy, France and Germany, which I gave: because it was easier to do them than to refuse. I was photographed, dutifully walking among my olive trees, playing with Labo and Daisy, and giving a series of pretty dull interviews. The atmosphere was pleasant and polite, there was a feeling that they were all interviewing the winner. One French team asked me to make a special speech in which I was to thank all those who had made it possible for me to win the most coveted prize at Cannes, the Palme d'Or, and were sullen with dismay when I declined, politely, to do so.

The final day of the whole idiotic affair was unsettling, in spite of my apparent unconcern; and the telephone became an instrument of dread. At ten a.m. it rang, and I was informed, unofficially, that I had certainly won the prize. The jury would make the official announcement at noon.

It rang again at eleven. A journalist from a London paper wanted to know how it felt "to win the most prestigious prize". I told him I didn't know, and hung up.

Lunch was oddly difficult to swallow. I began to think, against all my orderly instincts and my better judgement, that this time maybe, perhaps maybe . . . and went up to see if I had a clean white shirt; with buttons intact. Just in case.

At two o'clock the jury were still deliberating, but would I stand by because, I was assured, it was almost certain that I had won; with Marcello Mastroianni a close second.

I looked out my dinner jacket. Held it up to the light for moth-holes. I was in good shape there: no holes.

In the kitchen, washing up and preparing the dogs' dinners, I allowed myself to toy with the idea of a modest little speech of thanks in French: which was very silly indeed, for at two-thirty exactly I was told that I had lost to an American actor, John Voight.

I hung up the suit, put the shirt in the drawer.

It had been a good try. I'd almost enjoyed the suspense; and I wasn't in the least ashamed of my work on the film because I knew that it was, in truth, the best screen performance I had ever given. That in itself was reward enough.

When "Despair" eventually opened in New York to high critical acclaim and a box-office failure, Jack Kroll of *Newsweek* wrote of it: "Bogarde is superb: you seldom see such a sustained, moment-by-moment characterization on screen. . . . It's a performance by one of the best movie actors ever, at the peak of his talent." Which I really couldn't help thinking was pretty nice, and much more rewarding, to me, than a Palme d'Or.

Right or wrong, it made comforting reading; and reaching the peak of one's talent is, perhaps, no bad time to go out—for out I went, as things transpired.

Not from choice, for I have never at any time wished to abandon my chosen profession, but simply from a lack of acceptable material.

The cinema is often called The Seventh Art; and perhaps it

is. Certainly men like Resnais, Losey, Visconti and Fassbinder are artists (or sadly, were, in two cases) but their work has always been a desperate struggle against Big Business.

No longer do the great Jewish dynasties hold power: the people who were, when all is said and done, the Picture People. Now the cinema is controlled by vast firms like Xerox, Gulf & Western, and many others who deal in anything from sanitary-ware to property development. These huge conglomerates, faceless, soulless, are concerned only with making a profit; never a work of art. The Picture People have grown old, been bought out, sent scurrying to retirement in Palm Springs or Palm Beach, dismayed, displaced, bewildered by the loss of the cinema they once knew and which has probably gone for ever.

The Seventh Art is now but a small part of Big Business.

And Television Rules! Okay?

A question of profit and loss.

It is pointless to be "superb" in a commercial failure; and most of the films which I had deliberately chosen to make in the last few years were, by and large, just that. Or so I am always informed by the businessmen. The critics may have liked them extravagantly, but the distributors shy away from what they term "A Critic's Film", for it often means that the public will stay away. Which, in the mass, they do: and if you don't make money at the box-office you are not asked back to play again.

But I'd had a very good innings. Better than most. So what the hell?

# 14

A ND I was still creating, still inventing, still learning. To write.

I had reached a corner in my long corridor and made a deliberate change of direction, not a change of profession. It was simply an extension of the original job and there wasn't a STOP sign in sight. At least, as far as I could see.

Corners are not for hanging around at: they are for turning, for making a change; unless, of course, one loses heart and decides to lope off back the way one has come, which seems to me a very unadventurous thing to do.

Of course, the turning takes a bit of courage; the new way seems at first to be daunting and frightening after years of familiarity with the old, but there are some familiar facets along the new corridor.

The doors which had stood to the left and right of one before are repeated. There they stand: ajar, wide open, half-closed; filled with light, deep with sombre shades. But familiar. And there for the pushing open and discovery, perhaps, of very different contents, but they comfort one.

The final door, right down at the far end, is ever-present, just as before. You can't escape that, whichever way you decide to turn, so in the final analysis you might just as well take a risk in your journey, for that one door can never be avoided. It is there.

I have always been told that writing is a lonely, solitary, reclusive job. Very different, therefore, from acting, which is the absolute opposite. But even as a novice writer I have not found that to be true at all. It is neither lonely nor reclusive, and it is solitary only by virtue of the fact that one has to be alone and in silence in order to hear the voices which fill one's head. It is impossible to be lonely with so much conversation going on.

Some people, or so I am informed, can only write on a pad on their knees in a tumult of sound, or blasting music; others sit in a cell staring at blank walls so that the intensity of concentration is not broken.

Jane Austen apparently sat at a small table in the hall at the centre of the family house and wrote perfectly serenely, slipping her work discreetly under cover if she was disturbed; but this would not do for me.

I look out of my small window here above the woodshed, across the sloping tiled roof where lizards scuttle and chase, tails upraised in anger, and spiky geckos lie flat in the sun snapping at flies or bees. Beyond the sloping roof I can see the spires of four cypress trees, behind them a distant wood, beyond that the far hills. I see rain fall, sun blaze, snow pile, mist drift, the vine turn, the trees become bare in the wood, the hills stand stark and harsh against the light of winter.

But I am not distracted by these things, rather they comfort me; and although I am lost in time, secured against the outside world by a firmly closed door, I am never for one moment lonely.

How could I be?

The papers, letters, journals which one starts to research for work gradually fill the room with distant voices which grow ever louder the longer one reads. Voices drift out from all corners, from the ceiling, from the floor, from the shadowy shelves of reference books. Voices which one has loved, has laughed with, has even burst with fury at . . . but *voices*: and one is transported back to a past which becomes more vivid and alive than the present.

It is even stranger (and much noisier) when one is actually in the process of inventing people. It is then that the theatrical part of my life hastens to assist my writing-extension.

I sit, in a leather chair, and *talk* them into life. Ask them questions, work out with them how they lived, who they were, who they are going to be, what they will do, whom they will meet or couple with, and when they will die. I hear their laughter in my head, their accents in my ear: I know their sadness, their treachery, their kindness and their anxieties, for I have invented them all; and they are completely mine.

If anyone ever passed the door of this olive store, I reckon I'd be carted off as barking mad for talking to myself (it would seem) in different voices and dialects. For I play every scene I write, so as to be absolutely certain that the words are true and that the mood is correctly set. Dialogue can do this: and saves a lot of needless writers' explanation.

It is an extraordinary sensation, spending hours with my people. Exceptionally pleasant most of the time, irritating often; especially if a character takes off on his or her own path against my better judgement and I lose control of them. Then I rip them from the typewriter, screw them into a ball and chuck them away, insert a new sheet into the machine, and start again. "Now, this time get it *right!*" I say. Of course I suppose it is all a form of lunacy (so is acting come to that) but certainly it is not lonely.

And with autobiography, long-forgotten voices from the past return, jogging the memory, sometimes pulling at the heart cruelly, so that one walks in a daze, only very slightly aware of the present.

Occasionally, when she has been staying here, Elizabeth, who knows me all too well, will say, "Oh, he's off again. In one of his *moods.*" And of course she is right. Except that I am not in a mood in the terms which she means, I am mentally removed from the present with more than half of my mind far away. But I am not, for example, sulking. Just backtracking.

One of the things which makes writing magically different from acting is that I, and I alone, am responsible. In the theatre or in the cinema the actor is the interpreter of other people's words and work. His performance is directed by another: he has to balance his playing to other performances and other players, must at all times adjust, juggle, give way on occasion, so that he can find space for his own contribution to dazzle. If he can.

In the cinema there are a thousand technical things which he must take into account before he can even begin to offer a performance. The lights, the sound, the camera itself (a capricious beast to those whom it does not love) and there is focus, timing, other performers; a plethora of traps for the unwary.

But writing is your responsibility entirely. You are the writer of your script, the director of your play or film, the creator of your characters, you are every single technician, and you do all this quite alone. You are the boss, and for better or worse it is you who will have to carry the can in the end.

I have been surrounded at all times with advice, caution, suggestion, approval, and have been offered courage in abundance by my publishers, but I am perfectly well aware that what finally appears in print comes from my imagination, and it must be *I* who takes the rap. It's a solo performance all right; often nerve-racking.

At the beginning, I thought that one's Muse, for that is what I was always told it was called, just waited silently in the shadows, and all you had to do was to beckon her with one finger and she would arrive before you bearing a veritable cornucopia of riches in her arms.

A happy thought, but entirely false. At any rate in my case. *My* Muse sits slumped in the shadows, sulking. No amount of pleading, cajoling, tears, or begging and hand-wringing will drag her forth from her intense disinclination to assist me.

I have to go and grab her, wrestle with her, beat her about like a drunk, and force something from her grasp, however modest it might be. Mine holds no cornucopia of riches for me: a match-box at best, not more. And that is only offered resentfully. I have never been able to train her better: perhaps time will tell, but it is still a monstrous battle every single time I roll a sheet of paper into this machine. Sullen silence from my Muse. Anguished pleading from me as I stare in misery at the blank sheet before me.

Words, therefore, do not, as one kind woman in Australia wrote to me, "pour from your pen". They don't by a very long chalk. They are squeezed out one by one in sheer desperation, rather as one has to roll up and squeeze out the very last drops in an exhausted toothpaste tube; and no pen is involved, I regret to say, nothing nearly so romantic. It all goes straight down, flat and hard, from the typewriter at the very start. Mainly because I have an inbuilt belief that I have not written anything unless I actually see it printed before my eyes, also because my handwriting, reminiscent of unravelled knitting, confuses even me half an hour later. I am quite unable to decipher what I have set down: this is a clear case of the hand being faster than the mind, I suppose. I try to go too fast too soon. But then I have always done that: in as orderly a fashion as I can.

After the surprise success of *Postillion*, I realised that I would have to make a firm set of rules in order to write properly; or to write at all. If I was to take the business seriously then I must perform it seriously.

So from eight-thirty a.m. until twelve-thirty I write. The afternoons are clear then for the many jobs which await me on the land, but in the evenings from six until seven I re-read the morning's work and try to correct it, if I do not altogether destroy it (which I do all too often) and start off again the next morning.

It seems to me that I write each book twice; rejecting, correcting, destroying, cutting, adding, polishing. It's a long business. Sometimes I manage to get eight hundred words written, at other times I am very lucky if I manage eighty, and it's an exhausting, empty day: all the fault of my sulking Muse. I obviously got a dud.

Anyway: a lonely, solitary, reclusive job, I was assured by many who knew far more than I did, and I had been prepared for it, but it had proved to be untrue as far as I was concerned.

What I was *not* prepared for when I started writing was the appalling act of promotion. I had no idea that this vulgarity existed; no idea that once the book was finished, bound, and tidy, you had to go trotting off and flog it. For even if the word is unattractive it is exactly what you have to do: just as if your effort was plastic table-ware, a new brand of soap, or a Born-again Christian tract. I was astonished that such a gentlemanly (or so it had seemed to me) profession could stoop so low. I was well aware that in the cinema one had to work hard to sell the product, and I had had a great deal of experience in doing so; but I didn't expect it to happen in publishing. It is, however, essential today.

And, alas! it is exactly the same procedure as the cinema. The same interviews, the same chat shows which will guarantee sales, although I am certain that the people who watch chat shows don't buy books (but that's neither here nor there) and the same personal appearances in provincial cities. And what is perhaps the worst of all, the signing-sessions in bookshops. Those are the "crunchers": those really terrify me.

In the cinema at least I was always kept at a discreet distance from the audience. In writing I found, to my intense horror, that I was to be shoved right into its very arms. Stuck behind a desk or a table, with no way of escape, confronted far too closely by the people who had once been unseen, unheard, but who now were extremely visible, and vocal.

There one sat, pen in hand, selling one's wares like a pedlar at a fair.

"My dear, *do* look!" I heard a woman say in Harrods during one of these sessions. "Look what he's doing now, for God's sake! *Selling* himself in public!"

The second-generation Harrods' voice cut through the

book department like a rapier and pierced me to the depth of my quaking heart. My hand shook with anger, and someone got a very wobbly signature, but I couldn't possibly refute her remark: I was, as it happened, sitting only two feet away from the till, and every time we made a sale there was a shrill, chilling, "Ting!" to prove her point.

My first signing session ever was at Hatchards bookshop for *Postillion*. Elizabeth, Forwood, and I drove from the Connaught in silence. My voice had gone; my throat was dry, my tongue had become inextricably involved with the roof of my mouth and stuck there as if held by Jumbo Glue. Terror gripped me at the mere idea of having, as an actor, to leave the safety of my proscenium arch or the confines of my cinema screen and face an audience from a distance of feet, or less, stuck behind a table. If there *was* an audience. I knew that I would have to sit there for an hour at least, a blotter before me, pen in hand and smile inanely at perfectly ordinary customers, who had only come in to purchase an atlas perhaps, or the latest bestseller, in the desperate hopes that just one of them might be persuaded to buy a copy of my own modest offering, much as if I was selling flags for a charity, rattling my tin anxiously.

We didn't, therefore, speak to each other as we drove through Berkeley Square, and it was only as we started the down-run towards Piccadilly that I managed to croak something to the effect that I wished that I was dead and what the hell had I got involved in this potty business for anyway; then we swung left into the wide thoroughfare and I heard Forwood mutter the word, "Policemen".

"Where are the policemen? Has there been an accident? A bomb!" I said, suddenly alerted to near panic.

"Can't quite tell yet if they are outside Hatchards or Fortnum and Mason."

"Perhaps it's for the Queen. She's out shopping or something."

"It's Hatchards," said Elizabeth in a faint voice. She was as frightened as I was.

"What are they *doing*, for God's sake?"

"There's a queue, quite a big one too. And in this bitter wind . . ."

And there was.

And the morning was tremendous fun, warming, generous,

extremely touching and fully rewarding. I enjoyed myself to the full, it wasn't any different from my role as an actor: signing books was a breeze of a performance, and the audience, for want of a better word, who had waited so patiently in the cold March wind, were extraordinarily friendly to play to. It was an altogether happy occasion, and we sold a lot of copies, which, naturally, made everyone full of glee.

"Don't sign names," a discreet voice murmured in my ear. "Just your signature."

"But I *can't* just write my signature and nothing else!"

"Well, leave out the 'Best Wishes' part."

"It's not possible!"

"It's a question of time. *And* sales," said the discreet voice of authority resignedly.

But even though I insisted, and wrote the Maureens and Bettys and the Best Wishes as well, we had a record sale and everyone was smiling. A happy morning.

That evening I gave a small cocktail party to celebrate my new venture as a budding writer. The words which Mrs X had written with such firmness years ago came back to me in the midst of the pleasure and the laughter.

"*Force* memory!" she had insisted. And I had. And here we all were as a result.

The telephone rang. I clambered across small tables littered with glasses, olives, and bowls of scattered nuts. Charlotte Rampling from Paris.

"I wanted you to know. I've had a baby. He's six hours old and very beautiful."

"Oh Char! How super!"

"We're going to call him David."

"I've just had a baby today too; only it's got a slightly longer name."

"Oh! Your book. It's out! I forgot: what next; another one?"

I looked about the crowded room and the smiling faces, sensed the sweet smell of success, of belief supported and proved. Forwood refilled Norah's glass, they were laughing.

"Yes. I think so," I said.

What I didn't say was that I had already started on the first chapters of the next book. It would, I thought, be tempting fate to do so, and I'd done quite enough of that in the last few months.

"I think so, Char . . . but we'll just see how it goes. Cross your fingers?"

★    ★    ★

I had arrived at my mother's Edwardian hotel about half an hour late, a potted hoop of jasmin in one hand, a bag of trinkets and gifts in the other. Mr Brockway, the Manager, met me in the hall as I pushed open the front door, his pleasant, open face slightly tight with anxiety.

"Oh there you are! Good. She's got herself into a little state, nothing serious. I have been sitting with her. I think she thought that you'd had an accident . . . she's in her room, you know the way?"

I thanked him, asked him to tell my driver where to go for his lunch (for I knew no pubs in the area) and went down the corridor to her room.

She was sitting in a chair by the window, hands in her lap, her face puckered with distress, twisting her rings. Hyacinths in a pot, a jug of fading daffodils, a half-finished glass of wine beside her.

She bowed her head.

"Darling! I'm here . . . I'm sorry, we got lost. Came out of town the long way: Streatham, Purley . . . and then took the wrong lane here."

She made a strange, low, shuddering sound.

"Don't cry! For heaven's sake . . . your mascara will run! Come on now, it's all right."

She pulled herself together, sat upright, eyes wide, bright with unshed tears. "I thought you weren't coming."

"You *knew* I was . . . I'm late, I'm sorry."

"I'm all right. I'm all right. Just worried. What's that?"

"Jasmin, you can plant it in the garden later."

"From darling France."

It wasn't. It was from Maida Vale, but there was no point in saying so.

"I'm dying for a drink, I've brought my own. Are you having one?"

"Yes . . . oh yes. I'm having one. My Spanish."

I poured myself a stiff brandy and soda which I had brought with me in my hand-grip."

"Where's your bottle? You've almost finished that glass."

"It's here." Her hands were still restless, twisting the rings constantly.

"Let me fill it up . . . where is it?"

"Here."

In the wastepaper basket beside her chair.

"Why do you keep it in that?"

"The maids come in and out all the time."

"But they know that you have a bottle a day! Why hide it, darling?"

"That's my business."

I filled the glass: she took it eagerly, hands shaking a little, spilling some down her chin.

"Elizabeth brings you a crate of twelve every Saturday, doesn't she? I mean the maids know all that."

"I keep it in my room now. It was in the kitchen and I had to *ask* them when I wanted a bottle. They stole it."

"Oh Ma! Now come on . . . that's nonsense."

"Tell me why, pray?" Her eyes were enormous, angry, brilliant. "It's supposed to last me a week and I always run out by Thursday . . . now I keep it in here, hidden."

"Well: I've brought you a few bits and pieces, and look! A copy of my very first novel! How about that? I'm a novelist now. My third book!"

"Lovely." There was no interest. She screwed up her eyes. "What's this, on the cover? I haven't got my glasses."

"Bamboo, barbed wire, a butterfly. It's called *A Gentle Occupation*."

She placed it carefully on the coffee-table before her, took up her glass and drained it.

"Lunch is at one. Punctually. Do you like my hair?"

"Super. It's softer-looking."

"Had it done two weeks ago. I've combed it out. But it's going grey, isn't it?"

"No . . . pepper-and-saltish. Not grey, and after all you'll be eighty-one next month, I mean you ought to have a grey hair or two, surely?"

"You haven't."

"One or two."

"And you're about sixty. You take after my side of the family. My mother, Granny Nelson, had jet-black hair when she died; well into her eighties."

"We're lucky. Sometimes they say I dye mine."

"Who do?"

"Oh, the press."

"Jealous," she said, offering me her glass. "Fill it up, will you, before lunch."

"Will you take it in with you?"

"To lunch? With all those people looking on. Good God no."

A high-ceilinged, sunny dining-room. Separate tables round the sides; at one end a table of four, a son and daughter visiting, low murmurs of conversation. I called out, "Good morning" as I sat down. There was a small hush: "Good morning," they said, and continued murmuring and clinking cutlery.

A man at the table beside us finished his meal, pushed himself up with the aid of a white stick, adjusted a green plastic eye-shade over his forehead, and inched from the room in little shuffles.

"Cheerful, isn't it?" said my mother.

After lunch she refused to return to her room, so we went into the Residents' Drawing Room instead.

"I spend the whole bloody day in that place of mine, I want a change. No one ever comes in here after lunch, they all go to their rooms until supper time . . . at six."

The drawing-room was large, light, lined with books, a long window with a window seat, an open fire, logs smouldering, a potted plant trailing on the mantelshelf. A television set in a corner.

"Do you come in here often? To watch TV or something?"

"If you are 'on' I do. But I can't work it; the button things. I had a friend who used to come and watch with me if you were 'on'; she was a dear soul. They took her away one night and she's dead. Cuckfield Hospital."

Suddenly she laughed, a coarse, bitter sound. "They'll all finish up there, the lot of them: in Cuckfield-bloody-Hospital." She lit a cigarette with a flick of her lighter. "I never thought that I'd have to end up here. It's all coming true, you see."

"What's coming true?"

"That woman at the Cox's wedding, years ago; she saw my aura. Purple, violet. She said that I was a Tragedy Queen, that Ulric would die suddenly, that I'd be sent to a home . . ."

"Ma, for God's sake stop . . . it's all rubbish."

She smiled, snapped the cigarette lighter a couple of times. "This is really very interesting. You don't know *this* part." She looked at me with defiance. "She said that they would have to cut my legs off."

"Why?"

"Oh . . . because of something the soldiers got in the trenches. Begins with a G."

"Gangrene?"

"Gangrene."

"It's all silly rubbish, you know: it's simply none of it true. Now look here, listen to me: I'll do anything you like, *anything* you want. Would you like to come back with me to France? Live there?"

"God! No. I'd never make the journey. Anyway, we'd fight all the time; we're too alike, you and I."

"Would you like to move away from here then? To somewhere else, like Brighton; somewhere you could see a bit more of life. A town. Anywhere you say."

"No, no. I'll stick it out here."

"Would you like to go up to London, have a couple of weeks in the clinic, a real check-up, see what's what; would that be a good idea? A nice long rest in bed, lots of nurses and so on. Just to make sure you're all right, if you are worried."

"*I'm* all right. Don't bother about me. I've had my day, I'll stick it out. I'm tough, God knows I've had to be, all my life."

"You were walking almost normally today, all the way to the dining-room, and all the way back here. No stick, you didn't even need my arm, that's wonderful: and you *have* to walk, the doctors say so."

"I walk all right. I walk." She looked at me suddenly with a gleam of anger. "I made a big effort for you today. You are my first-born, after all." She threw the butt of her cigarette into the fire.

"I know that, and you really do look marvellous, the effort was well worth it. I haven't seen you look like this for ages and ages . . . you really look incredible."

And she did. Straight-backed, elegant, perfectly groomed, the high bones in her face catching a slant of sunlight through the window, her eyes enormous. She looked ten years less than her age.

"I always tried hard to look my best for Daddy: I never

wanted him to see me in an apron, you know. I had standards. I still have."

"Do you talk to Daddy?"

She looked at me suddenly, with a sharp, swift turn of her head as if I had caught her out or tricked her.

"Talk to him? Where?"

"In your room. His photograph is on your dressing-chest."

"Yes." She pulled a curl of hair behind her ear. "Yes, I talk to him. All the time, all the time."

"What do you say to him, Ma? Tell me what you say?"

With neat, small movements she began to rearrange a string of beads around her neck, smoothed the long tie of her brown silk shirt. And then she looked across at me with wide, clear, calm eyes, her hands folded on her thigh, the cigarette lighter clasped in slender hands.

"Come back," she said. "That's what I say to him."

★　　★　　★

I drove away, a couple of hours later, through the greening Sussex lanes in a state of grim depression to face what my Journal records as "a gruelling week: almost *too* much in fact."

In America I had done a number of promotional tours for various films; these were known in the business as Total Exposure, and started at eight in the morning until eight in the evening. Now and again, on the crammed schedule, I would notice a small bracketed "SC" which, I was informed, stood for "Shirt Change"; and that was the only break one got. What I was about to face was almost as bad. Publishing and the cinema were not so very far apart, after all. In both, one had to sell the product hard.

Work started the next morning with the BBC at eight-thirty and went on throughout the day with interviews on the hour, every hour: even lunch was an interview. But there was almost never time to change my shirt, a tie, or my jacket. The day came to a close with the Publishers' Party given in my honour, at which I remember shaking hands with Margaret Drabble dressed in snow boots and a brown woollen knitted hat, and then I got hurried to the Royal Command Performance where I shook hands with the Queen who was wearing white fox and emeralds: most of the day is a haze, and I just remember crawling into bed with a modest temperature and the firm conviction that I was beginning, at least a cold; at worst 'flu.

Which was all that I needed with five more days of "selling" to go. At the same time, it might as well be confessed, I was not feeling particularly well anyway.

A few weeks before, the excellent Dr Poteau had managed (after two wearying years) to diagnose a very tiresome malady to which I had become victim, as an intestinal parasite, which he assured me I must have contracted through drinking un-boiled water in southern Italy. (I hadn't been in southern Italy for years.) They could lie dormant for a long time, he said, and were tenacious, destructive, weakening and had shells: which made them extremely difficult to eradicate.

He prescribed a pill which was a brutal remedy and which, although it would surely destroy the beasts, was at the same time bringing me gradually to the edge of suicidal depression.

There was a very jolly added side-effect to all this: it was imperative that I should know exactly where to go, and how to get there speedily if, and when, disaster should strike; and with Dr Poteau's remedy one could never be certain. An altogether unnerving situation which necessitated a swift, and if humanly possible, discreet exit.

So I was hardly in the happiest state of mind to give interviews-in-depth, or really to enjoy the signal honour accorded me of a Foyle's Luncheon in the Blue Room at the Dorchester. I had a quick, to the point, chat with the Toast Master just before we all sat down, who assured me that my worries were at an end because what I might need most was situated exactly behind my chair, at the Top Table, through the door into the kitchens. It was marked, he said, clearly MEN. "Just one sign from you, Sir . . ." he said, and I relaxed. Well: almost. I still had to make an exit.

Neither did the situation help me to enjoy the signing-session, this time once again, thankfully, at Hatchards Book-shop, where they tactfully sat me miles away from the degrad-ing till and I managed to sign over six hundred copies, all of which carried Best Wishes and the personal names of the purchasers.

"You'd have sold over seven hundred if you'd left out the trimming: just written your signature," said the quiet voice of authority sadly. "*Sales* and *time*, remember . . ."

However, everyone seemed perfectly satisfied, the customers were warm and relaxing, and I was aware that if I had had to leave the session, for a few moments, I knew exactly where to go.

Forwood was brilliant at doing his reconnaissance in this particular field, and during the rest of the Promotional Week the ravishing P.R.O., Miss Bell, who had four years before seemed to me as if she was dressed from a Women's Institute stall, so strangely assorted were her garments ("Jumble sales, flea markets, yes: but *never* the W.I.," she had said firmly), quickly caught on to the problem with her usual efficiency and became as adept as he.

"Down on the left, second door, past the fire-extinguishers," she would murmur as I, with outstretched hand, a welcoming smile, and a happy greeting on my dry lips would go to meet another interviewer, or radio disc jockey, secured by my knowledge and usually managing to overcome the problem, by forgetting it. Apart from my two loyal scouts, no one else, of course, knew anything. And fortunately there were no bolts from the blue; or anywhere else.

Perhaps the happiest, and most relaxing event of the whole week was my own dinner party at the Connaught at the end of the fourth day: I was, I confess, pretty well flaked-out by this time, but the arrival around the big table of Norah Smallwood, John and his wife Susan, Charlotte and her husband Jean-Michel Jarre who had flown in from Paris especially for the celebration, and Angela Fox, the friend of many years, filled me with comfort by their own, obvious, pleasure: and after almost thirty years of staying at the Connaught I naturally knew the lay-out; so anxiety faded in the security of that vital information.

It was a little more unnerving the next day in Oxford when Blackwells gave me a splendid luncheon at the Randolph Hotel; but I knew the Randolph of old, having played in the theatre next door, and made a couple of films in the city, and knew that Forwood and Ros ("Miss Bell" had long ago been discarded for the more familiar name) would be well prepared, and able to do a cover-up job should the need arise and it would be discovered that I had, suddenly, left the gathering.

On the sixth day we flew to Amsterdam in the greatest style. Everything had been arranged and organised with extreme efficiency by Quentin Hockliffe, Chatto's Export Sales Director, reminding me of the times, years ago, when Betty Box and Ralph Thomas and I would tour the provinces promoting our films. I remember, distinctly, the extreme pleasure it gave me to feel the train slide slowly into the stations in Birmingham, Bristol, Manchester or wherever it might be; a sighing of steam, the compartment moving very gently along the platform until we absolutely, and *precisely*, stopped before the imposing figure of the Station Master, top-hatted, rose in buttonhole, who would then lead us proudly through his teeming domain to waiting cars, past rows of yelling teenagers waving hands, flowers and autograph books. I always managed to look back towards the engine and wave my thanks, receiving a salute back and a weary grin.

The Amsterdam trip was much the same, although done by air, and the day was one of extraordinary nostalgia and emotion. There, in the book shop, were gathered people who had come from all over Holland and whom I had known in the desperate days of our occupation of Java when we had liberated the civilian prison camps and released thousands of laughing, cheering, embracing skeletons from the Japanese.

Time had altered us: we were older, hair was white. At first I recognised no one; and then the photographs were produced. Brother officers I had forgotten. Myself aged twenty-four walking through a burning village. A laughing girl with a flower in her hair.

"That's me! Can you believe it? Annie . . . remember me? I'm a granny now!"

Programmes of the concerts which I had produced, my name indecently important across the top. "Pip van den Bogaerde Presents: 'Curtain Up!' " and we all laughed together.

"Oh, they were *funny* days! Of course you won't remember *us* after all this time, but we remember you."

"I'm older too. And I *do* remember."

"But we got through, didn't we? Most of us."

"Remember Jenny? She was in your show, but she didn't make it home. Typhoid."

"Bob stayed on for a time: but it was pretty hopeless. He's married now, in Breda."

The conversations were limited; I had a job to do, and the press to meet.

Polite, crisp, interested, because *A Gentle Occupation* was apparently the first book written about that period and those people and their courage.

The Left was a little cool, inclined to disbelieve that the book was fiction; the Communists (humourless, young, bearded, leather-jacketed) aggressive and at pains to explain that the word "terrorist", which I used, was incorrect. There had been *no* terrorists in Java, they insisted, only Freedom Fighters. They were indignant because, they said, it was the first time that the word had been publicly used in Holland, and it should be altered. Quite suddenly, at this conference, I was involved in Politics against my will, my modest novel became a tract; and cautiously abused. However, as all my interviewers at the session had been born many years after the events I had recorded, and had never, as far as I could gather, set a foot in the East Indies, I acceded to their insisting, refusing only to withdraw the word terrorist. It was pointless to argue. As I pointed out, all I had done was to write a fictional account of a tragic period which had cost us all many lives: I had not written a doctrine.

And then it was all over, the promotion campaign, and the next day I flew home to France, a bit haggard, down to eight and a half stone, but immeasurably happy all the same. I'd worked hard, as I should have done, and the book was selling. So that was all right.

A day or two later I discovered, to my mild surprise, that I was fifty-nine: an enormous pile of cards and telegrams confirmed this event, but I was far too tired to deal with them, I'd wait until I had settled down.

Walking with Labo, aging too, through the bright spring grasses, and the drifts of wild anemones, the sun warm on my back, the sea shining like a silver knife thrusting from the Estérel Mountains, I was curiously content: mainly because I was home again, but also because the fourteen months of solid slog which had produced *A Gentle Occupation* had not, it seemed, been in vain, and because a fourth book was already drifting about in my head: indeed I had taken the first completed chapter to Norah the day I arrived in London, and she had given me the green light to carry on. So . . . in a day or two, I'd be back at my trestles in the olive store talking to my new "people".

But for today, this first one of relaxation and peace in my paradise regained, I'd do nothing much. Just potter about:

dead-head the spent narcissus in the rough grass under the willow; perhaps trim the pomegranate, already spiked with scarlet buds among its thorny branches, and simply enjoy the irreversible fact that I was fifty-nine.

At least I'd got there.

And according to my own peculiar brand of arithmetic and logic, I determined that *tomorrow*, and not today, would mark the start of my sixtieth year.

I was not to know that tomorrow would also bring me the news that Ma had died.

When the two great tent-poles fall, which have, for so long, supported the fabric above the circus of one's life, the guy-ropes fly away, the canvas billows down, and there is nothing left to do but crawl out from under, and go on one's way alone.

"A Show For All The Family!" is over.

# EPILOGUE

They told me that flying at sixty-five thousand feet I would be able to see the curvature of the earth from Concorde.

But I don't. All that I can see is blue: an immensity of blue. Cornflower, to indigo, to darkest ink. Infinity.

I don't really want to see the curvature of the earth, to be perfectly honest; I am more than content with this view of infinity. I have long wondered what it looked like and now I know.

It is, quite simply, for ever.

I am so distanced in both mind and body that the earth is of no consequence.

Before me on this little table, in this most graceful, most elegant, most orderly of machines, my René Lalou hardly trembles in the crystal goblet, even though we are racing to New York at twice the speed of sound.

We left Paris a little over an hour ago: an amazing, heartlifting roar, and a tremendous upward, zooming, thrust; up, up, up, and away into this extraordinary cerulean atmosphere. Another change of direction.

We broke the sound barrier over Le Havre on Mach 1, and climbed higher and higher to reach Mach 2. It says so on the little illuminated panel ahead of me: otherwise I would never have known: naturally.

I am in limbo. An intermediate place between two extremes; perhaps the word "condition" is more fitting. At any rate I find limbo exceptionally pleasing.

Today New York, tomorrow Los Angeles, after a lapse of some twelve years, to make a film with Glenda Jackson.

My first time before a camera for over four years. That'll be interesting: but it is a cardigan-and-knitted-tie role, so I may not find it too taxing. Unless I have lost the trick. Could it be so? Always possible after a long time away.

I wonder? I wonder too how Miss Jackson will be. We have never met.

I saw her standing in one of the doorways, as I wandered along my corridor, four books finished and behind me; nothing much else to do. She didn't beckon me, or solicit my favour. She didn't even move. But she was Lorelei; and I, like the bewitched sailors on the Rhine, found myself unable to resist. I am told that she is very dedicated to her work, and doesn't suffer fools gladly.

So here I am. I do hope it doesn't lead to destruction?

No one else on earth but she could have got me back to Los Angeles. Should I tell her that? It might please her; and she might smile kindly on me. I do hope so. I have no reason to suppose otherwise, of course, but one is always uncertain; even in limbo. When I come home I think that I'll put Actor/Author on my Immigration Form, that would be right and proper surely?

We are about to begin our descent to New York; the Captain has just said so. Quite soon we shall be down on the prosaic earth again: limbo will give way to Customs and Immigration, to passports and work permits and, I hope, an enormous Cadillac to bear me off to my hotel. I can't help feeling that it is all going to be a tremendously exciting adventure, but I shall not let it go to my head.

I'm an orderly man.

Often pinched by doubt . . .

# INDEX